RHET OPS

PITTSBURGH SERIES IN COMPOSITION, LITERACY, AND CULTURE

DAVID BARTHOLOMAE AND JEAN FERGUSON CARR, EDITORS

RHET OPS

RHETORIC AND INFORMATION WARFARE

EDITED BY JIM RIDOLFO AND WILLIAM HART-DAVIDSON

UNIVERSITY OF PITTSBURGH PRESS

Published by the University of Pittsburgh Press, Pittsburgh, Pa., 15260

Manufactured in the United States of America
Printed on acid-free paper
10 9 8 7 6 5 4 3 2 1

Cataloging-in-Publication data is available from the Library of Congress

ISBN 13: 978-0-8229-4589-5
ISBN 10: 0-8229-4589-4

Cover photograph taken by tour guide at Greenbank Observatory, West Virginia, using Jim Ridolfo's polaroid camera, summer 2018.
Cover design by Melissa Dias-Mandoly

CONTENTS

PREFACE VII

INTRODUCTION: FROM THE DARK SIDE OF DIGITAL COMPOSING TO #RHETOPS 3

JIM RIDOLFO AND WILLIAM HART-DAVIDSON

PART I: RHETORICAL OPERATIONS AND EMERGING TACTICS

1. THE RHETORIC OF INFRASTRUCTURE: AMERICAN COLONIALISM AND THE MILITARY TELEGRAPH 19

ELIZABETH LOSH

2. REVISITING "A SOLDIER'S GUIDE TO RHETORICAL THEORY": INTELLIGENCE ANALYSIS IN THE OPEN 33

GARY MILLS

3. RHETORIC AND THE US INTELLIGENCE COMMUNITY'S MISUSES OF THEORY 54

NATE KREUTER

4. INSURGENT RHETORICS AND HISTORICAL MATERIALISM 67

MIKE EDWARDS

5. MINERVA RISING: THE PENTAGON'S WEAPONIZATION OF RHETORICAL KNOWLEDGE 78

JOHN GAGNON

6. INSURGENT CIRCULATION, WEAPONIZED MEDIA: WAGING THE LATE SIXTIES WAR WITHIN 90

BRAD E. LUCAS

7. GAMERGATE: UNDERSTANDING THE TACTICS OF ONLINE KNOWLEDGE DISRUPTORS 105

MICHAEL TRICE

PART II: DIGITAL PRACTICES

8. ISIS VERSUS THE UNITED STATES: RHETORICAL BATTLE IN THE MIDDLE EAST 125
WILLIAM M. MARCELLINO AND MADELINE MAGNUSON

9. STORMWATCH: MACHINE LEARNING APPROACHES TO UNDERSTANDING WHITE SUPREMACY ONLINE 142
RYAN OMIZO

10. DARK INTERACTIONS: INTERFACES AND OBJECT ARRAYS AS SURVEILLANCE IN DIGITAL RHETORIC 158
JOHN GALLAGHER

11. DIGITAL SURVEILLANCE OF GANG COMMUNICATION: GRAFFITI'S RHETORICAL VELOCITY BETWEEN STREET GANGS AND URBAN LAW ENFORCEMENT 170
SETH LONG AND KEN FITCH

PART III: PRACTITIONER STORIES

12. DIGITAL AGE EDUCATION: PREPARING WARRIORS FOR HYBRID CONFLICT AT AIR FORCE CYBERWORX 183
JEFFREY COLLINS AND GARY MILLS

13. MAPPING THE RHETORIC-OPERATIONS DIVIDE: CONSIDERATIONS FOR THE FUTURE 200
ANGIE MALLORY

14. SOCIAL MEDIA STRATEGY FOR THE MILITARY-ENGAGED AMERICAN RED CROSS 211
LAURA A. EWING

15. CHANGING TECHNOLOGIES AND WRITING FROM AND ABOUT WAR 219
D. ALEXIS HART AND CHERYL HATCH

16. MILITARY WIVES AS RHETORICAL INSURGENTS: RESISTING ASSIMILATION AS "FORCE MULTIPLIERS" 233
ELISE DIXON

AFTERWORD: INVENTING A CRITICAL PRAXIS OF ENGAGEMENT ON SOCIAL MEDIA PLATFORMS 246
JIM RIDOLFO AND WILLIAM HART-DAVIDSON

LIST OF CONTRIBUTORS 251
INDEX 255

PREFACE

WHEN THE WORLD BECAME AWARE OF RHET OPS

The world significantly changed while we were working with authors on the book you now hold. When we first conceived the project, the idea that online discourse might be a kind of weapon wielded by state or non-state actors in conflict was still relatively obscure. As we circulated our call for #RhetOps proposals in the summer of 2016, the US presidential election campaign was nearing its nadir. Both political parties had named presumptive nominees and were engaged in a highly contentious media campaign. There were already allegations in the mainstream press that Russian agents had sought to influence the outcome of the election by hacking, leaking confidential information, and influencing social media (Bessi and Ferrara) with what we label #RhetOps tactics, or rhetorical operations that make use of the latest digital and social networking technology to append, enhance, and amplify state and non-state conflicts. While our project felt important to us when we conceived it several years ago, by mid-summer 2016 the project began to feel *urgent* as we collected an increasing number of stories under #RhetOps, a hashtag to mark convergences between digital rhetorical theory and military operations, that pointed to broader militarization of social media and the concomitant questions concerning the vulnerability of democracy.

As we prepare this book's introduction, Facebook CEO Mark Zuckerberg has just completed his second day of congressional testimony, facing questions from elected officials regarding the potential misuse of their platform's user data by a British company, Cambridge Analytica. Less than two years after we launched the project that would become this book, the idea that words and images—memes, fabricated news stories, lifestyle quizzes, and digital games—can be weapons is now part of our daily public discourse. In the next seventeen chapters, contributors explore how this convergence of digital rhetoric and state/military operations has consequences for our field, pedagogy, and collective future.

In the scholarly essays collected here, authors present portraits of rhetorical knowledge deployed in scenes of conflict. Our objective as editors is to bring attention to what it means to study, teach, and learn rhetoric in a world that has been transformed by digital technology, but is also a world of wars alongside digital networks. This book is not, however, primarily about the mobile technologies and social networks that are now broadly acknowledged as human conflict vectors. The chapters collected in this volume offer readers a chance to focus, instead, on the human dimension of rhetorical practice: to reflect not only on the durable question of what it means to conduct oneself ethically as a speaker or writer but also what it means to *learn* the art of rhetoric as a means to engage adversaries in war and conflict.

RHET OPS

FROM THE DARK SIDE OF DIGITAL COMPOSING TO #RHETOPS

JIM RIDOLFO AND WILLIAM HART-DAVIDSON

The editors first began using the phrase *the dark side of digital composing* in the aftermath of the tragic Virginia Tech shootings in 2007. Reflecting on the difference between the 1999 Columbine shooting and the Virginia Tech shooting, we discussed the intentional effort on the part of the VT shooter to send a digital portfolio of media work to the press in an attempt to use the press to amplify his digital texts. This digital media work, combined with the shooter killing thirty-two people before committing suicide, deeply troubled us as teachers of digital writing. We saw a clear intention on the part of the shooter to think about the rhetorical delivery of his texts in a way that previous school shooters had, to our knowledge, not done. In between the two sets of attacks, the shooter stopped at the post office to mail a package. It was a digital portfolio of the shooter's photos, videos, and writing.[1] Sent to NBC news, the package contained photos of the shooter posing with weapons; several video clips, including one that became known as a "confession" video that now has over three million views on YouTube[2]; and other materials. He had spent quite some time planning not only the violent attack but also the way the words and images that characterize it and his own identity would be presented and circulated. The attacks themselves were "image events" meant to give the messages the shooter intended to circulate a massive media push. If the Virginia Tech shooter's use of media offered a shift in how digital media was used as a weapon of terror in school shootings, we also saw another shift happening in how media was being used by insurgencies in Iraq.

Around the same historical moment the Virginia Tech shooting happened, we were also reading about the growing compositional changes to how attack videos were composed and distributed. As Daniel Kimmage and Kathleen Ridolfo reported on Radio Free Europe/Radio Liberty: "Insurgents' willingness to forego a centralized brick-and-mortar production infrastructure and their reliance on the Internet as the primary distribution channel for their media products have led to the emergence of a decentralized, building-block production model in which virtually any individual or group can design a media product to serve insurgent aims and goals. . . . One or more individuals working anywhere in the world can create everything else."[3] As teachers of digital rhetoric, the Virginia Tech shooting and reports on how insurgents were using digital media digital struck us together with a force similar to the powerful example Steven Katz (1992) provides in his article on the ethic of expediency in technical communication.[4] As scholars, we saw that theorizing and understanding the ethical dimensions of digital composing must involve a careful examination of how digital composing intersects with violence. For us, questions arise from the massive increase in not only the available means of composition, but the potentially instant ubiquitous circulation of digital composition: what responsibilities do those of us who teach digital rhetoric and multimodal composing have to anticipate and prepare students to mitigate the dark side of digital composition and rhetorical operations that are imbued with digital media #RhetOps?

A question for us that emerged from our editorial conversations is how we should work toward articulating principles that guide our work as scholars and teachers of digital rhetoric as we see the ability for our disciplinary knowledge to become weaponized. These factors include new technologies and globalized markets, and we note that Laura Gurak's *Persuasion and Privacy in Cyberspace: The Online Protests over Lotus Market Place and the Clipper Chip* (1997) helped to open this line of inquiry.[5] Gurak's analysis, guided by the work of rhetorical theorists such as James Zappen and Michael Halloran and the science and technology studies scholar Langdon Winner, revealed that rhetorical ethics could and *would* be embedded into the mundane objects of our everyday lives. Another early monograph in this area is Bernadette Longo's *Spurious Coin: A History of Science, Management, and Technical Writing* (2000), a work that implicates technical writing pedagogy and textbooks in the project of the United States' global cultural dominance, a project that is equal parts industrialization and militarization. Today, we suggest that the militarized deployment of digital rhetoric is now part of our everyday lives—that is, the production and proliferation of mass disinformation campaigns, or what's been more recently called "fake news" in the popular press.

The line of inquiry into the broader social context of conflict Gurak and Longo helped to initiate continues today with works such as Mark Ward's *Deadly Documents: Technical Communication, Organizational Discourse, and the Holocaust* (2014).[6] Ward's book continues the conversation first begun by Steven Katz in 1992 when his article "The Ethic of Expediency" was among the first published pieces to include rhetorical analysis of primary source documents from the Third Reich. By including a contribution from Katz in the afterword to *Deadly Documents*, Ward emphasizes that the ethical issues Katz highlighted continue to be salient. The takeaway from this rich exchange between Katz and Ward is generative for our collection: rhetorical knowledge is a substantive, not merely an instrumental, component to both totalitarian regimes and to the means of resisting and dismantling them. We both make and unmake systems of domination with words. More recently in rhetorical studies, we've been influenced by scholarship such as Edwards and Hart's 2010 *Kairos* special issue on rhetoric and the military, William Marcellino's 2015 "Revisioning Strategic Communication through Rhetoric and Discourse Analysis" in *Joint Forces Quarterly*, both of which make a strong case for how rhetoric and the military converge.[7] By the time the call for papers went out in 2016, the work collected here was well underway as Philippe-Joseph Salazar published "A Caliphate of Culture? ISIS's Rhetorical Power" in *Philosophy and Rhetoric*, examining how an alternate global culture spreads its power.[8]

Outside of rhetorical studies, Zeynep Tufecki's *Twitter and Teargas: The Power and Fragility of Networked Protest* (2017) presents relevant case studies of uprisings and protest movements from Tahrir Square to Occupy Wall Street, drawing parallels between the strategies and politics of technologically mediated organizing. [9]*Twitter and Teargas* signals a shift away from the relatively benign portrayal of network technology as a force for positive social change typical in mainstream press coverage of events such as the Arab Spring. Tufecki's book raises important questions about technology and social networks in particular as a means to undermine democratic institutions and empower oppressive forces. These same themes lay at the center of Cathy O'Neil's best-selling *Weapons of Math Destruction: How Big Data Increases Inequality and Threatens Democracy* (2017).[10] O'Neil's account puts technology in the crosshairs. She examines algorithms used in various kinds of systems that incorporate data mined from user activity in digital spaces to divide people from one another, perpetuate inequity, and disenfranchise the vulnerable.

Across all of these sources, what we see is a burgeoning tradition of looking at the military implications of rhetoric and technical writing that goes back to at least to Katz. In this collection, we build on this work by assembling a diverse group of authors writing about the contemporary use of digital rhetoric by both state actors and military organizations as well as by non-state actors whose motives include carrying out violence.

Just as digital rhetoric amplifies compositional and rhetorical trends that existed in print and manuscript culture (i.e., composing for recomposition), it also enables new and inexpensive ways to weaponize rhetoric in support of face-to-face conflicts. As with composing with recomposition, the role of rhetoric in war is not new. Rhetoric has always had a well-documented role in arguments for and against war, arguments to acquire additional military resources, arguments to motivate and inspire troops, to strike fear in the heart of the enemy, and to spread disinformation and propaganda. However, what we think the evolving ways rhetoric can be digitally deployed, and how rhetoric or messaging is discussed as a critical tool worthy of military investment, is a new trend that the field should monitor.

Two broad themes therefore run through the chapters collected here: (1) increased interest in digital rhetoric by military organizations, and (2) the use of machine-learning and nonhuman agents in digital networks. To this end, we have assembled a broad group of researchers whose interests and experience range from scholars, researchers, and practitioners, including members of the RAND Corporation researching the Islamic State, a member of the Los Angeles County Sheriff's Department working on a project to track graffiti through databases, to the war reporter Cheryl Hatch reflecting on the media, to a former National Geospatial-Intelligence Agency employee examining the role of rhetoric and the intelligence community. By striking a balance between analysis and practitioner's stories, we think that this collection will help students, teachers, and researchers of rhetoric frame difficult conversations about the role of our field knowledge and its increasing use as a digital tool—not just to resolve conflict through deliberation but also to incite and exacerbate conflict. We have asked contributors to consider how should digital writers, teachers of digital writing and rhetoric, and scholars of rhetoric think about the world populated with networked, cyborg writers and their growing military applications? How should we talk about writing *with machines* as the ability of machines to deploy rhetorical strategies—often at humans' explicit request—grows more sophisticated? What should we teach these machines to do? *How* should we teach them? We have long recognized the perils of a rhetorical education for humans that is devoid of ethical reasoning, but we now must take seriously a new set of responsibilities to teach machines what to do and what not do with powerful rhetorical strategies.

WHY DIGITAL MILITARY RHETORIC?

While rhetoric has always been valuable to states and militaries, we want to make the claim that rhetoric's cost and use value to state and non-state conflict increases with the ubiquity and speed of digital delivery and large scale automated networks such as botnets. Ami Pedahzur, drawing on Theo Farrell, writes that the growth of special operations forces after World War II are due in part to their relative affordability, their ability to be constituted and disbanded quickly, and the way they are "alert, agile, and responsive to continual stimuli"—thus their human capital makes them an "ideal vehicle for exploration and innovation" of new tactics and capabilities.[11] Here, we see a parallel between how Pedahzur discusses the proliferation of special operations after World War II and the growth of #RhetOps in the twenty-first century. As we look at recent RhetOps campaigns, such as Russian interference in the 2016 US presidential election, this disruption work is relatively cheap when compared to advanced weaponry. As of February 2018, estimates are that Russia spent about $1.25 million a month on their efforts. Comparatively, the cost of one US Tomahawk missile is about $1.4 million. Building on Pedahzur's understanding of the growth of special operations after World War II, after 2016 we expect to see increasing state and non-state calls for #RhetOps initiatives that are short-lived, highly specific to a certain mission, agile, and rapidly created and disbanded. In short, #RhetOps may be understood as a kind of special work of its own, as we see in the chapters by Jeffrey Collins, Gary Mills, and Angie Mallory in parts 1 and 3.

For two examples of how #RhetOps imbues asymmetrical conflict, in an analysis of Islamic State (IS) media operations, the Soufan Group, a private intelligence firm founded by the former FBI agent Ali Soufan, offers a compelling example. The Soufan Group notes in their November 2014 report that "The Islamic State is crowd sourcing its propaganda . . . in a counterintuitive move, The Islamic State has maximized control of its message by giving up control of its delivery."[12] Six months later, on July 6, 2015, President Obama discussed his strategy for fighting IS after a Pentagon briefing by top commanders, outlining not only airstrikes and supporting local forces on the ground but also placing a strong emphasis on rhetorical strategy online: "As I've said before—and I know our military leaders agree—this broader challenge of countering violent extremism is not simply a military effort. Ideologies are not defeated with guns; they're defeated by better ideas—a more attractive and more compelling vision. So the United States will continue to do our part, by working with partners to counter ISIL's hateful propaganda, especially online."[13] President Obama's remarks suggest that to us what's happening at the level of how states wage war in the twenty-first century is an important call for digital rhetoricians to pay attention. The digital delivery tactics suggested by the Soufan Group are not completely new to rhetoric; however, their application and context point to some of the alarming ways that digital rhetoric may be leveraged to make and maintain war. And so it is time for our discipline to be more directly involved in highlighting not only how the knowledge is used but also what its application can teach rhetorical studies. From examples such as this, we argue that there is a large volume of practitioner activity taking place with relevance for our discipline. This is why in section 4 we've invited practitioner-scholars to talk about the work that's happening in their area of praxis. However, this is only the beginning of what we see as a much longer conversation. As a field, we still must systematically explore how this new era of #RhetOps impacts our pedagogy in terms of ethics, information literacy, and tool understanding and construction. How do we teach our students to be critical consumers and creators of weaponized social media? How do we teach undergraduates and graduates to spot and trace influence campaigns in real time? These are some of the questions we still need to explore.

On July 9, 2015, US Central Command published an announcement that the United States and the United Arab Emirates had launched an "online messaging, engagement center to counter ISIL" called the Sawab Center.[14] The center's mission is to "create and share its content, including text, graphics, video clips and animations. Since they were formed in 2015, the Sawab Center has produced dozens of infographics, short videos, and tweeted almost 15,000 times in Arabic and English to an audience of almost 665,000 followers.[15] Initiatives such as these were on former President Obama's mind. In his April 2016 interview with President Obama in the *Atlantic Monthly*, Jeffrey Goldberg writes that President Obama "thinks rhetoric should be weaponized sparingly, if at all, in today's more ambiguous and complicated international arena" although we've already seen some selective examples such as joint US-UAE initiative.

In current conflicts imbued with digital actors, it is sometimes difficult to discern the complexities of collaborative authorship and distribution, leading to what we call *a fog of digital rhetoric*. With this term, we aim to define the way that the digitally accelerated and distributed composing, delivery, and circulation of #RhetOps material by state and non-state actors creates literacy conditions ripe for doubt regarding the authorship, purpose, sponsorship, and motivation of digital texts, their compositionists, and amplifiers. A fog of digital rhetoric is a complicated set of digital circumstances related to volume of texts, speed of their travel, hazy ethos behind their delivery and circulation, and difficulty to track the full picture that require a combination of information literacy and understanding of digital rhetoric and compositional strategies to understand, decode, and potentially counter.

For example, in April 2018 the *Intercept* published a story about how the Guatemalan government has a "net center" that participates in concerted campaigns of "political social media manipulation."[16] For individuals on the newsfeed-receiving end of these "net center" influence campaign texts, the information literacy challenge to decode these texts is steep. Identifying the infrastructure of propagating messages, while only seeing a small sliver of a text's circulation, is a challenge itself. Beyond that, to identify who is composing and amplifying digital texts through human and nonhuman networks such as a combination of well-manicured social media accounts and botnets is even more daunting.

In addition, though not completely indistinct from military investments in digital rhetoric, we note here two specific trends that add urgency to the need for rhetoric studies to take up serious study of #RhetOps. The first is the massive, disruptive potential that social media provides to engage in what Jim Ridolfo has described elsewhere as a strategic act of delivery: composing for appropriation.[17] This may be disruptive in the sense of sowing confusion about authorship and doubt over political messaging, a fog of digital rhetoric, or it may also amplify violence and terrorism. In their article on "rhetorical velocity," Ridolfo and Devoss theorize the way networks provide not only the means to publish but also to push a message such that it spreads further and faster.[18] Seeking this "push" or textual amplification—aiming for others to see and share a message in whole or with some modifications—is an act of multimodal composition. There are a number of reasons for achieving a text's amplification, including the increasing appetite for sound and visual media in social media platforms such as Facebook, Twitter, and YouTube.

Critical to understanding the fog of digital rhetoric, and an important contributing trend we want to identify is one that Ryan Omizo explores in his chapter: the rise of automated scripts and machine-learning technologies—combined to create robots (or bots) capable of carrying out rhetorical operations. The capacity to conduct large scale and contemporaneous corpus analysis in real time on social networks and to write back into these evolving discourses creates significant disruptive potential. We note that since the late 1970s, rhetoric and writing studies has taken artificial intelligence and its influence on human rhetorical activity seriously, but *only* occasionally. Carolyn Miller[19] and Lynette Hunter[20] are two significant voices in this conversation, along with Kennedy.[21] Miller, in particular, has kept a very important question before us: wherein lies human rhetorical agency when machines and humans write together.[22] These once-theoretical questions seem pragmatic today as social media users must ask: Am I interacting with a real person? Related questions may well be encountered by graduates of university digital writing and rhetoric programs during a job interview: "Can you help build a bot for us that will influence public opinion?" These are just a few of the foggy and ethical digital rhetoric situations we imagine our students encountering and negotiating.

This new landscape of machine rhetorics encompasses not a future but, to borrow an oft-cited phrase from the cyberpunk fiction writer William Gibson, the unevenly distributed present-day circumstances of "assistive writing technologies"—commonly known as bots—that are increasingly incorporated into the writing process. Advanced bots are already in use by newswire services to draft sports and financial reports.[23] We may soon live in a world where most day-to-day writing tasks do not begin with a human creating a first draft, but with a machine assembling one from a personal archive of words. Robots may soon build new and rhetorically situated texts from a human's previous lifetime activity as a writer. While this has practical implications for assisting people with mundane tasks such as managing their email volume, there are also military applications. In conflict situations or even in sales and marketing campaigns, robots are impersonating human actors, employing what appear to be popular movements on social media (practices called *astroturfing* or *sockpuppeting*), aggregating into large botnets for psychological operations and influence campaigns. Machine learning, data mining, and user profiling can also be employed to find military targets by locating "influencers," human actors who hold significant persuasive power over others in a particular community, and target them with rhetorically tailored messaging.

The tactics employed in these kinds of operations can be familiar, but the tools to train these machine learners do not exist apart from the expertise and knowledge represented in this collection—both by the authors and those they cite. It is the formulations of rhetoric scholars and language researchers more broadly—our rubrics, our text corpuses, and our data sets—that are needed to proceed with a rhetorical education for malicious robots. The work we have done to monitor #RhetOps as a category of activity reported via social media tells us that rhetoric scholars may already be implicated in much of this activity by virtue of our work having influence and/or operational value in these contexts, whether most of us know it or not. As the contributors show in the next three sections, the application of rhetorical thinking to present-day conflicts, and, increasingly, our field knowledge, is already happening. For this reason, it is time for our field to be directly involved in how and if our disciplinary knowledge is used to wage war, engage in conflict, and clear the fog of digital rhetoric.

In chapter 8, for example, Michael Trice takes us on a tour of some of these related issues by closely examining the 2014 GamerGate hate campaign targeting leading women in video game development and journalism. Similarly, in chapter 9 William M. Marcellino and Madeline Magnuson examine how we may look at the digital social war talk footprint of the Islamic State as an aggregate corpus of texts in order to derive tactical and strategic countermeasures. In chapter 8 we see some of the tactical problems for those attempting to counter hateful internet speech. In chapter 9 we see a moment of hope in Marcellino and Magnuson's large-scale data analysis work in Twitter. In chapters 8 and 9 there's a common thread of how ubiquitous digital delivery and robots are creating new opportunities for state and non-state actors to compose and take advantage of confusion surrounding the origins and circulation of texts but also of how those techniques may be countered, albeit with a temporal disadvantage, by the same digital fog.

OVERVIEW OF CHAPTERS

In the next sixteen chapters, contributors with experience in academia, the US military, nongovernment agencies, and law enforcement discuss the role of digital rhetoric and conflict, not as a form of resolution but as an instrument with broad applications for how states project their power, police, fight wars, and engage symmetric and asymmetric adversaries. The book is organized into three parts.

In part 1, "Rhetorical Operations and Emerging Tactics," authors outline how the military and intelligence community understand rhetorical theory and information warfare. In chapter 1, "The Rhetoric of Infrastructure: American Colonialism and the Military Telegraph," Elizabeth Losh asks readers to consider the role the telegraph played in the coordination of intelligence, troop movements, resource management, and the suffering of Indigenous people that both built and were colonized by that infrastructure. In chapter 2, "'A Soldier's Guide to Rhetorical Theory': Intelligence Analysis in the Open," Gary Mills reflects on the publication of his *The Role of Rhetorical Theory in Military Intelligence Analysis* (2003). Drawing on Benjamin Fountain, Mills advocates for a critical consciousness or empowered critical thinking to "detect and defeat influence operations." In chapter 3, "Rhetoric and the US Intelligence Community's Misuses of Theory," Nate Kreuter argues that intelligence communities' use and weaponization of theory often backfires against their own mission. Looking at the "extraordinary rendition program" developed by the Central Intelligence Agency, Kreuter questions how the intelligence community (IC) adopts and puts into praxis theory from other disciplines. In chapter 4, "Insurgent Rhetorics and Historical Materialism," Mike Edwards asks readers to question the "blurring of the line between the open hand of rhetoric and the closed fist of force that occurs in rhetorical operations." In chapter 5, "Minerva Rising: The Pentagon's Weaponization of Rhetorical Knowledge," John Gagnon examines how the military is developing tools for "information capabilities" as part of their military research.

In chapters 6 and 7 authors look at some of the recent historical practices that inform digital information warfare. In chapter 6, "Insurgent Circulation,

Weaponized Media: Waging the Late Sixties War Within," Brad Lucas looks at Weather Underground and argues that social movement rhetorics in the 1960s serve "as a precursor for Rhet Ops." In chapter 7, "GamerGate: Understanding the Tactics of Online Knowledge Disruptors," Michael Trice takes readers into current events and outlines a concept called the *dissentivist* ethic, "a community ethic driven first and foremost by disrupting consensus" that's "driving much of the current deliberative environment online, an ethic that played directly" into recent state Rhet Ops campaigns.

For part 2, "Digital Practices," contributors provide a window into how digital tools may be used to gather, detect, and act upon or counter rhetorical operations. In chapter 8, "ISIS versus the United States: Rhetorical Battle in the Middle East," William M. Marcellino and Madeline Magnuson draw on tools from digital rhetoric and corpus linguistics to show how ISIS "war talk" may be analyzed and understood. In chapter 9, "Stormwatch: Machine Learning Approaches to Understanding White Supremacy Online," Ryan Omizo uses the faciloscope tool, a rhetorical analysis tool developed by Omizo and Hart-Davidson, to analyze discussion threads on a white supremacy website in order to see how hate is facilitated by white supremacist members. In chapter 10, "Dark Interactions: Interfaces and Object Arrays as Surveillance in Digital Rhetoric," John Gallagher looks at how self-reported data may be weaponized by intelligence agencies. Similarly, in chapter 11, "Digital Surveillance of Gang Communication: Graffiti's Rhetorical Velocity between Street Gangs and Urban Law Enforcement," Seth Long and Ken Fitch show how the Los Angeles County Sheriff's Department's graffiti-tracking database is used to map and police the city.

In the third and final section, "Practitioner Stories," we present practitioner stories of varying length from individuals and institutions that have experience with digital rhetoric and military conflict. We were especially interested in accounts that might serve as cases for further analysis, as well as situations that complicate conventional understanding of conflict and/or rhetoric. In chapter 12, "Digital Age Education: Preparing Warriors for Hybrid Conflict at Air Force CyberWorx," Jeffrey Collins and Gary Mills discuss the implications for hybrid warfare and "rhetorical arsenals" and the blueprint for the Air Force CyberWorx, an initiative to train future soldiers to be "responsible for the protection, maintenance, enhancement, and use of cyber technologies—weapons capable of swiftly complicating or calming down the doomsday narrative." Building on this theme in chapter 13, "Mapping the Rhetoric-Operations Divide: Considerations for the Future," Angie Mallory discusses her road to rhetorical operations and some of the future concerns for people working at the intersection of both areas. In chapter 14, "Social

Media Strategy for the Military-Engaged American Red Cross," Laura A. Ewing provides a compelling case example about how social media policy is created, enacted, and reconsidered in a nonprofit that works closely with the US military. In chapter 15, "Changing Technologies and Writing from and about War," D. Alexis Hart and Cheryl Hatch draw specifically from Hatch's own experience as a war correspondent, as well as her interviews with other conflict journalists. Finally, in chapter 16, "Military Wives as Rhetorical Insurgents: Resisting Assimilation as 'Force Multipliers,'" Elise Dixon examines the rhetorical instructions she was provided as the spouse of a Marine.

NOTES

1. M. Alex Johnson, "Gunman Sent Package to NBC News," NBCNews.com, http://www.nbcnews.com/id/18195423/ns/us_news-crime_and_courts/t/gunman-sent-package-nbc-news/#.WtO4KpPwb-Y.

2. As of April 17, 2018.

3. Kimmage and Ridolfo, "Iraqi Insurgent Media," 34–35.

4. Katz, "Ethic of Expediency," 255–75.

5. Gurak, *Persuasion and Privacy in Cyberspace.*

6. Ward, *Deadly Documents.*

7. Marcellino, "Revisioning Strategic Communication," 52–57.

8. Salazar, "Caliphate of Culture?" 343–54.

9. Tufekci, *Twitter and Tear Gas.*

10. O'Neil, *Weapons of Math Destruction.*

11. Pedahzur, "Military Entrepreneurs and the Evolution of Special Operations Forces."

12. Barrett, *Islamic State*, 51.

13. Obama, "Remarks by the President."

14. Redfield, "US, UAE Launch Online Messaging."

15. As of April 2018.

16. Currier and Mackey, "Rise of the Net Center."

17. Ridolfo, "Rhetorical Delivery as Strategy," 117–29.

18. Ridolfo and DeVoss, "Composing for Recomposition," n2.

19. Miller, "Technology as a Form of Consciousness," 228–36; Miller, "Opportunity, Opportunism, and Progress," 81–96; Miller, "Writing in a Culture of Simulation," 58; Miller, "What Can Automation Tell Us about Agency?" 137–57; Miller, "Should We Name the Tools?" 19–38.

20. Hunter, "Rhetoric and Artificial Intelligence," 317–40; Hunter, *Critiques of Knowing.*

21. Kennedy, "Textual Curators and Writing Machines"; Kennedy and Long, "Trees within the Forest," 140.

22. Miller, "Technology as a Form of Consciousness," 228–36; Miller, "Opportunity, Opportunism, and Progress," 81–96; Miller, "Writing in a Culture of Simulation," 58; Miller, "What Can Automation Tell Us about Agency?" 137–57; Miller, "Should We Name the Tools?" 19–38.

23. Van Dalen, "Algorithms behind the Headlines," 648–58; Ward, *Deadly Documents.*

REFERENCES

Barrett, Richard. *The Islamic State*. Soufan Group, 2014.

Currier, Cora, and Danielle Mackey. "The Rise of the Net Center: How an Army of Trolls Protects Guatemala's Corrupt Elite." *Intercept*, April 7, 2018. https://theintercept.com/2018/04/07/guatemala-anti-corruption-trolls-smear-campaign/.

Goldberg, Jeffrey. "The Obama Doctrine." *Atlantic*, April 2016, 70–90.

Gries, Laurie E. "Iconographic Tracking: A Digital Research Method for Visual Rhetoric and Circulation Studies." *Computers and Composition* 30, no. 4 (2013): 332–48.

Gurak, Laura J. *Persuasion and Privacy in Cyberspace: The Online Protests over Lotus Marketplace and the Clipper Chip*. New Haven, CT: Yale University Press, 1999.

Hart, D. Alexis, and Mike Edwards. "Rhetoric, Technology, and the Military." *Kairos: A Journal of Rhetoric, Technology, and Pedagogy* 14 (2010).

Hunter, Lynette. *Critiques of Knowing: Situated Textualities in Science, Computing and the Arts*. London: Routledge, 2002.

Hunter, Lynette. "Rhetoric and Artificial Intelligence." *Rhetorica* 9, no. 4 (1991): 317–40.

Kassel, Whitney. "The Army Needs Anthropologists." *Foreign Policy*, July 28, 2015. https://foreignpolicy.com/2015/07/28/the-army-needs-anthropologists-iraq-afghanistan-human-terrain/.

Katz, Steven B. "The Ethic of Expediency: Classical Rhetoric, Technology, and the Holocaust." *College English* 54, no. 3 (1992): 255–75.

Kennedy, Krista A. "Textual Curators and Writing Machines: Authorial Agency in Encyclopedias, Print to Digital." PhD diss., University of Minnesota, 2009.

Kennedy, Krista, and Seth Long. "The Trees within the Forest: Extracting, Coding, and Visualizing Subjective Data in Authorship Studies." In *Rhetoric and the Digital Humanities*, edited by Jim Ridolfo and William Hart-Davidson, 140–51. Chicago: University of Chicago Press, 2015.

Kimmage, Daniel, and Kathleen Ridolfo. "Iraqi Insurgent Media: The War of Images and Ideas: How Sunni Insurgents in Iraq and Their Supporters Worldwide Are Using the Media." Radio Free Europe/Radio Liberty, 2007.

Lee, Carol E. "Obama Says 'Progress Made' in Fight against Islamic State." *Wall Street Journal*, July 6, 2015. https://www.wsj.com/articles/obama-to-get-pentagon-briefing-on-islamic-state-1436197198.

Longo, Bernadette. *Spurious Coin: A History of Science, Management, and Technical Writing*. Albany: SUNY Press, 2000.

Marcellino, William M. "Revisioning Strategic Communication Through Rhetoric and Discourse Analysis." *Joint Force Quarterly* 76, no. 1 (2015): 52–57.

Miller, Carolyn R. "Opportunity, Opportunism, and Progress: Kairos in the Rhetoric of Technology." *Argumentation* 8, no. 1 (1994): 81–96.

Miller, Carolyn R. "Should We Name the Tools? Concealing and Revealing the Art of Rhetoric." In *Public Work of Rhetoric: Citizen-Scholars and Civic Engagement*, edited by John M. Ackerman, David J. Coogan, and Gerard A. Hauser, 19–38. Columbia: University of South Carolina Press, 2010.

Miller, Carolyn R. "Technology as a Form of Consciousness: A Study of Contemporary Ethos." *Communication Studies* 29, no. 4 (1978): 228–36.

Miller, Carolyn R. "What Can Automation Tell Us about Agency?" *Rhetoric Society Quarterly* 37, no. 2 (2007): 137–57.

Miller, Carolyn R. "Writing in a Culture of Simulation." *Towards a Rhetoric of Everyday Life: New Directions in Research on Writing, Text, and Discourse*, edited by Martin Nystrand and John Duffy, 58. Madison: University of Wisconsin Press, 2003.

Obama, Barack. "Remarks by the President on Progress in the Fight Against ISIL." National Archives and Records Administration, July 6, 2015. https://obamawhitehouse.archives.gov/the-press-office/2015/07/06/remarks-president-progress-fight-against-isil.

O'Neil, Cathy. *Weapons of Math Destruction: How Big Data Increases Inequality and Threatens Democracy.* New York: Broadway Books, 2017.

Pedahzur, Ami. "Military Entrepreneurs and the Evolution of Special Operations Forces." Working paper, University of Texas, 2016. DOI: 10.13140/RG. 2.1. 3485.0647.

Perelman, Les. "Construct Validity, Length, Score, and Time in Holistically Graded Writing Assessments: The Case against Automated Essay Scoring (AES)." In *International Advances in Writing Research: Cultures, Places, Measures*, edited by Jessica Early, Karen Lunsford, Suzie Null, Paul Rogers, and Amanda Stansell, 121–31. Fort Collins, CO: WAC Clearinghouse and Parlor Press, 2012.

Redfield, John. "US, UAE Launch Online Messaging, Engagement Center to Counter ISIL." US Central Command, July 9, 2015. http://www.centcom.mil/MEDIA/NEWS-ARTICLES/News-Article-View/Article/885201/us-uae-launch-online-messaging-engagement-center-to-counter-isil/.

Ridolfo, Jim. "Rhetorical Delivery as Strategy: Rebuilding the Fifth Canon from Practitioner Stories." *Rhetoric Review* 31, no. 2 (2012): 117–29.

Ridolfo, Jim, and Dànielle Nicole DeVoss. "Composing for Recomposition: Rhetorical Velocity and Delivery." *Kairos: A Journal of Rhetoric, Technology, and Pedagogy* 13, no. 2 (2009): n2.

Ridolfo, Jim, and Martine Courant Rife. "Rhetorical Velocity and Copyright: A Case Study on Strategies of Rhetorical Delivery." In *Copy(write): Intellectual Property in the Writing Classroom*, edited by Martine Courant Rife, Shaun Slattery, and Dànielle Nicole DeVoss. Perspectives on Writing. Fort Collins, CO: WAC Clearinghouse and Parlor Press, 2011. Available at https://innovationtest2.colostate.edu/books/perspectives/copywrite/.

Salazar, Philippe-Joseph. "A Caliphate of Culture? ISIS's Rhetorical Power." *Philosophy & Rhetoric* 49, no. 3 (2016): 343–54.

Sheridan, David Michael, Jim Ridolfo, and Anthony J. Michel. *The Available Means of Persuasion: Mapping a Theory and Pedagogy of Multimodal Public Rhetoric.* Anderson, SC: Parlor Press, 2012.

Tufekci, Zeynep. *Twitter and Tear Gas: The Power and Fragility of Networked Protest.* New Haven, CT: Yale University Press, 2017.

Van Dalen, Arjen. "The Algorithms behind the Headlines: How Machine-Written News Redefines the Core Skills of Human Journalists." *Journalism Practice* 6, no. 5/6 (2012): 648–58.

Ward, Mark. *Deadly Documents: Technical Communication, Organizational Discourse, and the Holocaust: Lessons from the Rhetorical Work of Everyday Texts.* London: Routledge, 2016.

PART I

RHETORICAL OPERATIONS AND EMERGING TACTICS

1

THE RHETORIC OF INFRASTRUCTURE

AMERICAN COLONIALISM AND THE MILITARY TELEGRAPH

ELIZABETH LOSH

Adolphus Washington Greely's importance to the history of American rhetoric had much more to do with his role supervising the installation of thousands of miles of telegraph cable than it did with his notable position as an author of speeches, correspondence, and a dramatic memoir about leading the polar expedition that first made him a national celebrity. He was chief of the disastrous Lady Franklin Bay voyage that devolved into firing squads and cannibalism, but Greely's career was recuperated after the debacle. He went on to receive the Medal of Honor for his service as an architect of electric communications infrastructure during the height of American colonialism when the United States occupied several formerly Spanish possessions in the Caribbean and the Pacific. Although initially greeted as potential liberators from Spain, US troops actively suppressed nationalist movements for Filipino independence. In battle with both Spanish and Filipino forces, the US military relied on telegraphic communication to convey intelligence, coordinate troop movements, and manage resources. So significant were Greely's contributions that in 1898 President William McKinley dedicated three paragraphs of his annual message to Congress to the achievements of the US Army Signal Corps in establishing the cable infrastructure that McKinley saw as vital to success in the Spanish-American War and realizing colonial ambitions in the decades that followed.

Greely's story as chief signal officer and the history of the military telegraph can be taken as a case study for framing a rhetorical theory of infrastructure. Such a theory recognizes how media studies and science and technology studies have become increasingly interrelated, and it deepens understanding of the canon of delivery. As Lisa Parks and Nicole Starosielski argue in their work on media infrastructures, it can be productive to pay less attention to "screened content" and more attention to "how content moves through the world and how this movement affects content's form."[1] By attending to media infrastructures rather than just media interfaces, it is possible to expand the concept of reception to include more aspects of distribution and to ask questions about what aspects of communication are intentionally assumed to be background conditions and consigned to positions of ideological invisibility.

The infrastructure of the military telegraph can be seen as a large-scale material assemblage of objects: cable, relay equipment, signal offices, warehouses, and specialized cable ships like the *Burnside* or the *Romulus*. However, the infrastructure of the military telegraph also required human labor and knowledge work involving specifications and standards. According to Leigh Star, infrastructure can be both concrete and abstract and composed of inanimate material objects and human actors. As Star and Ruhleder define infrastructure: "It is both engine and barrier for change; both customizable and rigid; both inside and outside organizational practices. It is product and process."[2] In the case of the expansion of the military telegraph in the Caribbean and Philippine archipelagos, Greely directed the human labor, material resources, procedural standards, and publication regimes that produced a contemporary communication infrastructure analogous—and in many ways—predictive of our own in establishing the path dependencies that still dictate much of the traffic of internet flows in a global network of submarine cables. From short connectors bridging components of mesh networks strung by activists high above modern cities to high-speed data fibers connecting real estate in the financial sector, the physical infrastructures of wired communications still matter. Furthermore, the ways in which notions of wirelessness from the Philippine occupation captivated the popular imagination suggest that fantasies of untethered connections can coexist with tangible reminders of deep infrastructural investments.

Of course, I am not the first to consider how predigital communication may have raised similar questions about sovereignty, subjectivity, and connection in earlier ages of electricity that remain relevant to our digital present. Katherine Hayles has claimed that telegraphy specifically altered "relations of language and code, bodily practices and technocratic regimes," and validated the "messages and cultural imaginaries" of "technogenetic feedback loops" that anticipated "the epigenetic changes associated with digital technologies, especially fast communication and the virtualization of commodities."[3] Building on the work of James Carey, who argued that telegraphy standardized time and separated communication and transportation, as well as information and physical goods, John Durham Peters has asserted that the telegraph also served as a powerful metaphor for "conjuring physical bodies and bodies politic"[4]—thus reconfiguring cosmology—and as a means for "numerical calculation and diagrammatic illustration" rather than just as a "storehouse for speech."[5] Unlike Carey, Peters considers this history of technology to be global and comparative by necessity rather than an expression of American exceptionalism. Recently, Grant Bollmer has posited a longer history of the "nodal citizen" in social media that dates back to conceptualizing railroad and telegraph infrastructures; he mines the use of the term *network* in nineteenth-century publications to bolster his claims. Bollmer also acknowledges the important contributions of Laura Otis to his thinking and cites her work on imagining "wired love" of various kinds in literary works as a way to conceptualize communicating with bodies and machines. In each of these rhetorical situations—poetic inspiration, financial manipulation, scientific speculation, philosophical investigation, political participation, or erotic intrigue—infrastructure serves as an important rhetorical actor. After all, access to the network could be constrained, connectivity could fail, and coding and encoding messages depend upon the technical expertise of trained knowledge workers.

SPEAKING FOR INFRASTRUCTURE

In speaking for his infrastructural accomplishments as a creator of official maps, reports, and manuals, Greely displayed politically savvy rhetorical strategies that marked him as an accomplished writer and document designer. His elaborate maps of cable networks for the military telegraph in "Porto Rico" and the Philippines were published by *National Geographic*, and these posters can still be purchased by cartographic enthusiasts today. The purple prose of Greely's reports often described perilous conditions for Signal Corps personnel in dramatic and heroic terms, whether it be in Alaska—which was characterized by "early springs, late autumns, enormous snowfalls, summer floods, impassable can[y]ons,"[6] or in Texas—where "Indians armed with their enemies' fire-power" dominated the landscape.[7] The foes of the military telegraph in the Philippines were particularly determined: "Destruction of sections of 2, 3, or even 5 miles of line was not unusual, but the climax was reached in the total destruction of 38 miles of line, every insulator being broken, every bracket destroyed or removed, every pole cut down and the entire wire carried away."[8] In contrast to his works written for legislators, Greely's manual on "the methods of laying and repairing cables, the installation of offices, the operations of cables, and their proper testing for faults and electrical conditions" imagined a clear ideal reader who was addressed as "an intelligent and resourceful officer" committed to "thorough and careful study."

FIGURE 1.1. Photograph from the Adolphus Greely Collection at the National Archives, Washington, DC.

As a rhetorical actor, the infrastructure itself generally tended to be a silent presence. Alan Liu and Matthew Gold have described such infrastructure as "normally mute." "Until something breaks, decays, or, as in heritage infrastructure, needs to be remembered or recapitalized. Then it speaks. Especially at moments of ruin or risk, infrastructure speaks eloquently about those who otherwise leave little textual evidence behind but instead a dreadful or artful material history—tracks at a border wall, inscriptions on the walls of the Angel Island immigrant cells, or graffiti on a bridge." In the account of Liu and Gold, infrastructure vocalizes in response to exigencies of duress and reveals vulnerabilities rather than strengths as sites of potential inscription. Similarly, in borrowing from the literature of art and design and the ideas of Manuel de Sola Morales about "urban acupuncture," Deb Verhoeven has suggested that the portmanteau *infrapuncture* might be a useful term to draw attention to how infrastructure reveals sites of "suffering and damage" and "where it hurts in society."

The suffering of the Indigenous people who often performed the most grueling infrastructural labor under Greely's supervision in laying the military telegraph beneath the sea, through the jungle, up stairways, and over mountain tops might be imagined indirectly by studying the large collection of photographs and documentary evidence that Greely donated to the National Archives. Clearly Native peoples were integral to the tasks of constructing the elaborate infrastructure, since they are shown in Greely's photographs stringing cable across waterways, riding boats on exploratory expeditions, unloading cable from cable yards and from the holds of ships, and climbing trees and steadying ladders. Of course, much of this labor was not voluntary. A caption informs us that one image shows "Insurgent Prisoners Trenching Shore-End of Cable."

Other tasks of infrastructural care and repair were often delegated to oppressed colonial subjects who were only nominally more free under American rule than the prisoners captured by Greely's army. A laudatory biography of Greely describes how the author demanded compliance from villagers who might resent having their land requisitioned for the US military's communication network. "As we had no means of protecting our line behind us, I let it be known everywhere we saw natives that if the wire was molested in any way, or if it was cut and not repaired at once, that the houses for two miles on each side of the road would be burned and all the cattle and horses killed. It was cut in a couple of places by retreating insurgents but immediately repaired by the inhabitants."[9]

American territorial claims over waterways were even more dramatic, since the Pacific Ocean was declared to be a "navigable water of the United States," and the commercial telegraph companies that succeeded the Signal Corps refused to request landing rights in the Philippines.[10] The tropical forests of Southeast Asia had already been despoiled by the clear cutting of trees for gutta-percha, a natural plastic widely used for insulation in submarine cables throughout the nineteenth century, which was "obtained by profligate, inefficient, and ultimately unsustainable methods of extraction, which killed the tree in the process."[11] By 1905 gutta-percha had been replaced by an amalgam of jute, tape, rubber, and armor wire to insulate telegraph cables, but the extractive economy that made undersea cable a valuable commodity remained in place.

As part of the tropical ecosystem, US military telegraphy was also attempting to rationalize and routinize natural forces. Weather stations had been dear to Greely's heart since his participation in the First International Polar Year (1882–1883), but these outposts also came to support technological practices like aerial reconnaissance and background state monitoring during colonial expansion. Thus it could be argued that even the most benign aspects of US telegraphy might have come to undermine both individual privacy and access to democratic participation in the public sphere. In this way James Fleming has argued that it is possible to construct an "alternative history of meteorological services by demonstrating that the primary postwar mission of the Signal Corps maintaining a national storm warning and telegraphic weather service was intimately linked to national strategies of domestic surveillance and social control."[12]

Certainly the infrastructures of communication technology were often seen as a facilitator of the colonial mission. However, Deep Kanta Lahiri Choudhury's work on "telegraphic imperialism" that focuses on the case study of the occupation of India by the British Empire questions the narrative of Indigenous recipients of telegraphy as "passive receptors of technology transfer."[13] In rethinking notions of center and periphery, Choudhury suggests that with new infrastructural conditions time, space, and language changed for the occupiers as well as for the occupied. Such "telegraphic imperialism," in Choudhury's terms, forced the colonizers to grapple with "information panics" of their own as they observed the workings of a surveillance state.[14]

In this way the military telegraph also represents an enormous chorus of complaints from potential injured parties: the Signal Corps officers described by Greely who endured difficult tours of duty, the Indigenous laborers who performed infrastructural labor under the duress of captivity or hostage conditions, the ecosystem that underwent the degradation of extractive technologies, the rule of law that was compromised by unchecked territorial expansion by the international community, and the remote citizens of the metropole who became the future subjects of the surveillance state that they enabled. These various forms of violence also became subjects for debate, discussion, and deliberation in a range of networked publics in the United States, where legislators, journalists, and members of the general public examined possible forms of compensation, remediation, and redress.

FIGURING THE TELEGRAPH IN POLITICAL DEBATES

Although the United States seemed to have dashed the hopes of revolutionaries in Cuba, the Philippines, and other formerly Spanish colonial possessions hoping for American allyship, assertions that technological development would reward colonial subjects for their patience under political subjugation were common. Such arguments were often advanced by pro-expansionist advocates, who were led by President McKinley, Vice President Theodore Roosevelt, and the newspaper tycoon William Randolph Hearst. The pro-expansionists portrayed conquest as a duty and asserted that the domination of Pacific island nations was a necessary stepping-stone to the markets of China that signified the coming of age of American global power. Anti-imperialists who championed "government by consent" included the presidential candidate William Jennings Bryan, the writer Mark Twain, the suffragist Susan B. Anthony, the labor leader Samuel Gompers, and the activist scholar W. E. B. Dubois. Members of the Anti-Imperialist League were dismayed by accounts of war crimes and human rights violations in an armed conflict that lasted for over a dozen years after it seemed to disappear from the headlines as newsworthy. The Anti-Imperialist League was often vilified in the press as an unpatriotic and seditious organization populated with traitors. Although the heated rhetoric of the period has subsided, only relatively recently has the Library of Congress heading for "Philippine Insurrection" been replaced by "Philippine Independence," and other legacies of the conflict have been memorialized by members of the continuing Filipino diaspora.

Pro-expansionist advocates often invoked technological progress as a way to justify US rule of territories liberated from Spanish occupation. For example, in 1898 Indiana senator Albert Beveridge rebutted the argument that US territories should be contiguous in order to maintain the necessary proximity of a coherent nation-state. He argued that "in 1819 Florida was farther from New York than Porto [*sic*] Rico is from Chicago today; Texas, farther from Washington in 1845 than Hawaii is from Boston in 1898; California, more inaccessible in 1847 than the Philippines are now." According to Beveridge, great oceans do "not separate us from lands of our duty and desire," because "the oceans join us," just as "electricity joins us," since "the very elements are in league with our destiny."

To see telegraphic networks of infrastructural connection as ones that reduced geographic scale and bridged distance was not uncommon in the colonial imaginaries of the period. For example, one famous 1892 *Punch* cartoon called "The Rhodes Colossus" showed the businessman, mining magnate, and politician Cecil Rhodes astride the continent of Africa with his legs spread wide and with his arms holding the telegraph line from Cairo to Cape Town. Although a similar 1898 cartoon called "The Colossus of the Pacific" in the *Chicago Tribune* that visualized a giant Uncle Sam bridging the bodies of water with his legs does not depict images of telegraphy, other images explicitly associated the iconic caricature of the United States with infrastructures of communication technology.

As the debate between pro-expansionists and anti-imperialists intensified in the United States, references to telegraphic infrastructure abounded in political cartoons. Often the bringing of the telegraph was shown as a sign of US generosity that was transported as part of what was commonly called the "white man's burden"—borrowing from Rudyard Kipling's anthem to British colonialism that was adapted by Americans on all political sides. Such burdens were supposedly shouldered altruistically by white saviors to help the less fortunate. In some cartoons, symbolic representatives of the United States uplifted, cradled, or supported the bodies of Native peoples; in other cartoons these ambassadors of goodwill bore a heavy load of gifts that symbolized American generosity. Even when Uncle Sam was not literally carrying telegraph poles on his shoulders, a similar progress narrative might be advanced in pro-colonial publications. For example, a *Judge* cartoon from 1900 showed telegraph poles in a white-tired automobile labeled "progress" driven by Uncle Sam. The US bounty in the cargo also included streetcars, locomotives, and tomes labeled "education." The vehicle was shown driving uphill on a mountain road blocked by a Chinese dragon. The cartoon's caption read "Some One Must Back Up."

In contemporary visual culture, Indigenous peoples in early twentieth-century American colonies were often portrayed as technologically backward and incompetent adopters of inventions arriving from the United States.[15] A cartoon from an 1899 edition of the *Philadelphia Press* titled "The Filipinos Adopt American Ideas" showed a grotesque organ-grinder attached to a monkey begging with a cup labeled "CASH" who was connected to his subhuman counterpart with a long wire next to a "SIGNAL SERVICE STATION" banner.[16] Other Filipinos in the scene are similarly shown cavorting with animals and engaging in ridiculous behavior.

At the same time, images of high-tech connectivity could also be shown to be a means for representing colonial sadism and unequal power relationships. A Charles Bartholomew cartoon from 1899 depicted the Filipino revolutionary politician Emilio Aguinaldo's torment while attached to a box labeled "DR. OTIS SEVERE ELECTRO-MILITARY TREATMENT."[17] Lightning bolts emanate from where Aguinaldo's hands are attached to the device and he begs for respite as he repeats the words "ENOUGH!! ENOUGH!! ENOUGH!! ENOUGH!" The illustration suggests that for the pro-independence leader of the Philippines, to be connected by wires was analogous to electrocution.

General Otis led troops engaged in the Battle of Manila and refused cease-fire negotiations with Aguinaldo; he was also known for maintaining tight control over access to the telegraph network. Journalists covering battles in the Philippines for publications like *Harper's Magazine* or *Collier's Weekly* were allowed relative freedom to travel and confer with troops far from the chain of command, but they had to contend with what they saw as excessive censorship under Otis's leadership when attempting to cable stories home to their news bureaus because the army controlled the one telegraph line out of Manila and reviewed all press reports. Reporters accused Otis of "fixing casualty reports, overrating military accomplishments, and underestimating the Filipinos' commitment to independence" by monopolizing access to communication networks.[18]

Alternative telegraph channels were unavailable to writers questioning the official story of war in the Philippines because Spanish authorities had limited the spread of the cable networks within their nineteenth-century possessions due to their fear of empowering revolutionaries.[19] In one 1899 cartoon in the *Record*, Otis's attempt to control access to telecommunications infrastructure was compared to blocking use of water infrastructure. The general is shown barricading the top of the "PHILIPPINE WELL OF FACTS" with the boards of "CENSORSHIP" while "GET ME OUT" messages leak out through the cracks.[20]

When represented as an apparatus of wired connections in political cartoons, the telegraph was presented as a tangible good indicating either the benevolence of the American charitable mission for development or the just consideration that might be expected in reciprocal exchanges with the United States for raw materials from the islands. As an investment-intensive assemblage of infrastructural components, the telegraph can be presented as concrete benefit to the Indigenous people of the Philippines, even if popular representations may perpetuate sadistic rhetorics of punishing insurgents, dehumanize Filipinos as potential users of the device, or reinforce the myth of the "white man's burden." Opponents of imperialist agendas could also demand access to the device as a utility channel for journalistic messages that could provide more truthful coverage of the brutality of tactics of total warfare or guerilla combat.

THE WIRELESS IMAGINATION

Strangely, many of these US political cartoons from the war with the Philippines showed futuristic wireless technologies rather than existing wired telegraphy. Cartoonists created images that assumed transmission techniques would soon carry signal broadcasts through the air without the technically challenging and costly cable infrastructures that President McKinley had praised in his message about Greely's accomplishments. Even though Marconi's famed wireless telegraph had claimed a greatly improved range from 80 miles to 2,000 miles by 1902, wireless transmissions were still often impracticably expensive and would have required relay ships to connect the US network to its colonial possessions. The 8,500-mile distance between Washington, DC, and Manila continued to be covered by the material infrastructure of suboceanic cables throughout the war. Yet in the popular imagination these remote territories could communicate with each other through transcendent invisible means auto-magically rather than via existing wired technologies.

The potential costs of connectivity to Indigenous people facing the US military were understood during this period, and risks of extermination from contact with the forces of Manifest Destiny could be represented with references to Marconi's wireless invention. Even in publications that supported the US colonial presence in the Philippines, such as *Puck* and *Judge*, telegraphy was understood to be capable of bringing messages about the prodigious capacities for violence from a more dominant military power. In an issue of *Judge* from 1899, a Victor Gillam cartoon shows a wireless telegraph being used as a communication device between tribal peoples in the United States and those in the Philippines facing extinction.[21] In front of a teepee with a sign indicating that the occupants are "THE LAST OF A ONCE POWERFUL RACE," a Native American chief in a feather headdress and buckskin clothes sends a message to a racially caricatured listener in the Philippines, who is shown wearing copious jewelry and armed with a shield, spear, and a quiver of arrows not likely to be effective against modern armaments. A grotesque pile of corpses has accumulated next to the telegraph pole, much like the images of trophy Filipino dead that Greely collected in his photo albums. Although the Native American chief is shown depressing a telegraph key, and the Native man from the Philippines is shown listening to his message, there are several references to optical rather than auditory technologies in depicting these futuristic devices. Reflectors atop the poles of the wireless devices shown in the cartoon made them look more like heliographs, which were still a commonly used technology among Signal Corps operators. In other cartoons that depict the colonial situation more benevolently, Filipinos are shown learning from the example of Native Americans in the educational or familial environments of classrooms or nurseries, and Filipinos, Hawaiians, and Caribbean islanders are often depicted as merely less mature newcomers in the process of development and assimilation. Yet in the *Judge* cartoon a message of impending death travels without the infrastructural apparatus of colonial rule invisibly through the air. Between and behind the two endangered groups of Indigenous people, Hawaii seems to be an intermediary observer.

Wireless telegraphy in cartoons could also be used to lampoon anti-imperialists. A 1902 image in *Puck* showed Massachusetts senator George Frisbie Hoar encouraging the insurrectionists thousands of miles away with a message transmitted through the air. The words "KEEP IT UP! WE ARE WITH YOU!" are sent in electric bolt letters from this often satirized anti-imperialist legislator from the Capitol dome to murderous Filipino insurgents creating mayhem and spreading death. In this way, those who express sol-

FIGURE 1.2. John S. Pughe, "WIRELESS TELEGRAPHY," *Puck*, February 26, 1902. Courtesy of Keppler and Schwarzmann, New York.

idarity with anti-imperialist opinions are imagined as remote boosters for insurgency campaigns. In this picture Marconi's device is shown somewhat more accurately with its wires and electromagnet, although the antenna in the image was considerably smaller than those necessary for long-distance communication.

As Adrian Mackenzie observes in *Wirelessness: Radical Empiricism in Network Cultures*, there is also a certain giddiness associated with twenty-first-century experiences of wirelessness. This new phenomenology promises "a state of effervescence" that "lies at the fringes of experience, but tinges experience with certain feelings of proximity and attentiveness that may very well not register consciously."[22] Although Mackenzie only mentions telegraphy briefly in a footnote, his theoretical grounding draws on the work of the late nineteenth-century psychologist and philosopher William James, who contended in his work on pragmatism that "Marconi telegrams" demonstrate that the "scientific tendency in critical thought" has now "opened an entirely unexpected range of practical utilities" that vastly exceeds "the scope of the old control" of nature "grounded on common sense."[23]

Mackenzie claims that as the infrastructural features of material connectivity recede, "an enveloping conjunction of relations coalescing around problems of spacing, departure, arrival, proximity, and being-with-others" takes precedence.[24] In contrast to Mackenzie's enthusiasm for what enters on the scene with the exit of visible tethers, Joanna Zylinska's video essay on "The

Vanishing Object of Technology" attempts to attend to the moment of disappearance before "mystifying the technological process even further," given that wireless technologies encourage "delegation of our everyday existence to the experts, designers and technocrats."

Just as other authors have argued that telegraphy from the turn of the twentieth century anticipated our current networked existence and attention to information flows, it may be useful to ask what the disappearance of telegraphic infrastructure meant in that past cultural conversation, particularly as members of the public debate the issue of the country's borders and the territories of the continental United States. Zylinska references expansive geopolitical investments in undersea cables being made by seemingly wireless apps for Facebook and Google, and in questioning the motives of American companies she calls for examining material reminders of "technological excess" and conducting an ethical inquiry into why many might want the spectacle of "objects connected to other objects" to disappear.

NOTES

1. Parks and Starosielski, *Signal Traffic*, 1.
2. Star and Ruhleder, "Steps toward an Ecology of Infrastructure," 111.
3. Hayles, *How We Think*, 12.
4. Peters, "Technology and Ideology," 142.
5. Peters, 145.
6. *Telegraph Age*, 610.
7. Ellis, "Lieutenant A. W. Greely's Report," 66.
8. US Army Signal Corps, *Report of the Chief Signal Officer*, 13.
9. Mitchell, *General Greely*, 192.
10. Headrick and Griset, "Submarine Telegraph Cables," 566.
11. Tully, "Victorian Ecological Disaster," 560.
12. Fleming, "Storms, Strikes, and Surveillance," 316.
13. Choudhury, *Telegraphic Imperialism*, 4.
14. Choudhury, 6.
15. See Sebring, "Civilization and Barbarism."
16. De la Cruz, Emmanuel, Ignacio, and Toribio, *Forbidden Book*, 90.
17. De la Cruz, Emmanuel, Ignacio, and Toribio, 126.
18. Brewer, "Selling Empire," 13.
19. Nye, "Shaping Communication Networks," 5.
20. De la Cruz, Emmanuel, Ignacio, and Toribio, *Forbidden Book*, 153.
21. De la Cruz, Emmanuel, Ignacio, and Toribio, 97.
22. Mackenzie, *Wirelessness*, 69.
23. Mackenzie, 68.
24. Mackenzie, 87.

REFERENCES

Beveridge, Albert. "The March of the Flag." Campaign speech delivered at Indiana Republican Campaign, Indianapolis. September 16, 1898. *Internet Modern History Sourcebook.* https://sourcebooks.fordham.edu/mod/modsbook.asp.

Brantlinger, Patrick. "Kipling's 'The White Man's Burden' and Its Afterlives." *English Literature in Transition, 1880–1920* 50, no. 2 (2007): 172–91.

Brewer, Susan A. "Selling Empire: American Propaganda and War in the Philippines." *Asia-Pacific Journal* 40, no. 1 (2013). http://apjjf.org/2013/11/40/Susan-A.-Brewer/4002/article.html.

Carey, James W. "Technology and Ideology: The Case of the Telegraph." In *Communication as Culture: Essays on Media and Society,* edited by James W. Carey, 201–30. New York: Psychology Press, 2009.

Choudhury, Deep Kanta Lahiri. *Telegraphic Imperialism: Crisis and Panic in the Indian Empire c.1830–1920.* Basingstoke, UK: Palgrave Macmillan, 2014.

"Close Images Collected by Brigadier General Adolphus W. Greely, Chief Signal Officer (1887–1906), 1865–1935." N.d. https://catalog.archives.gov/id/524379.

Cruz, Enrique de la, Jorge Emmanuel, Abe Ignacio, and Helen Toribio. *The Forbidden Book: The Philippine-American War in Political Cartoons.* Berkeley: Eastwind Books of Berkeley, 2014.

Ellis, L. Tuffly. "Lieutenant A. W. Greely's Report on the Installation of Military Telegraph Lines in Texas, 1875–1876." *Southwestern Historical Quarterly* 69, no. 1 (1968): 66–87.

Fleming, James Rodger. "Storms, Strikes, and Surveillance: The U.S. Army Signal Office, 1861–1891." *Historical Studies in the Physical and Biological Sciences* 30, no. 2 (2000): 315–32.

Greely, A. W. *Three Years of Arctic Service; An Account of the Lady Franklin Bay Expedition of 1881–84, and the Attainment of the Farthest North.* New York: C. Scribner's Sons, 1886.

Hayles, Katherine N. *How We Think: Digital Media and Contemporary Technogenesis.* Chicago: University of Chicago Press, 2012.

Headrick, Daniel R., and Pascal Griset. "Submarine Telegraph Cables: Business and Politics, 1838–1939." *Business History Review* 75, no. 3 (2001): 543–78.

James, William, and A. J. Ayer. *Pragmatism and the Meaning of Truth.* Cambridge, MA: Harvard University Press, 1978.

Liu, Alan, and Matthew K. Gold. "Session Description—Critical Infrastructure Studies." https://criticalinfrastructure.hcommons.org/session-description/.

Mackenzie, Adrian. *Wirelessness: Radical Empiricism in Network Cultures.* Cambridge, MA: MIT Press, 2011.

Mathieson, S. A. "Marconi: The West of England's Very Own Italian Wireless Pioneer." *Register,* February 23, 2015. https://www.theregister.co.uk/2015/02/23/geeks_guide_maroni_and_the_lizard_uk/.

Mitchell, William. *General Greely: The Story of a Great American.* New York: G. P. Putnam's Sons, 1936.

Nye, David E. "Shaping Communication Networks: Telegraph, Telephone, Computer." *Social Research* 64, no. 3 (1997): 1067–91.

Otis, Laura. *Networking: Communicating with Bodies and Machines in the Nineteenth Century.* Ann Arbor: University of Michigan Press, 2011.

Parks, Lisa, and Nicole Starosielski. *Signal Traffic: Critical Studies of Media Infrastructures.* Urbana: University of Illinois Press, 2015.

Peters, John Durham. "Technology and Ideology: The Case of the Telegraph Revisited." In *Thinking with James Carey: Essays on Communications, Transportation, History*, edited by Jeremy Packer and Craig Robertson, 137–55. New York: Peter Lang, 2006.

Sambourne, Edward Linley. *The Rhodes Colossus: Caricature of Cecil John Rhodes, after He Announced Plans for a Telegraph Line and Railroad from Cape Town to Cairo*. https://commons.wikimedia.org/wiki/File:Punch_Rhodes_Colossus.png.

Sebring, Ellen. "Civilization and Barbarism: Cartoon Commentary and 'The White Man's Burden' (1898–1902)." https://ocw.mit.edu/ans7870/21f/21f.027/civilization_and_barbarism/cb_essay03.html.

Star, Susan Leigh. "The Ethnography of Infrastructure." *American Behavioral Scientist* 43, no. 3 (1999): 377–91.

Star, Susan Leigh, and Karen Ruhleder. "Steps toward an Ecology of Infrastructure: Design and Access for Large Information Spaces." *Information Systems Research* 7, no. 1 (1996): 111–34.

The Telegraph Age. Vol. 20. New York: John B. Taltavall, 1903.

Tully, John. "A Victorian Ecological Disaster: Imperialism, the Telegraph, and Gutta-Percha." *Journal of World History* 20, no. 4 (2009): 559–79.

US Army Signal Corps. *Handbook of Submarine Cables*. Washington, DC: Government Printing Office, 1905.

US Army Signal Corps. *Report of the Chief Signal Officer, United States Army, to the Secretary of War*. Washington, DC: US Government Printing Office, 1901.

Verhoeven, Deb. "Identifying the Point of It All: Towards a Model of 'Digital Infrapuncture.'" Lecture delivered at the Digital Humanities at Oxford Summer School 2016, St. Hugh's College, Oxford University, Oxford, England, July 4, 2016. http://digital.humanities.ox.ac.uk/dhoxss/2016/lectures.

Zylinska, Joanna. "The Vanishing Object of Technology." *Catalyst: Feminism, Theory, Technoscience* 1, no. 1 (2015).

2

REVISITING "A SOLDIER'S GUIDE TO RHETORICAL THEORY"

INTELLIGENCE ANALYSIS IN THE OPEN

GARY MILLS

In this chapter we will look at some of the conversations surrounding and intersecting with "The Role of Rhetorical Theory in Military Intelligence Analysis: A Soldier's Guide to Rhetorical Theory." Although a minor touchstone for intelligence analysis and rhetorical theory, "A Soldier's Guide" still works as an effective vantage point from which to examine some of the scholarship addressing rhetorical theory, conflict, and intelligence analysis. Of note, readers will encounter a continuation and expansion of these conversations across each section of *Rhet Ops*. For my part, I sketch out a rough map of the intelligence analysis terrain while also sharing the context in which my work (more than fifteen years old) was written. This chapter also examines the growing disconnect between intelligence analysis and policy across conflicts ranging from the Korean War to the Iraq War. It is through this disconnect that the overarching narrative thread (story) is more readily compromised, and the ramifications of these narrative breaches are still actively at play.

The next section explores attributes of intelligence analysts since (like it or not—trained in the discipline or not) they are important rhetorical operators contributing to a wide range of narratives based on sources spanning highly classified sensitive compartmented information to open-source contributions. This leads to a quick look at how some intelligence communities are sharing more of their analysis processes with academe. The final section asks our community to consider open-source implications for not only intelligence analysts but also students in our writing and research classrooms.

Throughout this chapter I will try to add insight and texture to this topic from my perspective as the author of "A Soldier's Guide," a former military intelligence officer, and teacher of future Air Force officers whose job it may be to collect, analyze, assess, and communicate intelligence to decision-makers—not as a case study or an academic exercise, but as daily practices in response to real-world exigencies, often with lives being held in the balance. Effective military intelligence analysis hinges upon honest assessments of what is known and verified with evidence, what has yet to be resolved, and what perspectives exist that have yet to be considered. This desired outcome should persist, even if the underlying processes, technology, and analytical theories change. A critical anchor point is the ethical application of all of these tools in helping to enhance this complex narrative-building, truth-seeking practice

Addressing all these facets is a tall order, and this chapter will come up short in areas. Still, I want to add my vantage to the conversation expanding from the nexus of rhetoric and conflict. I hope to do this in the same spirit that I wrote "A Soldier's Guide," to spark conversation and, most importantly, encourage our community to help bring theory down from the ivory towers in order to spark a discussion about its potential benefits and pitfalls within military intelligence analysis. Importantly, we—the community represented (in part) by the contributors, sources, and readers of this collection—must take an active role beyond the safe and comfortable grounds of academe to point out both commendable (ethical and beneficial) as well as criminal (deceptive and destructive) rhetorical operations.

STILL "NOT UNPROBLEMATIC" AFTER ALL THESE YEARS

Before continuing, I want to share a recent email exchange I had with an active teacher, scholar, and former national-level agency intelligence analyst—Dr. Nate Kreuter. His chapter, "Rhetoric and the US Intelligence Community's Misuses of Theory," which follows, examines the intelligence community's (ICs) misuse of theories, specifically psychological theory and the resulting "tension" generated between these areas of study and operators placing these academic tools into practice in intelligence collection operations.[1] Kreuter explores IC and Department of Defense–level applications of academic theory by the CIA's extraordinary rendition program, transfer of US detainees to foreign governments for interrogation, and the US Army's Human Terrain System (HTS), designed to gain a better understanding of local populations and their cultures in combat zones in order to enhance counterinsurgency operations.[2] This level of social and cultural awareness is vital, according to Marr et al., "in Iraq and Afghanistan, where the [local] people are centers of gravity . . . [and Army soldiers] must take the necessary steps to really understand and know them."[3]

Kreuter's research in both areas is fascinating. More directly, it is our common look at theory that puts our chapters in proximity. The theoretical foundations serving to justify the extraordinary rendition and HTS programs have employed social science theories to wide-ranging effect. Clearly, the extraordinary rendition program uses these academic tools in an attempt to place a legitimate sheen on blatantly unethical and inhumane practices. The HTS program is different, and it interests me for several reasons. It promises to show a complex, nuanced, and ethical application of theory in an effort to enhance counterinsurgent operations through intelligence collection and sharing. I expect Kreuter to spotlight some productive, though still not unproblematic, applications since it fosters engagement and interactions with the local leaders and the general population to build a functional understanding of complex and shifting political, economic, ethnic, and cultural contexts within areas of operation in order to defeat insurgents and promote stability. Also of interest is Colonel Jack Marr. Marr is now retired from the US Army, but in 2008 he was the ranking officer and lead out of the four authors of "Human Terrain Mapping: A Critical First Step to Winning the COIN [counterinsurgency] Fight," published in *Military Review* in 2008. I expect this to be one of Kreuter's touch points since it addresses how Colonel Marr and his staff reportedly built upon best practices of successful military units already in Iraq prior to the arrival of their task force in 2007, which helped to shape the design of HTS: "Overwhelmingly, the units that seemed to be winning the [COIN] fight had made significant inroads with local leaders, had found proactive ways to understand and respect local cultural norms, and had addressed specific community needs."[4]

The Human Terrain System's positive implications are immense—"respect local cultural norms" and "addressed specific community needs"—potentially fostering individual as well as area-wide growth, health, and stability. The authors go on to highlight that the process of daily interactions and exchanges with Iraqis secured "even greater dividends" than the resulting map.[5] I see a building of empathy and humane support, right? This application of social theories is certainly justified . . . or is it? The potential pitfalls, abuses, or misapplications, however, remain. Marr and his team were moving into dangerous rhetorical waters: "Developing the HTM process amounted to creating a tool for understanding social conditions."[6] I can see the panic on social scientists' faces after hearing army infantry (combat arms) officers talk about creating a tool for gaining awareness of the Indigenous population.

Staying with HTS, I'd like to scare some rhetoricians too: "As it collected and cataloged pertinent information, the task-force staff tailored its plan in order to capture a broad range of details. An important aspect of the process involved putting the data in a medium that all Soldiers could monitor and understand."[7] Technical writing, design, and Human-Computer Interaction (HCI) implications aside, what happens to all these potentially real, compassionate experiences responsible for building local respect and support of Indigenous populations when they are then turned into a matrix, map, or narrative? I look forward to Kreuter's discoveries on HTS, and his take on Marr's application of theory.

My point with HTS, and in degrees with "A Soldier's Guide," is that we must consider not just the use (or potential abuse) of the theory but also examine the agents creating and activating these hybrid, situated, context-driven, exigency-shaped approaches. In some cases, giving any one person agency (narrative or process-shaping power) without appropriate oversight must raise immediate public concern. But, in other cases, the benefits of opening up agency (theoretical license) may far outweigh the complete avoidance of or delays waiting for a pristine, discipline-approved application of existing theory in that specific context. One of my frustrations is academe's near-automatic assumption that military use is going to isolate and weaponize any theory (Foucault in my case—social theory in Marr's case) as a quick fix, no matter the consequences. Ethics and integrity are integral parts of the military community, so much so that it is accepted as a baseline assumption since most writings are intended for readers within the community. This may generate confusion across other discourse communities drawing from these works. It may help if military contributors to these conversations explicitly address ethical expectations and safeguards.

In my exchange with Kreuter, we discussed this point of ethics, which is important to both of us. Of note, he brings up the issue of oversight: "All of which [misuses in the ER program and potential misuse of theory with the HTS] is a lead up to something I think you agree with, which is that we need a rhetorical theory of intelligence. My big fear though is that that needs to be an ethical theory and implementation, and I am concerned for how we ensure such a thing, given how vulnerable rhetoric is to misuse."[8] So, how do we ensure the theoretical intent is maintained and hold users accountable for the ethical implementation? My goal, and Kreuter's, is to spark a conversation about whether any transfer potential is there. Kreuter goes further by pushing for communities to provide guidance and oversight. He sees the need for even more conversations on theoretical transfer and their associated issues: "I agree with you that it's never a clean transfer (moving theory from one place to another), and I also agree that sparking those conversations is really important, because I don't think they happen often or deeply enough for those actually working in the IC (for a host of reasons)."[9] Continuing, Kreuter addresses the concerns generated by the distance between disciplines: "IC analysts are sometimes too removed from the communities where theory is developed and tested, and that as a result their deployment of theory is sometimes unhelpful, actively harmful to US interests even."[10]

In terms of my work, Kreuter shared a concern in terms of my use of Foucault in "A Soldier's Guide": "While I am 100% in support of your effort to develop a rhetorical theory of intelligence, I did find your reading and suggested deployment of Foucault troubling."[11] Of key note, Kreuter echoes concerns expressed by Hamilton Bean in 2010. Bean claims that "A Soldier's Guide" weaponizes (he uses "incongruous attempt to 'operationalize'")[12] Foucault's theories through a forced alignment with the military's "preconceived intelligence doctrine": "Mills himself acknowledges that Foucault would frown upon this 'institutional' use of his power analysis," yet this situation does not prevent him from praising Foucault as a "'very reluctant, unintentional military tactician' (pp. 22–23). Certainly, Foucault's ideas are open to wide interpretation. But Foucault's theoretical program was focused on social change. So, at its very core, Major Mills's application necessarily distorts aspects of Foucault's theories in order to make them amenable to preconceived intelligence doctrine."[13] From Bean's, and then later Kreuter's, vantage, it is understandable why they expressed concerns about my proposed application of Foucault.

My development of what I saw then as a useful primer or guide on the analytical opportunities of theory for intelligence officers (my work's audience) likely appeared more like a move to simply coopt then intentionally recalibrate Foucault to serve as justification for any number of potential military intelligence and IC abuses, which by the time Bean and Kreuter joined my conversation were already well established as part of the national and disciplinary conversation. As part of our email exchange, Kreuter addresses his perspective on my work's pitfalls and promises: "I would characterize my perspective toward 'Soldier's Guide' as similar [to Bean's], in that I very much disagree with your reading and conclusions there, but I think the larger, more important endeavor is really laudable and important, which is your effort to return intellectual rigor to the IC, which I would argue is not currently present in the ways Kent [advocate for CIA's development of its own literature] had hoped for it to be."[14] I appreciate Kreuter's honest evaluation of my work's theoretical flaws. He does, however, see my attempt to scaffold the study of rhetorical theory within the military intelligence community. Kreuter has the advantage of having been an intelligence analyst in the IC, so he is attuned to the academic origins and intertextual struggles the discipline faces while also understanding the exigencies driving the search for new approaches in the IC.

In light of these conversations, I often reflect on whether Foucault was the right choice for "A Soldier's Guide." I would still use Foucault, not exclusively, as a spotlight theorist. He understood the all too complex nature of discourse and conflict. More so, he knew how to frame issues through targeted questions. I love how Michael Dillon and Andrew Neal explain it in *Foucault on Politics, Security and War*, "Michel Foucault is not there to tell you what to think. He is there to provoke you into thinking."[15] Dillon and Neal assert Foucault leaves space for others "to do your own work, especially where that work may also engage and re-figure the problematisation [of the topic]."[16] In an interview with Alessandro Fontana and Pasquale Pasquino, Foucault responds to a question concerning military depictions of power: "Does the military model seem to you, on the basis of your most recent researches, to be the best one for describing power; is war here simply a metaphorical model, or is it the literal, regular, everyday mode of power?"[17] Foucault responds with deep-rooted questions that open new lines of inquiry: "One is driven to ask the basic question: Isn't power simply a form of warlike domination? Shouldn't one therefore conceive all problems of power in terms of relations of war? Isn't power a sort of generalized war which assumes at particular moments the forms of peace and the state?"[18] Foucault goes on to express the importance of questions about class, military and civil institutions, tactics, political structures, and power relations.[19] Foucault and others have much to add, even if it is simply awareness that there is no one answer, but a range of contingencies and complications that only more questions can help explore.

INTELLIGENCE ANALYSIS CAUGHT IN THE MILITARY AND POLICY DIVIDE

I received the publisher's mock-up for final approval of "A Soldier's Guide" while I was in Norfolk, Virginia, attending Joint Forces Staff College (JFSC)—three months of formal joint doctrine training and exercises that took me away from my North Atlantic Treaty Organization (NATO) intelligence assignment in Belgium. "A Soldier's Guide" was originally slated to go to press in 2001 or 2002, but a string of plot complications generated delays. So, "A Soldier's Guide" was written before 9/11, received some revisions, and was then published a few months after the start of the Iraq War. As a result, its references to the first Gulf War and Balkans conflict were still relevant, but dated in light of recent events. I was considering major edits with the start of the Iraq War, but minor changes were all I could muster. I had accepted that any real look at the intelligence fueling the Iraq invasion would call for a substantial rewrite—actually, a completely different type of work.

As the Iraq War advanced, questions and concerns about intelligence analysis spurred new research into the gaps and shortfalls across the intelligence community as well as disconnects and deception across national policy. Within a year of the war's start, international security researchers would expose the plan for regime extreme makeover that had been underway for several years. Chaim Kaufmann highlights "regime change in Iraq" as a key agenda item for the Bush administration in early 2001, with public hype for a "preventative war" starting in 2002.[20] Kaufmann effectively argues how "the marketplace of ideas failed to correct the administration's misrepresentations or hinder its ability to persuade the American public."[21] He explains the marketplace of ideas as a safety net of sorts: "median voters have strong incentives to scrutinize expansionist arguments and reject those that . . . risk weakening, rather than strengthening, national security."[22] This open forum is supposed to deter threat inflation, but Kaufmann examines issues ranging from the Bush administration's ability to frame the issue (Saddam as not only a regional threat but also a direct threat to the United States) to its leveraging of the residual, but still palpable, public fear of another 9/11–style attack.[23]

Threat inflation is a powerful form of manipulation engaging up to four rhetorical mechanisms. Kaufmann details these manipulations starting with claims that would quickly collapse if examined with a reasonable degree of due diligence. Second, the rhetor routinely claims "worst-case assertions" with little, if any, justification. Third, rhetors use biased, revolving standards to evaluate intelligence sources in order to amplify the "worst-case threat assessments," and finally, claims are based on circular logic "such as Bush administration claims that Hussein's alleged hostile intentions were evidence of the existence of weapons of mass destruction (WMD) whose supposed existence was used as evidence of his intentions."[24] These rhetorical moves serve not only as warning signs of manipulation of intelligence analysis but also the manipulation of how the public calibrates what is real, what is of value, and how a nation is ultimately perceived by the international community—still areas of contention today.

In *Why Intelligence Fails* Robert Jervis addresses the unjustified belief—not evidence—that fueled confidence at the highest levels prior to the invasion.[25] "Compounding the problem, the IC did not realize how much depended on so few individuals, especially where biological weapons were concerned."[26] Adding to the danger was "conformity and consensus" across the major intelligence contributors,[27] which resulted in "analytical judgements," not authentic intelligence assessments, which "should have been expressed with much less certainty, [and] the limitations on direct evidence should have been stressed."[28]

In his postmortem of the Iraq invasion intelligence assessments, Jervis points explicitly at the IC's failure to apply "standard social science comparative methods"[29] and to consider alternatives, such as the routine chaos (randomness and mistakes) of everyday life on the Iraqis' part.[30] This in turn was all hampered by "preexisting beliefs, and implicit views of Saddam's goals and outlooks."[31] The overarching, layered pressure for the IC to "solve" the artificially accelerated "mystery of the hidden WMDs [weapons of mass destruction]" was felt by agency directors on down to the individual analysts. This overpowering politicization of the intelligence process complicated analysts' ability to provide objective assessments.[32]

In addition to these concerns, both the IC and policymakers failed to employ human-centric approaches/cultural lenses (empathy, source and IC perspective calibration, etc.), which would have given a clearer look into the ruptures present in Saddam's administration.[33] The fixation on technical/engineering nuances of aluminum tubes and illusive chemical vans generated a fixation on individual (technology-centric) data points, and not the entire mosaic.[34] The inclusion of Iraqi-centric intelligence collection, and an actual adherence to the required intelligence/policy divide, might have generated a deeper examination revealing that the Iraqi regime was not a rational system with a unified mindset, but one like our own, made up of imperfect, flawed individuals.[35] To help counter some of these issues, Jervis proposes adoption of more peer review and analyst cross talk during the assessment building process.[36] IC oversight must start from within.

The conflict between policy, intelligence analysis, and the conduct of military operations is nothing new. But, what if we had a better understanding of how policy and warfare interact as part of a continuum, not an artificial divide? This too might remove some of the adverse pressure on intelligence analysis. In this case, the narrative behind the war might have at least rung with truth, even if the objective of regime change remained the same. Specifically focusing on the military/policy divide, Thomas Waldman advances a new interpretation of Clausewitz's *On War* that moves us from a focus on war's subordination to policy to an understanding of war and policy as interwoven part of a conflict continuum.[37] Politics and warfare are linked by the irrational, contingent, and fluid attributes of each.[38] This co-catalyzing effect is best recognized for the chaos that it brings, which ultimately calls for even greater awareness of policy objectives and warfighting strategies. Any successful orchestration of these two areas also requires ethical and rational leadership. It also draws in the personalities, agendas, and flaws of key agents in each camp. A lack of awareness of this entropy can result in destabilization and needless destruction: "Where extraneous political concerns impinge on strategic decisions, soldiers can find themselves being sacrificed for the sake of a politician's position, industrial contractor's profits, or the continuance of amicable relations with allies."[39]

Waldman's analysis of "the political web of war" highlights the potential for an irrational, "paradoxical impact" as policy and war either dance together in step or struggle against one another while remaining permanently tethered in the web.[40] One needed result is elimination of an illusion of subordination or actual control: "On one hand, policy provides war with a rational structure, whereby belligerents seek to attain their ends through the reasoned use of force. On the other hand, it is embedded in what we have termed the political web of war, and this constitutes one of the greatest barriers to rational strategic behavior."[41] This messy depiction of how the web of war works aligns well with our real-world engagement of politics and military force across the globe, most notably in conflicts following World War II. Examples of these tensions between military and policy highlight the pivotal role key agents in both the military and political camps play in hijacking, and, ultimately, derailing desired outcomes.

In Korea General McArthur's military success following the Inchon landings encouraged his push past the 38th parallel into North Korea. The original United Nations (UN) mandate called for the reestablishment of existing borders—not an invasion of North Korea. Although Truman ultimately approved "pursuit of forcible reunification," the continued encroachment north brought China into the conflict.[42] This in turn removed the potential of the UN bringing the North Koreans to negotiations from a position of strength. Further complicating this context, McArthur's adversarial and public defiance of policy following China's entry resulted in his being fired by Truman. The mythic "unconditional surrender" narrative of World War II was broken, resulting in armistice.[43] But the myth of the mighty, iron-willed American general endured, even after military peers revealed in closed sessions that any expansion in Korea would ultimately weaken the United States' global military footing.[44] In essence, expansion of the war had the potential to create greater political and territorial losses across Asia, including a risk of drawing the Soviets into the conflict.[45] McArthur's ambitions on the Korean peninsula hampered the ability for military and policy alignment.

In Vietnam, General William Westmoreland's force-on-force attrition strategy had shown little results, and he was ill-prepared for the hybrid warfare used by the North Vietnamese.[46] Even with the technical victory over the North Vietnamese during the Tet Offensive, instability in policy and strategy rapidly devolved into multiple operations, most counterproductive or only partially employed. Westmoreland was replaced in 1968 by General Creighton Abrams. In *Westmoreland: The General Who Lost Vietnam*, Lewis Sorley asserts one of the general's key failings was his overestimation of American tolerance of US troop losses.[47] Another was the lack of confidence generated by Westmoreland's inaccurate estimates (intentionally distorted intelligence) of enemy force strength sent to senior policy officials, presenting an optimistic footing when the opposite was true.[48] Of note, it was the ICs, the Central Intelligence Agency, and the Defense Intelligence Agency that initiated a call for new order of battle assessments (enemy strength reports) following the Tet Offensive that revealed Westmoreland's estimates were artificially low.[49] His strategy privileged employment of US forces instead of extensive training and involvement of South Vietnamese troops, which, in turn, left the enemy free to conduct hybrid warfare operations.[50] Additionally, Westmoreland's micromanagement leadership approach stifled debate (internal review/oversight) raised by his most capable and creative unit commanders.[51]

In Iraq the major ground and air war was accomplished in a matter of months, with President Bush claiming "Mission accomplished" on May 1, 2003.[52] Military objectives were swiftly taken, but the policy reaction in Washington, DC, and on the ground upended progress. Later the same month, Paul Bremer's decision to completely dismantle the Iraqi Army—not part of the White House policy plan—opened the door to extended instability and seeded the rise of sectarian insurgencies.[53] Powell explains the misalignment in an interview on May 17, 2016: "I called Dr. Rice as soon as I saw it, [open source reporting of the dismantlement of the Iraqi military] and I said: 'Condi, do you know about this? Does the president know about this?' She said no. I said: 'What's going to be our action? What is he going to do about it?' The answer was, the decision has been made by the people on the ground, Bremer, and so we will not overturn his decision; that would be very awkward. So we lived with it."[54] In the same interview, Powell calls Bremer's actions, and policymaker's failure to correct it, as "a major, massive strategic error."[55] These were complex interactions between policy and warfare that needed the aid of a continuum choreographer.

Waldman's novel revisioning of Clausewitz's view of politics and conflict is steeped in a rich understanding of human interactions—a real look at our (often lack of) communication practices. Continuation as used by Waldman opens a vantage on conflict as "perpetually shifting relations within, between, and beyond individual groups will shape the course of war."[56] This sounds like Foucault in practice. According to Michael Dillon and Andrew Neal, "War and politics, by Foucault's account, therefore always seem to form complex, mutually informing and strategically interactive, grids of intelligibility for one another."[57] "Policy-makers and commanders are inevitably entwined in this political web. The cynical reasons for which force is often employed may degrade the purity of policy, but it remains policy nonetheless and will invariably impact war, potentially to its detriment."[58] The point here is that we balk at the idea of rhetorical theory being a part of the exploration of warfare, and its associated intelligence analysis. Yet, rhetorical theory is at the heart of all these interactions in many ways and forms. As the historical examples help to highlight, one of the best applications of rhetorical theory would be to take a closer look at our own interactions and the resulting pushback and resistance active within the US military/political continuum.

INTELLIGENCE ANALYSIS TEMPLATES: PAST AND PRESENT

Of key interest is the fact that all the aforementioned policy, intelligence, and strategy failures were, and should have been, subject to debate by its key players. We tend to allow discourse about intelligence analysis and strategy to (at least initially) go unchecked (or maligned by conspiracy theory) because it is assumed the critical mechanisms are hidden away in safes and Secret Compartmented Intelligence Facilities. The reality is the foundational analysis processes have always been public. I must admit, it was not until being prodded by questions from others about open-source access to military issues that this point really sank in. Open-source discourse has even encouraged the once highly secretive ICs to embrace higher degrees of collaboration with outside organizations.

We have had open-source templates for intelligence analysis all along, providing historical, cultural, and strategic perspectives. Homer was one of the first with his portrayal of Odysseus as strategist and intelligence analyst extraordinaire in the *Iliad* and *Odyssey*. Odysseus, arguably, was the original Jack Ryan, with the strength of a warrior and the analytical/rhetorical prowess of a philosopher. From another vantage, Sophocles also uses Odysseus as a problematic pivot point in *Philoctetes*. In this work Odysseus is a different kind of intelligence analyst—darker and duplicitous. "The plot of this play requires that Odysseus, for all his oratorical skills, be a failure . . . must be a failed rhetorician. . . . Sophocles has invested the ethos of Odysseus with such a horde of negative traits that he forfeits any possibility of winning the victory."[59] In *Philoctetes* Odysseus hides behind the authentic and virtuous ethos of Achilles's son—Neoptolemus. This interesting disparity underscores the tightrope of credibility and trust vital to leadership and authentic narratives, or the result is an epic fall: "This Odysseus is a failure both as a doer of deeds and as a speaker of words."[60] Homer and Sophocles open their audiences to the potential of deceptive and duplicitous practices initiating and sustaining war.

Homer gives audiences a global and communal (epic) examination of policy and military discord, while Sophocles provides an intimate look at an individual agent's ethical collapse, all in a quest to win at all cost, even if it means sacrificing, abandoning, and actively deceiving your own warriors.

Sun Tzu's *The Art of War* remains a touchstone for intelligence analysis for military and business strategoi, a list that also includes Machiavelli, Shakespeare, Clausewitz, among others. The senior intelligence analyst Jeffrey White's "Shakespeare for Analysts: Literature and Intelligence" shares the bard's open source contributions to intelligence professionals: "Reading and studying literature expands the imagination, and analysts need imagination to make inferences, to bridge gaps in information, to see patterns, in other words, for discovery. Those who study literature learn to interpret. This is the essence of 'sense making.' Literature can assist us in the area of 'storytelling.'"[61] Shakespeare's focus on "human behavior in contexts" ranging from cultural asymmetries and civil wars to coalition warfare and political legitimacy provides an excellent lens to view intent and behavior.[62]

Focusing on academic training grounds, in *Cloak and Gown: Scholars in the Secret War, 1939–1961*, Robin Winks explores the origins of analysts establishing the Office of Strategic Services (OSS), the precursor to the CIA, during World War II. Recruits were drawn from college campuses for their ability to think in unconventional ways, generating novel solutions to war's complex challenges.[63] Their broad liberal arts educations made recruits capable of "abstract and objective thought," [64] which was driven by an "unfettered sense of curiosity."[65] Winks also describes the need for these analysts to always look past the initial or obvious solution: "The scholar knows that one ought to feel uncomfortable when in the field, or at research, and certainly in the classroom, for one ought to be aware of the elements of one's own confusion."[66] He goes on to explore the importance of seeking and understanding context, change, and contingency: "Disciplines like history and anthropology, philosophy or law, are also about what did not happen, or does not happen, and by extension might well happen differently or have happened differently on a given set of facts."[67] Although Winks does not provide a master template for the ideal intelligence analyst, we do see the overarching pattern of well and broadly studied creative thinkers able to envision alternatives and their implications.

To gain a fresh vantage from a current, experienced intelligence analyst, I asked Jack (a pseudonym) a few questions. Jack is a retired military intelligence analyst with enlisted and officer corps experience. I have worked with Jack in the past. As a civilian intelligence specialist, Jack is currently deployed to an unspecified location. I opened a dialogue with him in February 2018. In order to protect Jack's identity, some of his responses have been redacted, and some minor editorial changes have been made in order to enhance narrative flow.

> GM: How do you approach being moved to a new topic, region, or focus area? What are some initial steps/processes as you move from analyzing country A to B . . . or topic X to Y?
>
> JACK: If I don't have a baseline knowledge of a topic, I generally begin with unclassified open sources to build up an initial understanding of a problem set. There is an abundance of good sources such as Stratfor, Google Scholar, etc. (yes, to include Wikipedia if the information is properly sourced) to outline a detailed framework from which to derive (usually) about 80 percent of the information I need to understand a problem set. Many times outlining the information needs is more important than actually collecting the data that is needed, or, to quote my old Wing Commander Col [deleted], "Answers are easy, it's getting the questions right that is difficult!"[68]

Of key note, Jack was not asked about open sources at any point in our exchange, so it is fascinating to see not only his focused application of open sources but also his drive to outline information needs in order to craft essential questions as part of the process.

Open sources serve as a scaffold for deeper analysis. Jack also underscores the power within the analysis process itself. He highlights the advantages of scaffolding at the lowest level of classification: "Once I have exhausted those publicly available resources, I usually 'work my way up' from collateral systems (SIPRNET) to SCI (JWICS) sources; but to be honest given the inability to share the information as the classification climbs, I try to keep my sources as 'low' as possible to ensure I can provide it to the largest possible audience."[69] Here Jack stresses the value of collaboration with peers to foster analyst-level review.

Another question focused on what Jack does differently in terms of intelligence analysis techne (source use) as a senior analyst:

> JACK: I find that after I learn what I can from open sources, the collaborative sources such as iSpace not only provide a good portion of the information and analysis but also are rich in the fact that—if done properly, i.e., not working toward a general consensus but focused on truly understanding the issue at hand—the analytical results of the collective effort far outweigh the sum of knowledge of individuals involved. Again, it must be done properly as I have seen "groupthink" poison more than one collaborative effort, and firmly believe it's what undermined the Iraqi WMD effort (i.e., the October 2002 *National Intelligence Estimate*).[70]

Again, we see open-source scaffolding but also online mediated collaboration with other senior experts—all while ensuring the dialogue remains productive, resulting in new perspectives—not the "poison" of groupthink.

Finally, I asked Jack about what he was searching for when he was conducting intelligence analysis:

> GM: Are you looking for the truth, reality, or what when you are conducting analysis?
>
> JACK: It is a mixture of ground truth and perception. The delta is usually the most difficult part, trying to delineate between the two and determine why one is not the other. Otherwise, I usually follow the formula set by GEN Colin Powell who had three basic requirements for his intel: tell me what you know, tell me what you think, and tell me what you don't know. [Unfortunately, Powell did not apply this same criteria for his address to the UN Security Council.] To be honest I learned more about formal analytic processes ([Jonathan] Lockwood's *The Lockwood Analytical Method for Prediction,* [Richards] Heuer's "Analysis of Competing Hypotheses," etc.) from the [deleted] master's program I took than I ever got in any DoD intelligence courses I completed.[71]

Jack must not only triangulate the truth/facts but also be able to understand the wide range of perceptions generated from each source. He also addresses the difference between truth and perceptions—and the cause behind the misalignment. In closing his response, Jack asserts that his most valuable training actually came from academe, not the military. Importantly, as educators, we can use many of these same processes to teach our students how to search for the "delta" between ground truth/facts and perception/deception. Jack's responses highlight the critical role open source research plays in current, ongoing intelligence analysis and assessment. For Jack, it is a critical baseline that can serve as scaffolding to layer complexity—and as needed, add increasingly higher source classifications. He values the inputs of other analysts and is comfortable having this exchange mediated online.

ANTHROPOMORPHIC ANALYSTS, CIA'S TRADECRAFT NOTES, AND CAROLYN MILLER

In the late 1990s the IC as a whole was sharing more through open-source works, even the ultra-secretive National Reconnaissance Office (NRO), whose thirty-one-year existence was not declassified until 1992,[72] was sharing once-classified Cold War Corona Satellite imagery with the world in 1995.[73] The equally secretive National Security Agency (NSA) was sharing some items, but not much. Even its history, "The Origins of the National Security Agency: 1940–1952," was classified top secret when it was published in 1990, and it wasn't until 2007 it was released as an open-source document, with some redactions.[74] The NSA's public presence is much different today. Their homepage allows visitors to solve fun puzzles (the NSA is known as the "Puzzle Palace") created by NSA mathematicians.[75] Parents and children are encouraged to learn about their K–12 STEM outreach programs, including a CryptoKids® page with anthropomorphic animals serving in different roles in the NSA such as engineers, signals intelligence analysts, and linguists.[76] The NSA has gone from a cloaked "no such agency" and "never say anything" narrative to one of open recruiting and sponsorship of STEM education.

Back in the 1990s, the CIA offered more. I still have my copy of "A Compendium of Analytic Tradecraft Notes" mailed to me back in 1998. The Compendium includes ten notes on analytic tradecraft, which equate to best practices for intelligence analysts to apply. The CIA had also sent me copies of notes 11–17 published in February 1996. This open sharing of key analytic processes was a rare move by any intelligence organization, especially the CIA. In the February 1997 reprint, deputy director of intelligence John Gannon underscores this rare opportunity: "We are making the *Compendium of Analytic Tradecraft Notes* available to scholars to shed light on how we support intelligence consumers. This release, although unusual for an intelligence agency, reflects our renewed commitment to reach out to academia and the public, as defined in the Directorate's new Strategic Plan."[77] Gannon's reprinting of Jack Davis's "Tradecraft Notes" was a boon for my thesis. I had sources on intelligence processes that went beyond my own Air Force intelligence training and experiences to explore.

The collection described many of the same issues I was studying in my rhetorical theory courses in the mid-to late 1990s. The CIA had its own audiences, literature, and more—just with different labels. "The word 'tradecraft' comes from our colleagues in the clandestine service, who use it to embody the special skills and methods required to do their business. We have borrowed it to capture our special skills and methods."[78] The CIA's tradecraft notes (TN) lead us straight to rhetorical doppelgängers such as techne, genre, discourse communities, and many other points on the rhetorical map. The parallels are vivid. Here are the first five of the ten notes: (TN 1) analysts need to anticipate the needs of the audience; (TN 2) evaluate sources and maintain credibility; and (TN 3) clearly and logically manage uncertainty, variables, and complexity. (TN 4) they must anticipate and communicate alternate (unlikely or unexpected) events; (TN 5) communicate precisely about what is known (e.g., fact vs indirect information); and explore the potential for deception and disinformation.[79] The CIA expressed a drive to generate audience-focused analysis and products, which demanded a shift in rhetorical situation, modes of persuasion, and communication mediums depending on customers' needs: "Long analytic papers largely focused on the Soviet threat worldwide that were the norm 10 years ago have given way to a combination of briefings and short but insightful writing and multimedia products covering a broad range of regional and transnational issues."[80]

Back then, even the CIA's limited transparency was startling. The growth of the discussion of techne had been on the periphery of my library and web searches as I tried every permutation of *rhetorical theory* and *intelligence analysis* with my dial-up modem. Of all the government agencies, the CIA was the most actively engaged in developing a literature-aligned methodology and techne for analysts. Within the CIA as early as 1955, Sherman Kent asserts intelligence analysis as a "discipline," and in desperate need of a literature of its own.[81] Additionally, beyond solidifying the CIA's corporate knowledge, fundamental principles, and vocabulary, it should also prompt an "elevated debate" across different analysts, departments, and organizations.[82]

At the same time, I was beginning to learn about Carolyn Miller's insightful works. "Genre as Social Action" made me rethink the role of intelligence assessments as genre—"a rhetorical means for mediating private intentions and social exigence."[83] In a recent return to this topic, in "Genre as Social Action (1984), Revisited 30 Years Later (2014)" Miller asserts "genre has become a much more complex, multidimensional social phenomenon, a structurational nexis between action and structure, between agent and institution, between past and future."[84] Amid the complexity, genre remains effective because it "characterizes communities, offers modes of engagement through joint action and uptake, connects the flux of experience to our sense of the past and the future, makes recurrent patterns significant, and provides satisfactions and pleasure."[85] Miller's "Learning from History: World War II and the Culture of High Technology" reveals how we can better view technology, culture, and institutional relationships, especially in terms of how knowledge (by extension intelligence analysis) derived from technology-intensive sources (from my vantage, drones, satellites, and sensors) can "pervade other cultural arenas"[86] and "acquire cultural power."[87] Miller's look at rhetorical mechanics, specifically "rhetorical studies of technology"[88] at play in a nation before and after World War II helped me to better understand the IC's, and my own, footing with issues such as "dissemination, diverse applications, and the cultural potency."[89]

OPEN-SOURCE IMPLICATIONS AND CHALLENGES

Intelligence analysis is an open art form across civilian and military organizations—its key rhetorical mechanisms are becoming more of a part of our collective conversation about conflict. What is less known is how open-source and classified domains inform and influence each other. I see this tension between source communities as a productive arena for exploration—aligned with the warfare/policy struggle addressed by Waldman. With his work with the CIA, Jervis has demonstrated one avenue of collaboration via agency-invited postmortem reviews. However, a better solution might entail more collaboration across intelligence communities with a focus on evidence-based knowledge-building without political pressure to find a specific answer—or the privileging of uncorroborated, single-source information coming from technology (satellite imagery, drones, etc.) and the analysts overly reliant on those same sources. If the conversation continues to grow, perhaps in the not too distant future one of the major intelligence agencies might include a "rhetorical operations specialist" in their cadre, inspiring young rhetoricians to join the fight, making assessment techne, collaboration, and understanding of the political/warfare continuum better.

What can we do? As educators we can advance these analytical and research processes with our own students. These skill sets have fallen under different names over the years, such as *critical technological literacy*,[90] *electric rhetoric*,[91] and *critical literacy*,[92] fusing functional, cultural, and rhetorical implications of writing with technology.[93] *Cyberliteracy* captures an understanding of "the relationship between communication technologies and ourselves, our communities, and our cultures."[94] Combined, these monikers encapsulate awareness of not only the effects and consequences of technology in the communication process but also the rhetorical implications of what we draw in and create as a result of these interactions, even how we triangulate truth. Students must be prepared.

I'll close this chapter with insight from a war literature exemplar—Benjamin Fountain. He calls the main opponent to an awareness of grounded truth the "Fantasy Industrial Complex" (FIC).[95] He refers to this type of targeted, distorted, and commercialized marketing of influence as America's unique and pervasive perversion of language: "Words that had nothing to do with reality, words whose purpose was to distort, to sell an agenda, to numb the audience—or to put it another way, the language of advertising. . . . The sum effect of all this was to take us farther and farther from the reality of war."[96] This distance intentionally and forcefully hampers the negotiation of meaning. Fountain warns America to wake up and escape the self-imposed cultural dream state to embrace "the facts of the situation—what happened, and who acted, and why. Not the fantasy version, the numbed-out and dumbed-down version, but the true version, or as close to the truth as clear thinking and seeing can get us."[97] It is our responsibility to not only call out FIC across public, especially official, domains but also to teach students how to identify FIC/deception to become informed, empathetic, and ethical citizens.

NOTES

The views expressed in this work are those of the author and do not reflect the official policy or position of the US Air Force, Department of Defense, or the US government.

1. Nate Kreuter and Gary Mills, email exchange, "Re: Facilitating a Connection on Your Contributions to RhetOps," September 5, 2018.
2. Kreuter and Mills, email exchange.
3. Marr, Cushing, Garner, and Thompson, "Human Terrain Mapping," 18.
4. Marr, Cushing, Garner, and Thompson, 18.
5. Marr, Cushing, Garner, and Thompson, 24.
6. Marr, Cushing, Garner, and Thompson, 19.
7. Marr, Cushing, Garner, and Thompson, 19.
8. Kreuter and Mills, email exchange.
9. Kreuter and Mills, email exchange.
10. Kreuter and Mills, email exchange.
11. Kreuter and Mills, email exchange.
12. Bean, "Foucault's Rhetorical Theory and U.S. Intelligence Affairs," 20.
13. Bean, 20.
14. Kreuter and Mills, email exchange.
15. Dillon and Neal, *Foucault on Politics, Security and War*, introduction, Kindle.
16. Dillon and Neal, 2–220, Kindle.
17. Rabinow, *Foucault Reader*, 64–65.
18. Rabinow, 65.
19. Rabinow, 65.
20. Kaufmann, "Threat Inflation and the Failure of the Marketplace of Ideas," 6.
21. Kaufmann, 6.
22. Kaufmann, 7.
23. Kaufmann, 32.
24. Kaufmann, 8–9.
25. Jervis, *Why Intelligence Fails*, 127.
26. Jervis, 140.
27. Jervis, 130.
28. Jervis, 149.
29. Jervis, 152.
30. Jervis, 153.
31. Jervis, 155.
32. Jervis, 131.
33. Jervis, 14.
34. Jervis, 149.

35. Jervis, 153.
36. Jervis, 188–89.
37. Waldman, "Politics and War," 5.
38. Waldman, 5.
39. Waldman, 8–9.
40. Waldman, 9.
41. Waldman, 9.
42. Matray, "Revisiting Korea."
43. Matray.
44. US State Department, "MacArthur Hearings Report: Part 2," 2–3.
45. US State Department, 4.
46. Birtle, "PROVN, Westmoreland, and the Historians," 1220–21.
47. Sorley, *Westmoreland*, chap. 11, loc. 95 of 397, Kindle.
48. Sorley, 163, 187, Kindle.
49. Sorley, 188, Kindle.
50. Sorley, 91–92, Kindle.
51. Sorley, chap. 10, 83, Kindle.
52. Sehgal, "Eight Years Ago, Bush Declared 'Mission Accomplished' in Iraq,"
53. Pollack, "Seven Deadly Sins of Failure in Iraq."
54. Breslow, "Colin Power."
55. Breslow.
56. Waldman, "Politics and War," 8.
57. Dillon and Neal, *Foucault on Politics, Security, and War*, loc. 1 of 220, Kindle.
58. Waldman, "Politics and War," 8–9.
59. Austin, *Sophocles' 'Philoctetes' and the Great Soul Robbery*, 32.
60. Austin, 33.
61. White, "Shakespeare for Analysts," 1.
62. White, 4.
63. Winks, *Cloak and Gown*, 58.
64. Winks, 28.
65. Winks, 54.
66. Winks, 57.
67. Winks, 57.
68. "Jack" (former military, now civilian, intelligence analyst), email exchange with Gary Mills, February 16, 2018.
69. "Jack," email exchange with Mills.
70. "Jack," email exchange with Mills.
71. "Jack," email exchange with Mills.
72. National Reconnaissance Office (NRO), "Who We Are," http://www.nro.gov/about/nro/who.html.
73. National Reconnaissance Office (NRO), "President Orders Declassification of Historic Satellite Imagery."
74. Burns, "Origins of the National Security Agency."
75. National Security Agency (NSA), "NSA's 2018 Puzzle Periodical."
76. National Security Agency (NSA), "Digital Media Center."
77. Gannon, "Foreword," v.
78. Gannon, v.
79. Davis, "Compendium of Analytic Tradecraft Notes," 41.

80. Gannon, "Forward," v.
81. Kent, "Need for an Intelligence Literature."
82. Kent.
83. Miller, "Genre as Social Action," 163.
84. Miller, 69.
85. Miller, 69.
86. Miller, "Learning from History," 307.
87. Miller, 310.
88. Miller. 310.
89. Miller. 310.
90. Selfe, *Technology and Literacy in the Twenty-First Century*, 149–50.
91. Welch, *Electric Rhetoric*, 6.
92. Warnick, *Critical Literacy in a Digital Era*, 6.
93. Selber, *Multiliteracies for a Digital Age*, 25.
94. Gurak, *Cyberliteracy*, 16.
95. Fountain, "Soldiers on the Fault Line," 3.
96. Fountain, 6.
97. Fountain, 4.

REFERENCES

Austin, Norman. *Sophocles' 'Philoctetes' and the Great Soul Robbery.* Madison: University of Wisconsin Press, 2011.

Bean, Hamilton. "Foucault's Rhetorical Theory and U.S. Intelligence Affairs." *Poroi* 6, no. 2 (2010): 15–32. https://doi.org/10.13008/2151-2957.1067.

Birtle, Andrew. "PROVN, Westmoreland, and the Historians: A Reappraisal." *Journal of Military History* 72, no. 4 (October 2008): 1213–47.

Breslow, Jason. "Colin Power: U.N. Speech "Was a Great Intelligence Failure." *Frontline,* May 17, 2016. https://www.pbs.org/wgbh/frontline/article/colin-powell-u-n-speech-was-a-great-intelligence-failure/.

Burns, Thomas. "The Origins of the National Security Agency: 1940–1952 (U)." National Security Agency, 1990. https://www.nsa.gov/news-features/declassified-documents/cryptologic-histories/assets/files/origins_of_nsa.pdf.

Davis, Jack. *A Compendium of Analytic Tradecraft Notes.* Edited by F. Douglas Whitehouse. Washington, DC: Government Printing Office, 1997.

Dillon, Michael, and Andrew Neal, eds. *Foucault on Politics, Security and War.* Basingstoke, UK: Palgrave Macmillan, 2008. Kindle.

Fountain, Benjamin. "Soldiers on the Fault Line: War, Rhetoric, and Reality." *War, Literature & the Arts: An International Journal of the Humanities* 25 (2013). wlajournal.com/wlaarchive/25_1/fountain.pdf.

Gannon, John. "Forward." In *A Compendium of Analytic Tradecraft Notes*, by Jack Davis, v–vi. Washington, DC: Government Printing Office, 1997.

Gurak, Laura. *Cyberliteracy: Navigating the Internet with Awareness.* New Haven, CT: Yale University Press, 2001.

Jervis, Robert. *Why Intelligence Fails: Lessons from the Iranian Revolution and the Iraq War.* Ithaca, NY: Cornell University Press, 2010.

Kaufmann, Chaim. "Threat Inflation and the Failure of the Marketplace of Ideas: The Selling of the Iraq War." *International Security* 29, no. 2 (Summer 2004): 5–48.

Kent, Sherman. "The Need for an Intelligence Literature." Central Intelligence Agency. https://www.cia.gov/library/center-for-the-study-of-intelligence/csi-publications/books-and-monographs/sherman-kent-and-the-board-of-national-estimates-collected-essays/2need.html.

Marr, Jack, John Cushing, Brandon Garner, and Richard Thompson. "Human Terrain Mapping: A Critical First Step to Winning the COIN Fight." *Military Review* (March–April 2008): 18–24.

Matray, James. "Revisiting Korea: Exposing Myths of the Forgotten War." *Prologue* 34, no. 2 (Summer 2002). https://www.archives.gov/publications/prologue/2002/summer/korean-myths-2.html.

Miller, Carolyn. "Genre as Social Action." *Quarterly Journal of Speech* 70, no. 2 (1984): 151–76.

Miller, Carolyn. "Genre as Social Action (1984), Revisited 30 Years Later (2014)." *Letras & Letras* 31, no. 3 (July 2015): 56–72.

Miller, Carolyn. "Learning from History: World War II and the Culture of High Technology." *Journal of Business and Technical Communication* 12, no. 3 (July 1998): 288–315.

National Reconnaissance Office. "President Orders Declassification of Historic Satellite Imagery Citing Value of Photography to Environmental Science." February 24, 1995. http://www.nro.gov/news/press/1995/1995-01.pdf.

National Reconnaissance Office. "Who We Are." http://www.nro.gov/about/nro/who.html.

National Security Agency. "Digital Media Center." https://www.nsa.gov/resources/everyone/digital-media-center/publications/cryptokids/.

National Reconnaissance Office. "NSA's 2018 Puzzle Periodical." https://www.nsa.gov/news-features/puzzles-activities/puzzle-periodical/2018/puzzle-periodical-02.shtml.

Pollack, Kenneth. "The Seven Deadly Sins of Failure in Iraq: A Retrospective Analysis of the Reconstruction." *Brookings*, December 1, 2006. https://www.brookings.edu/articles/the-seven-deadly-sins-of-failure-in-iraq-a-retrospective-analysis-of-the-reconstruction/.

Rabinow, Paul, ed. *The Foucault Reader.* New York: Pantheon, 1984.

Sehgal, Ujala. "Eight Years Ago, Bush Declared 'Mission Accomplished' in Iraq." *Atlantic*, May 1, 2011. https://www.theatlantic.com/national/archive/2011/05/mission-accomplished-speech/350187/.

Selber, Stuart. *Multiliteracies for a Digital Age.* Carbondale: Southern Illinois University Press, 2004.

Selfe, Cynthia. L. *Technology and Literacy in the Twenty-First Century: The Importance of Paying Attention.* Carbondale: Southern Illinois University Press, 1999.

Sorley, Lewis. *Westmoreland: The General Who Lost Vietnam.* New York: First Mariner Books, 2012. Kindle.

US State Department. "MacArthur Hearings Report: Part 2." September 22, 1951. https://www.trumanlibrary.org/whistlestop/study_collections/koreanwar/documents/index.php?documentdate=1951-09-22&documentid=ma-3-25&pagenumber=1.

Waldman, Thomas. "Politics and War: Clausewitz's Paradoxical Equation." *Parameters: The US Army War College Quarterly* 40, no. 3 (2010): 48–60.

Warnick, Barbara. *Critical Literacy in a Digital Era: Technology, Rhetoric, and the Public Interest.* Mahwah, NJ: Lawrence Erlbaum Associates, 2002.

Welch, Kathleen. *Electric Rhetoric: Classical Rhetoric, Oralism, and a New Literacy.* Cambridge, MA: MIT Press, 1999.

White, Jeffrey. "Shakespeare for Analysts: Literature and Intelligence." Defense Intelligence Agency, July 2003. http://ni-u.edu/ni_press/pdf/Shakespeare_for_Analysts.pdf.

Winks, Robin. *Cloak and Gown: Scholars in the Secret War, 1939–1961.* New York: William Morrow, 1987.

3

RHETORIC AND THE US INTELLIGENCE COMMUNITY'S MISUSES OF THEORY

NATE KREUTER

The post–9/11 US intelligence community (IC) sometimes deploys the theoretical knowledge of academic disciplines in cynical and instrumental ways, and in ways directly contrary to the purposes for which the theories were originally developed. Such "weaponizations" of theory and disciplinary expertise potentially invalidate the IC's work, and almost certainly, when exposed, reduce the IC's ethical standing such that it becomes more difficult for the IC to secure the trust of policymakers and the public and carry out its work of protecting US citizens and US interests.

The most egregious recent example of the IC's backfiring weaponization of theory arises from its abuse of prisoners in the extraordinary rendition program run by the Central Intelligence Agency (CIA), and since investigated and exposed in the *Senate Committee Report on CIA Torture*.[1] Once the program, which exploited research from the field of psychology in order to enact "effective" torture, became public, the reactions from both government and academe were damning, and criticism was directed not only at the CIA but also at the American Psychological Association (APA), whose officers had in some cases collaborated with the CIA to enable the torture program.[2] Controversy also surrounded the IC's Human Terrain System (HTS), which sought to map cultural, linguistic, and political allegiances in Iraq and Afghanistan by deploying anthropological practices and trained anthropologists, many of whom held PhDs in the field.[3] The HTS was similarly condemned by the American Anthropological Association, whose executive board stated that it "views the HTS project as an unacceptable application of anthropological expertise"[4] and subsequently condemned the HTS in a comprehensive report.[5] In these two examples we see the IC deploying the theories of psychology and anthropology, respectively, but deploying them in ways that run counter to the professional ethics that govern both disciplines and the disciplines' practitioners. In both cases the professional organizations condemned the IC, and some of their own colleagues, for corrupting theory by deploying it in unethical ways in the service of national security interests.

The extraordinary rendition program was developed by Bruce Jessen and James Mitchell, two psychologists contracted by the CIA to develop interrogation techniques for "high-value" detainees. Drawing upon their experience teaching in the Air Force's Survival, Evasion, Resistance, and Escape (SERE) training program, as well as research in their own field, the two developed the infamous interrogation technique known as waterboarding, as well as strategies for "softening" detainees through sleep deprivation and aural assaults with loud music. The various techniques that Jessen and Mitchell developed were a perversion of research in psychology, which warned of the dangers of such high-pressure interrogation techniques so that they would be avoided, not utilized,[6] and which many psychologists and lawmakers already considered torture.[7] In response to revelations about the extraordinary rendition program, the American Psychological Association has since developed their "Policy Related to Psychologists' Work in National Security Settings and Reaffirmation of the APA Position against Torture and Other Cruel, Inhuman, or Degrading Treatment or Punishment." Among other things, the policy states that "psychologists shall not provide knowingly any research, instruments, or knowledge that facilitates the practice of torture or other forms of cruel, inhuman, or degrading treatment or punishment."[8] The Senate Intelligence Committee, the APA, and a federal court all decided that Jessen and Mitchell had deployed the theory arising from the field of psychology in unethical and illegal ways.[9] The Hoffman Report further found that "the APA Ethics Director joined and supported at times by other APA officials, colluded with important DoD officials to have APA issue loose, high-level ethical guidelines that did not constrain DoD in any greater fashion than existing DoD interrogation guidelines. We concluded that APA's principal motive in doing so was to align APA and curry favor with DoD."[10] In the case of the Human Terrain System (HTS), the American Anthropological Association's executive board specifically cited misuse of anthropological *expertise*, a synonym for theory in some respects, in its objections. Both disciplines were in a sense betrayed by disciplinary insiders whose collaborations with the IC facilitated the IC's unethical adoptions and implementations of disciplinary-specific theory.

From these two examples of theory that were given praxis within the IC, an obvious paradox emerges: theorist-practitioners in a variety of knowledge fields commonly hope that their expertise will be applied to make the world a better, safer place. But disciplinary expertise divorced from the theorist-practitioners who develop that expertise, and who are simultaneously bound through disciplinary culture, and sometimes the law, to uphold their respective fields' ethical norms, is subject to abuse and exploitation. Further, the case of the extraordinary rendition program shows that even disciplinary experts who are not members of the IC are susceptible to the corrosive effects of secrecy, and an accompanying lack of public accountability, when their expertise is applied in the intelligence environment, rather than in traditional disciplinary venues.

In order to ask how the IC uses and potentially abuses theory, we must have some working definition of what constitutes *theory.* I offer here a general, but unconventional, definition, one that can apply to all of the various knowledge fields upon which the IC might draw as it undertakes its multidisciplinary work. My definition is: theory is epistemology plus ethics, and is manifested in praxis, in the theory's application in real-world problem solving. The theory of my own discipline, rhetorical theory, has always been surrounded by concerns about the ethics of how we give rhetoric praxis. Following Cicero and Quintilian, theorists have asked whether or not a good rhetor needs also to be a good person, a good actor. We could ask the same question of institutions such as the IC. Good in this case means *ethical* before it might mean *effective.* In essence, this question reduces questions of ethics to an initial question of whether or not we believe in the "goodness" or "badness" of the rhetor. In the modern era, Richard Lanham has dubbed this dilemma the "Q question."[11] The Q question is often skirted through "the weak defense," which "argues that there are two kinds of rhetoric, good and bad. The good kind is used in good causes, the bad kind in bad causes. Our kind is the good kind; the bad kind is used by our opponents."[12] The weak defense might apply to all types of theory. But the weak defense is an evasion, and while it possibly helps in forensic situations to determine the past ways in which a theory was deployed, it offers no deliberative promise to help deploy theory ethically in the future.

That the IC adopts theory from external sources is not itself worrisome. The IC's deployment of theories developed by outsiders is a potential source of efficiency. Importing knowledge from outside of the IC serves as a force multiplier, freeing IC analysts to do other work. The IC cannot be expected to, for example, independently develop its own theories of psychology. Nor do the fast-paced demands of intelligence production allow for the leisure required to develop new theory. Kairos functions in a more rapidly evolving, compressed time scale in intelligence than it does in academe, and the speed with which intelligence must be produced places an additional pressure on theory. There are many reasons, then, for the IC to import theory from disciplinary experts in academe and industry. However, unethical adoptions or applications of theory by the IC, when they occur, produce a conflagration between epistemology (our methods for creating knowledge), ethics (our collective sense of right and wrong, often defined through norms and custom but also sometimes through law), and praxis (the ways in which we apply theory in the world). The two examples of the extraordinary rendition program and the HTS indicate that when the IC adopts theory out of a knowledge field and gives that theory praxis in the intelligence production environment, the theory is subject to misunderstanding, misapplication, or abuse. The theory is easily corrupted in the absence of the oversight created by disciplinary procedures, norms, and expectations, and by the secretive environment inherent to the IC's work, which also occludes public and institutional accountability for individuals. Such erosions of theory (whether intentional or not is immaterial) do a disservice to the intelligence goals that the theory was intended to support, potentially reduce the standing of the theory within the knowledge field where it originated, and more largely erode the ethos of the IC, and of the United States itself, at a time when international credibility and collaboration are essential for preventing weapons of mass destruction proliferation and confronting international terrorism.

To its credit, the IC and its professionals have increasingly devoted time and text struggling to develop a theory of intelligence analysis that can fully account for the data collection, analysis, and dissemination work that the intelligence community undertakes.[13] The efforts to establish a method, an epistemology of intelligence production, were initiated by Sherman Kent over seventy years ago,[14] but have intensified considerably since the failure to anticipate the terrorist attacks of September 11, 2001, and the inaccurate intelligence that facilitated the invasion of Iraq in 2003.[15] Following Kent, the intelligence community sees itself primarily as a social science,[16] and primarily seeks to draw upon theory from the social sciences to inform its work: "there are numerous theoretical approaches within social science that can be deployed to increase our understanding of intelligence."[17] Attempts to define a theory specifically of intelligence analysis have been primarily epistemological endeavors, with far less consideration given to ethics. The intelligence community's theory of itself and its own work is not the subject of this chapter though. Rather than focus on the IC's epistemology, I focus our attention on the other primary, but often less visible, component of theory—ethics—too often neglected by the IC itself.

What, then, is the IC's relationship to the ethical components of theory, writ large? What ought to be the nature of the relationship? Regardless of which knowledge discipline it arises from, it is a mistake to see theory as strictly or only an epistemology, as only a way of seeing the world. All disciplinary bodies of theory contain within them ethics, which is sometimes explicitly a part of the theory, but often is implicit. In general, those disciplines that deal directly with human subjects are most likely to make ethical expectations explicit within their articulations of theory. For example, the fields of psychology and sociology have explicitly articulated ethical norms, norms that, as we have seen, the IC has violated in the recent past. Even the claim made by some practitioners in some disciplines that a theory is ethically neutral is itself a type of ethical claim, and one that tends to favor the ethical status quo, rather than being truly ethically neutral, a neutrality that long ago ethicists realized might be impossible.[18] Nonetheless, theory from a wide variety of knowledge fields, or disciplines, influences the IC's work at various stages of the intelligence production process. The ethical components of those theories do not always appear to transfer with the disciplinary knowledge that they govern in their home disciplines.

There are generally thought to be three phases of intelligence production—collection, analysis, and dissemination[19]—and each of these phases contain opportunities for the IC to interact with theory, and with the ethical components of theory. In the first phase, collection, information and data are gathered. Data might come from human sources (HUMINT), intercepted signals (SIGNINT), overhead imagery (IMINT), or other collection disciplines, but regardless of the collection method, the first step to intelligence production consists of gathering data. Previously written intelligence products might also contribute data to an intelligence question. The second phase, analysis, might take dozens of forms, from the chemical analysis of air samples collected near a suspected nuclear weapons production facility, to a highly speculative analysis of a foreign leader's mental stability. After the analysis phase, and often after many pieces of analysis are combined into a larger analytical product, the third phase, dissemination, takes place, and the finished intelligence product is disseminated to policymakers, military leaders, and depositories within the IC where the analysis can be referenced in the future. All three phases of intelligence production require praxis, the application of theory, and also then interact with explicitly adopted or implicitly accepted ethical norms and practices. The extraordinary rendition program and the HTS are examples of psychological and sociological theory that were given praxis primarily at the collection stage of intelligence production and, to a lesser extent, at the analytical stage.

In simpler, but perhaps more polemical terms: to engage in the intelligence production process is to engage in ethics. All intelligence work has ethical implications, even if those ethical considerations are unknown to, or ignored by, the intelligence professionals and communities of professionals engaged in acts of collection, analysis, and dissemination. A primary question, which this question seeks to initiate, but that requires many contributions, is: how can the IC adopt theory from academe while remaining accountable to the public for the ethical application of said theory, and particularly when the IC's work is necessarily secretive?

Within academic disciplines, the ethics of theory and praxis are persistently worried and scrutinized, as scholars continually examine, critique, modify, dismiss, and invent theory, and standards for the application of theory through praxis. In this regard, academic disciplines are essentially self-policing, with complex, redundant systems for monitoring what counts as knowledge, and for what is acceptable in the attempt to expand human knowledge. Individual scholars are accountable for their uses of theory. Both the products and processes of knowledge production are subjected to persistent review. Such scrutiny examines both the epistemology and ethics of theory within disciplines. The credentialing of experts by conferring degrees, the processes of publishing, the peer review of books and articles, and institutional review boards (IRBs), all serve as mechanisms for monitoring what knowledge is being produced, how worthy it is of recognition, the ethics of how it is produced, and the ethics of how knowledge is then reapplied to create new knowledge. Such policing in its modern form is generally effective within academe. However, the pace of such work in academe is glacial, particularly when compared to the rates at which the intelligence community must move through the processes of intelligence collection, analysis, and dissemination. Time pressure, coupled with the need to produce intelligence much more quickly than academe produces knowledge, presents another pressure that may contribute to the sidestepping or overlooking of ethical norms. The ethical safeguards developed over time to oversee academic knowledge production are robust, but are inadequate for the intelligence community. Such gatekeeping does not operate fast enough for IC needs, and IC analysts are not individually or institutionally accountable for their deployments of theory in the ways individual scholars are. Unfortunately, the IC appears not to have developed alternate methods for policing itself that also keep pace with the rapid timelines of intelligence production.

Self-policing is also facilitated in academic disciplines by relative transparency. While secrecy might in some cases surround a project during its development, academic culture and economics always push toward publication, toward sharing and authorial accountability. Knowledge is not considered to exist until it has been preliminarily vetted (through some form of peer review) and published, upon which it is further vetted as fellow experts analyze, argue with, and test what has been published. Academic culture is simultaneously open and dispersed. Because, for example, physicists are spread across thousands of institutions, one physicist can critique the work of another without fear of reprisal at her own institution. The intelligence community, though, is characterized by secrecy, and secrecy not just with the outside world but also within itself. The necessary secrecy of IC work is perhaps the major factor in allowing analysts and their agencies to avoid accountability when theory is misapplied. As a hierarchical culture, critiques of colleagues' work might also create fear of reprisal for analysts. The need-to-know policy dictates that intelligence sources, data, and analytical processes are kept secret not only from the public but also from most other elements of the IC. Again, the extraordinary rendition program provides a cautionary example. The program was able to be established and continue only because relatively few interrogators and analysts knew about it, which prevented potential whistle-blowers from exposing the program sooner, before its damage could become so widespread.

Elected policymakers also seem to exert their oversight only too late. Such was precisely the case when the Senate investigated the CIA's extraordinary rendition program. Only after the program had done its damage to prisoners and the United States's international standing was the problem revealed and subsequently investigated. Given their separation from the IC, and the many other duties of elected policymakers, we cannot realistically expect them to oversee the sorts of day-to-day operations where theory is given praxis within the IC.

In addition to the possibility of misusing theory through misunderstanding or misapplication, corruption also invites the abuse of theory. Within the United States, the vast amounts of money set aside for intelligence activities potentially invite the corruption of theory in pursuit of financial gain. Infamously, the public version of *The Senate Intelligence Committee Report on Torture* notes that the two contractor psychologists responsible for developing the CIA's enhanced interrogation program were awarded a contract worth over $180 million, $80 million of which they received before the program was revealed and the contract terminated.[20] Jessen and Mitchell, the architects of the enhanced interrogation techniques, eventually were forced to settle with some victims of the program for an undisclosed sum.[21] Simply creating contact between the discipline of psychology and the CIA program was not enough to prevent abuses. Many conferences between the APA and the CIA were held, but while the joint conferences between intelligence professionals and APA researchers did result in a movement of knowledge and expertise from the field of psychology into the intelligence community, they did not have the effect of producing oversight. The conferences resulted in a transfer of epistemology, arming the IC with new ways of acquiring information (perhaps of dubious reliability) from prisoners; however, they did not facilitate a similar transfer of accompanying ethics from APA guidelines and practices. If anything, the lack of ethics in the CIA appears to have eroded the ethical obligations of APA officers. The APA report on its own complicity in the extraordinary rendition program cites lucrative funding opportunities offered by the CIA as one motive that overwhelmed its officers' ethical standards. Money threatens to corrupt disciplinary knowledge almost as easily as it threatens to corrupt individuals' ethics.

Relatively recently the IC has begun to look to my own field—rhetoric—as a body of theory that might inform IC practices, particularly in the phases of analysis and dissemination but also in offensive and counterintelligence operations. This volume exists to examine the recent operationalizing or weaponizing of rhetoric. The turn by some within the IC toward rhetoric is a break from the institution's past. Sherman Kent specifically eschewed rhetoric.[22] This eschewal was not made out of ignorance. As a Yale history professor prior to his work in the Office of Strategic Services (OSS) and role in founding the CIA, Kent appears to have been at least familiar with the rhetorical theories of his day. He rejected a potential role for rhetoric within the IC on the grounds of his perception that rhetoric is inherently relativistic. Contemporary intelligence professionals, however, are reexamining the possible relationship between rhetoric and intelligence production. One way to glimpse the IC's reengagement with rhetorical theory is through master's theses written by IC practitioners. Such documents provide a rare window into the opaque, secretive world of intelligence production. However, we need to be careful when considering such theses as evidence of intelligence community thinking. On the one hand, these theses carry the predictable and required disclaimers that their contents do not reflect IC policy. And yet, these theses are written by the current and future practitioners of intelligence work.

Gary Mills's thesis, "The Role of Rhetorical Theory in Military Intelligence Analysis," is an exceptional example.[23] Not only does it deploy rhetorical theory in an argument about how intelligence work might and should be undertaken, it has also elicited a reply from within the academic discipline of rhetoric. Hamilton Bean's article "Foucault's Rhetorical Theory and U.S. Intelligence Affairs" seeks explicitly "to understand the meaning, accuracy, and implications of Major Mills's statement."[24] As Bean discovered, Mills's thesis is significant because it is one of few "publicly available document[s] produced by the U.S. military that discusses the role of rhetorical theory," and because the thesis was published by the Air Force's Air University as "a 'Fairchild Paper,' which serves as a mark of distinction within the Air University system."[25]

In his thesis Mills is quite sensitive to the resistance his work is likely to encounter with its military audience, and he frontloads his argument with a combination of requests to suspend judgment and advocacy on behalf of rhetoric, writing, for example, that "typically, as a mission-oriented community, we tend to shun concepts and theories that do not appear to directly support the war fighters (soldiers, sailors, and airmen) in the completion of a broadening array of duties ranging from direct, conventional combat to peacekeeping operations" and that "an operationally tailored application of rhetorical theory can make the intelligence community—more importantly, your day-to-day work—even more effective."[26] Like myself, Bean agrees with Mills that a rhetorical theory of intelligence analysis is necessary, and that the intelligence community would benefit from the development of a viable rhetorical theory of intelligence analysis. Mills's thesis, though, rests on an unconventional reading of Michel Foucault's *Discipline and Punish*. Mills's argument is essentially that the intelligence community needs a rhetorical theory of intelligence, that Foucault can provide that theory, that Foucault theorizes rhetorical power through the metaphor of the panopticon, and that the intelligence community can become the panopticon. The misapplication of theory that Mills commits occurs when he argues that the intelligence community can, if it applies itself diligently, essentially become the panopticon of which Foucault speaks. In a typical reading, Mills argues that "from controlling who has information access through panoptic background investigations to centralized control of access mediums—message traffic, encrypted Internet Web sites, and compartmented programs—intelligence agencies carry many of the same watermarks of Bentham's original panopticon blueprint."[27] As Bean writes, "Mills suggests that intelligence analysts are akin to the guards in Bentham's 'panoptic prison,' able to observe and control subjects from a central position."[28] Bean criticizes Mills's readings of Foucault—who seems in the first place an especially unlikely choice on which to base an entire theory of intelligence, because Foucault is only tangentially considered a rhetorician, but more importantly because Foucault's career was devoted to disrupting centralized wielders of power like the intelligence community, not aiding their pursuits. Bean is correct to point out the liabilities of Mills's proposed rhetorical theory of intelligence. "Through bold assertions," Bean observes, "Major Mills builds a counter ethos to Foucault that, ideally, allows Mills to circumvent the anticipated objections of his readers."[29] Mills even goes so far in his attempt to curry his military to leadership as to call Foucault a "very reluctant, unintentional military tactician."[30] Bean is critical of Mills's attempt, pointing out that: "Certainly, Foucault's ideas are open to wide interpretation. But Foucault's theoretical program was focused on social change. So, at its very core,

Major Mills's application necessarily distorts aspects of Foucault's theories in order to make them amenable to preconceived intelligence doctrine."[31]

Mills's attempt to provide a rhetorical theory of intelligence—primarily because it is based on an instrumental reading of a single author who certainly was not a "very reluctant, unintentional military tactician," only maybe even a very reluctant rhetorician—cautions us about the risks of misapplying theory, even when well-intentioned. Mills's thesis—accidentally or not—proposes an unethical application of Foucault's theory. Mills attempts to instrumentally deploy Foucault's theory while divorcing Foucault's metaphor of the panopticon from Foucault's ethics, with a resulting inversion of both Foucault's meaning and his purpose.

One issue that Bean does not address in his own critique is the role of academic advisers and academic gatekeeping. Responsibility for such an inversion of Foucault, submitted and approved as the final document toward a master's degree, rests as much with those advising the student as it does with the student himself. Theorists operating within academe have a critical responsibility when dealing directly with the IC, or with its constituents, when they return to our universities to develop expertise that they will then deploy within the IC after their period of study. One does wonder how such a construal and decontextualized application of theory in this case was approved.

Mills's thesis contrasts sharply with that of Nathan Woodard, another intelligence professional, who wrote "Preaching Truth to Power: Toward a Rhetorical Framework of Intelligence Analysis," in 2009 for the National Defense Intelligence College.[32] Woodard foregrounds ethical issues in his thesis, writing that he seeks to examine "how ethically constrained persuasion can be combined with intelligence analysis to significantly improve the usefulness of the intelligence for its consumers."[33] Woodard recognizes that intelligence products are "inherently persuasive,"[34] which is actually a bold argument within the IC. Additionally, Woodard argues that intelligence analysts should not strive for neutrality in their analysis or language, but instead for an ethically developed and transparent position that the intelligence consumer can then accept or reject.[35] There is much to debate in Woodard's thesis in terms of which rhetorical theory in particular might best serve the IC, and how best to give that theory praxis in the IC's work. Most important, though, is Woodard's refusal to instrumentalize theory in the way that Mills does by attempting to bend it toward his own purpose—a resistance that is almost certainly based in Woodard's foregrounding of rhetoric in terms of ethics. Woodard stresses the need for ethics, before even the need for rhetoric.

Woodard has happened upon Lanham's "Strong Defense" of rhetoric, the idea that rather than judge rhetoric forensically based on the goodness or badness of the ends it achieves, rhetoric needs referents in certain truths, which are not universal but "determined by social dramas, some more formal than others but all man-made," and, "Truth once created in this way becomes referential, as in legal precedent."[36] The task—and it is a tall one—for the IC is to create opportunities for the "social dramas" of critique, monitoring, and oversight that will in turn safeguard the ethics of the work it undertakes. The social dramas of academe—peer review and such—do not fit, but some version of them will be necessary, or the corruption of the rhetorical theory that the IC deploys will be almost certain, pressured by the exigencies of life and death with which the IC regularly deals and which tempt dramatic modifications of long-standing ethical norms.

The fact that multiple, independently operating intelligence professionals have begun to consider rhetorical theories of intelligence production suggests that rhetorical theory is being imported into the IC, not only in applied ways but at a theoretical level, at the level upon which intelligence work is being conceived and framed and prior to work actually being undertaken.

Throughout its history, the persuasive potential of rhetoric has been criticized for its potential to cause harm, a concern that places ethics at the center of rhetorical undertakings. Unfortunately, past instrumentalizations of theory from psychology and sociology suggest that the IC may be prone to abuse the very qualities that give rhetorical theory force. Incumbent upon IC professionals and the rhetoricians who collaborate with them will be developing a system of ethics and ethical monitoring in order to ensure that the past abuses of theory and expertise from psychology and sociology are not repeated with rhetoric. Scholars and intelligence analysts must collaborate to answer a question that is simple to state, but complex in its implications: How do we move useful theory into the IC without instrumentalizing it, and ensure that it is applied ethically? How do we do this particularly given the secrecy and velocity that govern intelligence analysis? The integrity of theory, writ large, and the institutional credibility of the IC both depend upon finding systemic, institutionally applicable answers to these questions.

NOTES

1. Senate Select Committee on Intelligence, *Senate Select Intelligence Committee Report on Torture.*

2. Hoffman et al., "Independent Review Relating to APA Ethics Guidelines."

3. Sims, *Human Terrain System.*

4. AAA Executive Board, "Statement on Human Terrain System."

5. AAA Commission on the Engagement of Anthropology with the US Security and Intelligence Communities, "Final Report."

6. Hoffman et al., "Independent Review," 44–48.
7. Senate Select Committee on Intelligence, *Report on Torture*, 5–6, 16–17, 19–20, 44–49.
8. APA, "National Security Settings."
9. Fink, "Settlement Reached in C.I.A. Torture Case."
10. Hoffman et al., "Independent Review," 9.
11. Lanham, *Electronic Word*, 155.
12. Lanham, 155.
13. Gill, "Theories of Intelligence." See also Bean, "Intelligence Theory from the Margins."
14. Kent, "Need for an Intelligence Literature."
15. Lowenthal, *Intelligence*, 5–8; Gill, "Theories of Intelligence"; Wirtz, "Sources and Methods."
16. Kent, *Strategic Intelligence*, 60–61.
17. Gill, "Theories of Intelligence," 45.
18. Fries, "Ethical Neutrality of Science."
19. Lowenthal, *Intelligence*, 50–51.
20. Senate Select Committee on Intelligence, *Report on Torture*, 16.
21. Fink, "Settlement Reached in C.I.A. Torture Case."
22. Kent, "Words of Estimative Probability." For discussion see, Kreuter, "US Intelligence Community's Mathematical Ideology of Language."
23. Mills, "Role of Rhetoric."
24. Bean, "Foucault's Rhetorical Theory," 15.
25. Bean, 19.
26. Mills, "Role of Rhetorical Theory," 2, 1.
27. Mills, 31.
28. Bean, "Foucault's Rhetorical Theory," 21.
29. Bean, 20.
30. Mills, "Role of Role of Rhetorical Theory," 22–23.
31. Bean, "Foucault's Rhetorical Theory," 20.
32. Woodard, "Preaching Truth."
33. Woodard, "Preaching Truth to Power," 2.
34. Woodard, 3.
35. Woodard, 22–32.
36. Lanham, *Electronic Word*, 156.

REFERENCES

American Anthropological Association (AAA). "American Anthropological Association Executive Board Statement on the Human Terrain System Project." October 31, 2007. http://www.americananthro.org/ConnectWithAAA/Content.aspx?ItemNumber=1952.

American Anthropological Association Commission on the Engagement of Anthropology with the US Security and Intelligence Communities. "Final Report on the Army's Human Terrain System Proof of Concept Program." October 14, 2009. http://s3.amazonaws.com/rdcms-aaa/files/production/public/FileDownloads/pdfs/cmtes/commissions/CEAUSSIC/upload/CEAUSSIC_HTS_Final_Report.pdf.

American Psychological Association (APA). "Policy Related to Psychologists' Work in National Security Settings and Reaffirmation of the APA Position Against Torture and Other Cruel, Inhuman, or Degrading Treatment or Punishment." August 2013. http://www.apa.org/about/policy/national-security.aspx.

Bean, Hamilton. "Foucault's Rhetorical Theory and U.S. Intelligence Affairs." *Poroi* 6, no. 2 (2010): 15–32.

Bean, Hamilton. "Intelligence Theory from the Margins: Questions Ignored and Debates Not Had." *Intelligence and National Security* 33, no. 4 (2018): 527–40.

Fink, Sheri. "Settlement Reached in C.I.A. Torture Case." *New York Times*, August 17, 2017. https://www.nytimes.com/2017/08/17/us/cia-torture-lawsuit-settlement.html?mcubz=0.

Fries, Horace. "On the Unity and Ethical Neutrality of Science." *Journal of Philosophy* 39, no. 9 (1942): 225–34. http://www.jstor.org/stable/2017625.

Gill, Peter. "Theories of Intelligence." In *The Oxford Handbook of National Security Intelligence*, edited by Loch K. Johnson, 43–58. New York: Oxford University Press, 2010.

Hoffman, David H., et al. "Independent Review Relating to APA Ethics Guidelines, National Security Interrogation, and Torture." American Psychological Association, July 2, 2015. https://www.apa.org/independent-review/APA-FINAL-Report-7.2.15.pdf.

Kent, Sherman. *Strategic Intelligence for American World Policy*. Princeton, NJ: Princeton University Press, 1949.

Kent, Sherman. "The Need for an Intelligence Literature." In *Sherman Kent and the Board of National Estimates*, edited by Donald P. Steury, 13–19. Washington, DC: Central Intelligence Agency, 1994.

Kent, Sherman. "Words of Estimative Probability." In *Sherman Kent and the Board of National Estimates*, edited by Donald P. Steury, 127–41. Washington, DC: Central Intelligence Agency, 1994.

Kreuter, Nate. "The US Intelligence Community's Mathematical Ideology of Language." *Technical Communication Quarterly* 24, no. 3 (2015): 217–34.

Lanham, Richard. *The Electronic Word: Democracy, Technology, and the Arts*. Chicago: University of Chicago Press, 1993.

Lowenthal, Mark M. *Intelligence: From Secrets to Policy*. Washington, DC: CQ Press, 2000.

Mills, Gary H. "The Role of Rhetorical Theory in Military Intelligence Analysis: A Soldier's Guide to Rhetorical Theory." Master's thesis, Air University, 2003.

Senate Select Committee on Intelligence. *The Senate Select Intelligence Committee Report on Torture*. New York: Melville House, 2014.

Sims, Christopher. *The Human Terrain System: Operationally Relevant Social Science Research in Iraq and Afghanistan*. Carlisle, PA: US Army War College, 2015. http://ssi.armywarcollege.edu/pdffiles/pub1308.pdf.

Wirtz, James J. "Sources and Methods of Intelligence Studies." In *The Oxford Handbook of National Security Intelligence*, 59–69. New York: Oxford University Press, 2010.

Woodard, Nathan P. "Preaching Truth to Power: Toward a Rhetorical Framework of Intelligence Analysis." Master's thesis, National Defense Intelligence College, 2009.

4

INSURGENT RHETORICS AND HISTORICAL MATERIALISM

MIKE EDWARDS

Consider two juxtaposed moments. First, the climax of China Miéville's 2004 science fiction novel *Iron Council*, wherein the titular insurgent train is frozen in time as an eternal monument to coming revolution in its voyage toward the armed forces of a hegemon metropolis, with this fictional moment owing an ideological debt to the historical materialist writings of Karl Marx: "The perpetual train," the socialist Miéville writes in this novel themed around war, labor, and imperialism; "The Iron Council itself. The renegade, returned, or returning and now waiting. Absolutely still. . . . The train, its moment indurate."[1] Second, the 2006 publication of the US Army's *Field Manual 3-24 on Counterinsurgency* (*FM 3-24*),[2] a document that updated and historicized military counterinsurgency doctrine with insights from scholarship in sociology and anthropology but had the citations for those insights excised in the production process prior to publication.[3]

Those two juxtaposed moments embody the widely differing digital rhetorical tactics and strategies of the US military and its declared insurgent opponents in the evolution from President Bush's "global war on terror" to President Obama's "targeted efforts to dismantle specific networks of violent extremists" to President Trump's rhetoric opposing "radical Islamic terrorism."[4] This chapter examines two sets of doctrinal documents concerned with and embodying the digital rhetorical strategies of those two groups—the US military and its declared insurgent opponents—in order to raise questions about the nature and consequences of the profound difference in those strategies. Those strategies are metonymically represented in the example that opens this chapter. In *FM 3-24*, the US Army attempted to historicize its doctrine toward counterinsurgency, only to have those attempts stripped of citations and historical context in favor of a dehistoricized and instrumental present- and future-focused attempt on tactics of winning hearts and minds. In *Iron Council* the frozen train is a reminder of the material accumulation of historical labor and resources committed to the revolutionary effort, providing a strategic horizon toward which future revolutionaries might continue to strive.

These tendencies—one a hegemonic dehistoricized instrumentalism, the other a revolutionary historical materialism—are visible in the rhetorics that Western media use to characterize the conflicts between the US government and the variously described insurgent or terrorist targets of its military operations, and particularly in the motivations that Western media ascribe to groups such as the Islamic State of Iraq and the Levant (ISIL) and Al Qaeda. The *Washington Post* reporter Jim Tankersley, for example, paraphrases a November 24, 2015, argument from the economist Thomas Piketty that "inequality is a major driver of Middle Eastern terrorism . . . and Western nations have themselves largely to blame for that inequality," pointing to a historical economic circumstance as one significant driver of terrorist activity, to the point where "the Middle East's political and social system has been made fragile by the high concentration of oil wealth into a few countries with relatively little population. . . . Those economic conditions . . . have become justifications for jihadists."[5]

Other authors refuse such historicizing rationales. The *Quartz* blogger Tim Fernholtz argues against Piketty, citing empirical studies by the economist Alan Krueger to "suggest that poverty and inequality aren't behind terror attacks."[6] Fernholtz points to Piketty's observation "that Middle East economies with high inequality are typically the semi-or-outright authoritarian regimes backed by the West, including Egypt, Saudi Arabia, Iraq, and the Gulf States" in order to acknowledge that "inequality is a very real factor in these corrupt countries, but so too are crackdowns on civil liberties and political participation. The studies cited here find that terrorism has a significantly tighter correlation to states without functioning political processes (due mainly to dictators or political collapse) than to poverty. The linkages Piketty sees between terrorists and Western foreign policy in the Middle East may very well exist, not just because it has led to economic disparities but because it has contributed to the political dysfunction that appears to drive radicalization."[7] While one may acknowledge the overdetermined nature of motivations for terrorism, the way Fernholtz broadly characterizes Middle Eastern countries as politically nonfunctional or dysfunctional is an Orientalist rhetorical move characteristic of colonial perspectives.

Such an Orientalist move permits its authors and audiences to perceive the motivations of groups from whom terrorist and insurgent activities emerge as simply an existing evil, requiring obliteration rather than attention or rhetorical response. The rhetorical move on the part of the West, then, becomes a hegemonic dehistoricized instrumentalism: destroy the enemy and their rhetorical capability, using the tools presently available to hand. Terrorism relies on the same strategy, but in the rhetorics associated with terrorist movements, there is also a more complex revolutionary historical materialism, an ideological mode most often associated with Marxism, proposing that the material aspects of history related to producing and reproducing the conditions of existence fundamentally affect all aspects of a society's development, including its politics and culture.

We can see both those tendencies—toward hegemonic dehistoricized instrumentalism and toward revolutionary historical materialism—on display in two sets of documents associated with the United States and its insurgent opponents. On the one hand, the US military publications examined later in this chapter outline sets of digital practices (rhetorical and otherwise) for US forces to undertake to gain a tactical and strategic upper hand in combating global extremism and insurgency. On the other hand, Al Qaeda in the Arabian Peninsula's magazine *Inspire*[8] and the magazine *Dabiq*,[9] published by ISIL, both depict long-standing global traditions of oppression and inequality and in response advocate for tactics of terror and assassination while offering historicized rationales for the long-term rhetorical and material legitimacy of their movements.

The US military presents its rhetorical operations as either information consumption (intelligence) or information production and distribution (the combination of psyops, public affairs, and strategic communications now termed *military information support operations*) taking place in the continuous present-time rhetorical battlespace. Such an ahistorical orientation is visible in the military documents examined later in this chapter, and stands in contrast to the material-historical arguments represented with carefully attuned cross-cultural rhetorical appeals in *Inspire* and *Dabiq*. Analysis of the digital rhetorics on display in *Inspire* and *Dabiq* suggests an awareness that rhetorical labor aggregates over time—historically and materially—into circulating rhetorical capital. In working toward peace, digital-rhetorical strategies in arenas of global conflict might seek to combine cross-cultural rhetorical listening and postcolonial rhetorical perspectives with a deeper awareness of the economic, intellectual, and historical-material foundations of those arenas of conflict.

The US military's investment in a dehistoricized and instrumentalist rhetoric is itself part of a broader Western cultural turn observed by James Arnt Aune, who describes a historical progression in which economic changes resulted in the classical hierarchies associated with connections between individual expression and community values being superseded by more modern hierarchies associated with emerging technologies of communication and circulation and their links to "how discourse functions as power" in market economies.[10] Some instances of military rhetoric have attempted to acknowledge this phenomenon, as noted above in regard to *FM 3–24*, and as illustrated by Colin Gray's observation in a US Army War College publication that "the United States waged war (in Vietnam, Afghanistan, and Iraq) with too little effort being devoted to the whole narrative and context of conflict."[11] That attention to material and historical context, on the other hand, is characteristic of the rhetorical endeavors represented in *Dabiq* and *Inspire*.

In Marx's formulation of the materialist conception of history, "the mode of production of material life determines the general character of the social, political and spiritual processes of life.[12] It is not the consciousness of men that determines their existence, but, on the contrary, their social existence determines their consciousness."[13] In other words, we can only understand the present by viewing it through its material conditions and the history of those conditions, and our political, cultural, and social lives are tied to the relations of production and material relations particular to our cultures and lived histories. However, those who refuse such formulations, particularly in Western hegemonic cultures, have the rhetorical luxury of perceiving themselves as natural and beyond question—the default.

Therein we see an answer to the question posed by Raka Shome: "How do Western rhetorical discursive practices, in their representation of the world and of themselves, legitimize the contemporary global power structures?"[14] Shome's essay later offers its own answers, observing "that while other kinds of analyses were done on George Bush's Gulf War rhetoric, there were hardly any analyses of how the U.S. rhetoric on the Gulf War constructed the Middle Eastern people (and different Muslim cultures) as uncivilized and immoral, and always already inclined towards barbaric terrorist activities"[15]—not only uncivilized but premodern, embedded in a backward past. Ulrich Beck observes a similar tendency serving instrumental ends, noting that "terrorist enemy images are *deterritorialized, de-nationalized and flexible state constructions that legitimize the global intervention of military powers as 'self-defence.'*"[16] In other words, according to the Western representations investigated by Beck and Shome, terrorism comes from a place beyond and prior to that of the modern nation and its borders and strategies.

Despite or perhaps because of such a circumstance, contemporary military doctrine suggests that Information Age terrorism—particularly in the circulation of its rhetorical operations—must be met by abstracted and ahistorical tactics. Those tactics often operate in the gray areas between *ratio* and *elocutio*; between the closed fist of reason and the open hand of persuasion;

between what the army terms the kinetic and the cognitive domains. On the more rhetorical side, the advice offered by the army in its *Social Media Handbook* is fairly innocuous, although representative in its synchronous and instrumental positioning of rhetorical context: "As communicators, we operate in a 24-hour news cycle with the news moving faster than ever before. . . . As communicators, we need to be the first with the truth, whether it's good or bad. Social media allows us to do that. . . . In today's media environment, understanding social media, especially as it relates to time, can help you excel as an Army communicator."[17] A similar attention to what Ridolfo and DeVoss have described as "rhetorical velocity"[18] is visible in an assertion from the US Army War College that "the United States is buffeted by hostile, inhospitable, or uncertain networks, movements, and/or environmental disturbances manifesting as organized and purposeful resistance (e.g., Islamic State of Iraq and Syria [ISIS] and Al Qaeda) on the one hand and leaderless instability (e.g., Arab Spring) on the other. The former threatens core US interests and enduring defense objectives directly, the latter by implication. All are part of a generalized disintegration of traditional authority structures . . . , fueled and/or accelerated by hyperconnectivity."[19] In these observations, we see military authors at least aware of the kairotic components of the rhetorical situations they address, particularly as they address delivery in digital contexts.

Those digital contexts have changed the military's perception of its rhetorical approaches and its attitudes toward those approaches. Prior to the broad adoption of internet-based communication technologies, the military saw its rhetorical roles as existing either in public affairs (communicating in a reasonably straightforward manner to largely friendly audiences) or psychological operations (PSYOPS, or propaganda and other tools aimed at hostile audiences). In the "hyperconnectivity" of the Information Age, however, "largely free-riding on the back of a metastasizing global cyber superstructure, [terrorist] actors are increasingly weaponizing information, disinformation, and popular disaffection in order to by-pass the traditional defenses of target states and institutions."[20] When deployed by nonterrorist or friendly forces, such approaches are termed Information Operations (IO) or Military Information Support Operations (MISO).[21] These tactics are readily recognizable as rhetorical, as evidenced by some of the "examples of joint military information support operations activities" provided by a joint chiefs of staff MISO publication:

> Modify the behavior of selected target audiences toward US and multinational capabilities . . .
>
> Promote the ability of the host nation to defend itself against . . . insurgencies and terrorism by . . . encouraging empathy between host nation armed forces and the civilian populace . . .

> Mobilize support for US and multinational military operations . . .
> Gain and sustain popular belief in and support for US and multinational political systems . . .
> Attack the legitimacy and credibility of the adversary political systems . . .
> Shift the loyalty of adversary forces and their supporters to the friendly powers . . .
> Arouse foreign public opinion or political pressures for, or against, a military operation . . .
> Undermine confidence in the adversary leadership . . .
> Counter hostile information activities . . . [22]

However, it should be emphasized that the military considers such rhetorical tactics only a subset of what it terms IO or MISO. The US Army War College *Information Operations Primer* states that "Information Operations seek to influence the behavior of target audiences by changing their ability to make decisions, while simultaneously defending the friendly capability to make proper decisions. This is no different from the exercise of the other forms of national power. In this instance the means is information, but the resulting outcome is the same. . . . While frequently referred to as 'soft-power' or 'non-kinetic,' IO includes the use of physical attack against adversary information systems or directly against decision makers."[23] Here, then, is the transition from the open hand to the closed fist; from the cognitive domain to the kinetic—and the blur between the two.

Some military authors acknowledge these complexities. The authors of *FM 3–24* rejected the input of US military personnel who argued that the manual did not go far enough to "out-terrorize the terrorists."[24] Similarly, the authors of the *Primer*—in working to untangle the nonequivalencies of the dichotomies between "kinetic" and "non-kinetic" weapons and "lethal" and "nonlethal" effects—observe that "what gives a PSYOP capability its effect is careful selection of a convincing message that gains access to the logic or emotions in the mind of the target. Application of kinetic weapons requires only physical access to the target."[25] Terrorists and generals alike understand that bombs have PSYOP effects and thus could be considered ultimately persuasive, though such definition might seem problematic to rhetorical scholars. The *Cyber Warfare Lexicon* acknowledges further terminological difficulties as well, noting that "terms associated with traditional weapons are based on the assumption of materiel or personnel as the target and damage as the effect. Materiel is defined as the 'equipment, apparatus, and supplies used by an organization.' Although this description could cover adversary computer networks, it would be a linguistic stretch to say that the information on those networks is also materiel. Since cyber targets are very often non-materiel, and since cyber weapons can create non-damage effects, it stands to reason that the language of traditional munitions will be inadequate if we try to force it to cover offensive and defensive cyber operations."[26]

At the same time, recent accounts of actions carried out in Iraq and Afghanistan detail lethal kinetic attacks against personnel as a component of information operations intended to degrade enemy infrastructures and networks of rhetorical circulation and delivery, raising further questions for rhetorical studies about the division between the open hand and the closed fist. Sean Naylor's history of the US Joint Special Operations Command (JSOC) describes the post–9/11 growth of the Computer Network Operations Squadron (CNOS) as an aspect of JSOC dedicated to kinetic cyber operations—killing insurgents who constituted the human networks of rhetorical and informational delivery.[27] According to Naylor, "a strike force would hit a house based on signals intelligence that there was a cell phone linked to an insurgent leader inside. Once the strike force found the phone, analysts would load its contents into computers. . . . The NSA had built a query that alerted it whenever the same username and password information were entered in different countries . . . allowing [US operatives] to upload software onto computers in Mosul's Internet cafés that would alert them whenever someone typed in one of these username and password combinations. Analysts soon knew that they were tracking a senior Al Qaeda leader in Iraq from the contents of one of the accounts."[28] The human networks of rhetorical distribution through which these insurgent cell phone and email networks were connected were simultaneously infrastructural and social, requiring a history of interpersonal trust and individual rhetorical transactions built up over time: in other words, history.

One role of rhetorical activity can be to attempt to establish that history. While the US military is demonstrably uninterested in such rhetorical purposes, the insurgent publications *Dabiq* and *Inspire* pursue them in interesting ways. According to its first 2014 issue, dated 1435 in the Hijri calendar, the English-language *Dabiq* is concerned primarily with matters of theology, to include encouragements for migration (*hijrah*) and community (*jama'ah*) in service of the issue's theme, "The Return of Khilafah" (the Caliphate).[29] The ISIL authors assert, for example, that "the Islamic State has an extensive history of building relations with the tribes within its borders in an effort to strengthen the ranks of the Muslims, unite them under one imam, and work together towards the establishment of the prophetic Khilafah"[30] and justify their arguments through the use of references to the Hadith and Quran, to recent speeches by religious leaders, and to thematic and metaphorical connections between contemporary events and historical examples. Such rhetoric is recognizable to Western eyes both in its content—a conservative valorization of an imagined past golden age and wish for its return—and in its form, with a well-designed and consistent visual identity, striking and attractive layout and typography, and skilled and dramatic use of color and original and stock photography.

The form of the Al Qaeda magazine *Inspire* is similarly polished in its visual appearance. Like *Dabiq*, it was published as a full-color PDF for English-language audiences. Using methods primarily associated with digital technologies in the first and subsequent issues, the editors and authors use drop shadows, textured backgrounds, metallic or reflective or otherwise seemingly three-dimensional effects on text, page layout and typographic effects, carefully chosen stock and news photography and imagery, and sophisticated alphabetic effects including the Unicode ligature for the calligraphic character for the Arabic honorific *jalla jalalahu* ("may his glory be glorified") after every use of the name of God.[31]

They combine these digital methods with sophisticated rhetorical appeals: one op-ed style article by Shaykh Usama Bin Ladin cites James E. Hansen's 1988 Congressional testimony during Hansen's time working for NASA on the dangers of global climate change in order to make an argument about global warming, economic inequality, and the subsequent increasing radicalization of the Islamic world, while at the same time invoking religious texts, thereby linking recent Western events to arguments from the shared history of Islam.[32] A section on "Open Source Jihad"[33] includes instructions on "How to Make a Bomb in the Kitchen of Your Mom" and instructions on how to send and receive secure communications email using the "Asrar al-Mujahideen 2.0" email encryption application. The magazine references figures, debates, and rhetorical topoi prominent in the contemporary media throughout, while also linking them to historical examples, as with Anwar al-Awlaki's contention regarding the perceived European cartoonists' slanders of the prophet Muhammad that "if you have the right to slander the Messenger of Allah, we have the right to defend him. If it is part of your freedom of speech to defame Muhammad it is part of our religion to fight you."[34]

Unlike *Dabiq*, however, *Inspire*'s rhetorical purposes extend beyond historical justification in disturbing ways, to the point of having murderous consequences. One example: the instructions in the "How to Make a Bomb in the Kitchen of Your Mom" section are thought to have been used by the Tsarnaev brothers to manufacture the pressure-cooker bombs used in the April 2013 Boston Marathon terror attack.[35] A second example: *Inspire* invokes the French newspaper *Charlie Hebdo*'s publication of cartoons mocking the prophet Muhammad as a contributing factor to its publication of a kill list of public figures associated with the cartoons, a public argument that may have contributed to the shootings at the newspaper's offices in Paris on January 7, 2015.[36] The form and substance of the magazine's arguments and delivery function as technologies of attention—as contributors to its rhetorical velocity—and so help to incline some who encounter it in various contexts to perform the attentional labor required for the magazine's distribution, use, and reproduction, and perhaps also helped to incline some of its readers to intervene in the formation of history themselves. Again, the line between the open hand and the closed fist is blurred, both in the arguments made by the magazine and by the terrorist acts its arguments may have inspired. *Inspire* cannot be fully understood simply as a synchronic moment of competing and conflicting cultural values among which its multiple audiences must choose, but requires a more complete historical understanding of its material contexts.

Bo Wang paraphrases the 2009 suggestion made by Sue Hum and Arabella Lyon[37] "that a comparative historicized approach that attends to moments, texts, and political situations within and across cultures would allow us to foster a dialogical engagement with other rhetorics."[38] Such a comparative approach might suggest that the blurring of the line between the open hand of rhetoric and the closed fist of force that occurs in rhetorical operations is itself a cross-cultural phenomenon. The explicit attention to history in the Al Qaeda and ISIL documents is Miéville's revolutionary train: "Years might pass and we will tell the story of the Iron Council and how it was made, how it made itself and went, and how it came back, and is coming, is still coming."[39] Samir Khan, *Inspire*'s editor, and Anwar al-Awlaki, one of the magazine's authors, were both US citizens. They were killed by a US drone strike in Yemen on September 30, 2011. In such operations and their historical and rhetorical antecedents, is there a place for Krista Ratcliffe's "ethical responsibility to argue for what we deem fair and just while simultaneously questioning that which we deem fair and just"?[40]

NOTES

1. Miéville, *Iron Council*, 542.
2. US Army, *Field Manual 3–24*.
3. Edwards, *Postcapitalist Economics and Technologies of Composition*.
4. All three phrases have been used widely by their authors in multiple contexts.
5. Tankersley, "This Might Be the Most Controversial Theory."
6. Fernholtz, "Poverty in the Middle East."
7. Fernholtz.
8. Khan, *Inspire* 1, 2010.
9. *Dabiq* 1, 2014.
10. Aune, "Historical Materialist Theory of Rhetoric," paragraph 4. It bears noting here that scholarship in the field of Islamic economics frequently represents such economic systems as

neither capitalist nor socialist due in part to the economically significant ways *riba* (usury) and *zakat* (alms) are governed within such systems.

11. Gray, *What Should the U.S. Army Learn from History?* 10.
12. Some translators here prefer "intellectual."
13. Marx, *Contribution to the Critique of Political Economy*, 11–12.
14. Shome, "Postcolonial Interventions in the Rhetorical Canon," 558–71, 559.
15. Shome, 564.
16. Beck, "Terrorist Threat," 39–55, 44; emphasis in original.
17. US Army, *Social Media Handbook*, ii.
18. Ridolfo and DeVoss, "Composing for Recomposition."
19. Freier, Bado, Bolan, Hume, and Lissner, *At Our Own Peril*, 59.
20. Freier et al., *At Our Own Peril*, 55.
21. Some documents relating to IO and MISO, like the US Army's 2013 *Field Manual 3-53*, while not classified as Secret, are unavailable to civilians. Others, like the US Department of Defense's 2013 *Instruction on Human Intelligence* are classified as SECRET and the copy I obtained was so heavily redacted as to provide no usable information.
22. US Joint Chiefs of Staff, *Joint Publication 3-13.2*, iv–8.
23. US Army War College Department of Military Strategy, Planning, and Operations, *Information Operations Primer*, 44.
24. Edwards, *Postcapitalist Economics and Technologies of Composition*.
25. US Army War College Department of Military Strategy, Planning, and Operations, *Information Operations Primer*, 5.
26. USSTRATCOM, *Cyber Warfare Lexicon*, 5.
27. Naylor, *Relentless Strike*, 261.
28. Naylor, 344–45.
29. *Dabiq* 1, 2014.
30. *Dabiq*, 12.
31. Khan, *Inspire* 1, 2010.
32. Khan, 8–9.
33. Khan, 31–47.
34. Khan, 26.
35. Khan, 33–40.
36. Khan, 24.
37. Hum and Lyon, "Recent Advances in Comparative Rhetoric," 162.
38. Wang, "Rethinking Feminist Rhetoric and Historiography," 32.
39. Miéville, *Iron Council*, 564.
40. Ratcliffe, "Rhetorical Listening," 203.

REFERENCES

Aune, James Arnt. "An Historical Materialist Theory of Rhetoric." *American Communication Journal* 6, no. 4 (Summer 2003). http://ac-journal.org/journal/vol6/iss4/iss4/mcmcgee/aune.pdf.

Beck, Ulrich. "The Terrorist Threat: World Risk Society Revisited." *Theory, Culture & Society* 19, no. 4 (2002): 39–55.

Dabiq 1, 2014.

Edwards, Mike. *Postcapitalist Economics and Technologies of Composition*. Pittsburgh: University of Pittsburgh Press, under contract.

Fernholtz, Tim."It's Not the Poverty in the Middle East That's Driving Terrorism—It's the Politics." *Quartz*, November 30, 2015. https://qz.com/561848.

Freier, Nathan P., Christopher M. Bado, Christopher J. Bolan, Robert S. Hume, and J. Matthew Lissner. *At Our Own Peril: DoD Risk Assessment in a Post-Primacy World.* Carlisle Barracks, PA: US Army War College, 2017.

Gray, Colin S. *What Should the U.S. Army Learn from History? Recovery from a Strategy Deficit.* Carlisle Barracks, PA: United States Army War College, 2017.

Hum, Sue, and Arabella Lyon. "Recent Advances in Comparative Rhetoric." In *The SAGE Handbook of Rhetorical Studies*, edited by Andrea A. Lunsford, Kirt H. Wilson, and Rosa A. Eberly, 153–65. Thousand Oaks, CA: SAGE, 2009.

Khan, Samir, ed. *Inspire* 1, 2010.

Marx, Karl. *A Contribution to the Critique of Political Economy.* Translated by N. I. Stone. Chicago: International Library, 1904.

Miéville, China. *Iron Council.* New York: Del Rey, 2004.

Naylor, Sean. *Relentless Strike: The Secret History of Joint Special Operations Command.* New York: St. Martin's, 2015.

Ratcliffe, Krista. "Rhetorical Listening: A Trope for Interpretive Invention and a 'Code of Cross-Cultural Conduct.'" *CCC* 51, no. 2 (December 1999): 195–224.

Ridolfo, Jim, and Dànielle Nicole DeVoss. "Composing for Recomposition: Rhetorical Velocity and Delivery." *Kairos: A Journal of Rhetoric, Technology, and Pedagogy* 13, no. 2 (2009). http://kairos.technorhetoric.net/13.2/topoi/ridolfo_devoss/velocity.html.

Shome, Raka. "Postcolonial Interventions in the Rhetorical Canon: An 'Other' View." In *Contemporary Rhetorical Theory: A Reader*, 2nd ed., edited by Mark J. Porrovecchio and Celeste Michelle Condit, 558–71. New York: Guilford, 2016.

Tankersley, Jim. "This Might Be the Most Controversial Theory for What's behind the Rise of ISIS," *Washington Post*, November 30, 2015. https://www.washingtonpost.com/news/wonk/wp/2015/11/30/why-inequality-is-to-blame-for-the-rise-of-the-islamic-state/?utm_term=.44a5be96441c.

US Army. *Field Manual 3-24: Counterinsurgency.* Washington, DC: Department of the Army, 2006.

US Army. *Social Media Handbook.* Washington, DC: Department of the Army Office of the Chief of Public Affairs, 2016.

US Army War College Department of Military Strategy, Planning, and Operations. *Information Operations Prime.* Carlisle Barracks, PA: United States Army War College, 2011.

US Joint Chiefs of Staff. *Joint Publication 3-13.2: Military Information Support Operations.* Washington, DC: United States Department of Defense, 2011.

US Strategic Command (USSTRATCOM). *The Cyber Warfare Lexicon.* Version 1.7.6. Offutt Air Force Base, NE: United States Department of Defense, 2009.

Wang, Bo. "Rethinking Feminist Rhetoric and Historiography in a Global Context: A Cross-Cultural Perspective." *Advances in the History of Rhetoric* 15 (2012): 28–52.

5

MINERVA RISING

THE PENTAGON'S WEAPONIZATION OF RHETORICAL KNOWLEDGE

JOHN GAGNON

In June 2017 the Strategic Studies Institute and the US Army War College published *At Our Own Peril: DOD Risk Assessment in a Post-Primacy World* as a point of reference for the secretary of defense, the chairman of the joint chiefs of staff, Department of Defense (DoD) leadership, and military commanders in the field. *At Our Own Peril* highlights changes in the international system, the collapsing authority of the United States within that system, and the ways in which those changes require fundamental shifts in strategic and military decision-making. The authors write, "Now, it is becoming increasingly clear that the United States is either at the doorstep or in the midst of a . . . wave of foundational strategic change. This study labels this period 'post-primacy.' For the DoD, post-primacy is marked by . . . : hyperconnectivity and weaponization of information, disinformation, and disaffection . . . ; proliferation, diversification, and atomization of effective counter-U.S. resistance . . . ; and finally, violent or disruptive dissolution of political cohesion and identity."[1] In their view, within this period the uncontrolled spread of information "threatens core U.S. interests and enduring defense objectives" and is "part of a generalized disintegration of traditional authority structures fueled by hyperconnectivity."[2] The authors call for greater investment in surveillance, enhanced propaganda through strategic manipulation of public opinion, and increased control of information content and information flows. This emphasis on "the bloodless battlefields of information and influence" to counter the "forces of social disintegration and virtual mobilization and resistance" is the inevitable outgrowth of long-standing concerns within the Pentagon and throughout the military about the dulling of the dual-edged sword of strategic and military primacy in the years since the invasions of Iraq and Afghanistan.[3]

Investments in information capabilities stand front and center in the Pentagon's attempts to position itself to contain, manage, and win both traditional and nontraditional (e.g., asymmetric) conflicts throughout the world, and to maintain domestic support. Programs like the now-defunct Human Terrain System and the ongoing Minerva Research Initiative have spearheaded this effort. While not stated as such, the DoD's interest in information control and manipulation intersects with rhetoric studies in very particular and important ways. Within the academy, we tend to prefer to think of rhetorical scholarship and study as tools to build bridges between people, communities, and cultures, emphasizing commonality rather than division. But, from the perspective of military decision-makers, now as throughout history, rhetoric—and its attendant capacity to provide insight into hyperconnectivity, disinformation, and disaffection—is viewed as another weapons system to be studied for deployment throughout the battlespace. Recent investments in funding academic research into potentially weaponizable rhetoric are perhaps best seen in the Pentagon's Minerva Research Initiative, a military-to-academia funding pipeline designed to explore areas of interest to ongoing and future conflicts.

In taking a closer look at Minerva, this chapter considers one avenue through which the Pentagon has increasingly sought to weaponize rhetorical knowledge to increase its information capabilities across the battlespace and sheds light on the work product derived from academic research funded by the Minerva Initiative during its first decade. A substantial number of projects funded by Minerva are of direct interest to the work of those involved in rhetoric studies because of the Initiative's emphasis on information control and influence in an increasingly hyperconnected world.

THE MINERVA INITIATIVE: AN OVERVIEW

The Minerva Initiative is a research program, founded in 2008, which is sponsored and solely funded by the DoD. Envisioned by former secretary of defense Robert Gates, the initiative sought to "repair" relations between the military and the academy while spearheading studies on areas of strategic interest to national security. As it describes itself, the Minerva Initiative "brings together universities, research institutions, and individual scholars and supports multidisciplinary and cross-institutional projects addressing specific topic areas determined by the Department of Defense."[4] Since its founding, the initiative has made more than $75 million available in direct research funding.[5]

This joint military-academic venture was described by James Petras, in a 2009 editorial, as a "military-academic empire building strategy" using "academics in uniform" to divide, destroy, and control—engaging researchers "in some of the more brutal aspects of colonial warfare."[6] Henry Giroux similarly questioned the growth of military-funded research in academia, writing, "as in other spheres of American civic life, the institution of higher education is being militarized."[7] Giroux echoed Petras' concerns about the ways in which military-to-academia funding pipelines exercised "subtle, though influential, pressure in shaping the priorities" of academic programs and departments.[8]

At the time of its creation, and immediately after, academics expressed deep concerns about the design, motivations, and potential influences of the Minerva Initiative. Yet, despite considerable shared skepticism across the academy about the creation of the Minerva Initiative, little has been done to interrogate, in the years subsequent to its founding, its research priorities and the actual uses to which its funds have been put. Since the initial outcry in 2008–2009, very little has been publicly put forward about the efficacy of the program, or its impacts on both academic research and military operations. Indeed, criticism of the program has gone more or less silent. It seems appropriate, then, to cast the lens of inquiry back in the Minerva Initiative's direction at the decade milestone since its founding.

Historically speaking, the Minerva Initiative is not exactly a new idea. Indeed, it is commonly accepted that academic research played a crucial role in helping the United States develop the modern weaponry necessary for winning World War II and establishing postwar military superiority across the following decades. The STEM fields remain the beneficiaries of robust Pentagon-sourced funding. But the Minerva Initiative stands apart from such programs in the fact that it is specifically designed to fund research outside of the realm of "hard" science, instead situating its focus on areas of interest to those conducting research in the humanities and social sciences.

The closest parallel program in recent history—Project Camelot—was a 1964 research initiative managed by the Special Operations Research Office at American University. Project Camelot was designed to understand the "sources of revolutionary movements and insurgencies in Latin America and to develop strategies of 'insurgency prophylaxis.'"[9] The project eventually self-destructed when a researcher misrepresented the initiative, concealing the military's financial backing.[10] Hugh Gusterson, who added his voice to that of skeptics of the Minerva Initiative early after its creation, wrote: "The Pentagon seeks to recuperate the implosion of Project Camelot and its estrangement from the [research] community in the Vietnam years by establishing a community of [researchers] who will be drawn into the training of soldiers and intelligence officers, who will serve as adjudicators of research proposals for others, and who will train students and direct them to careers as military [researchers]. Project Minerva is an attempt to restore the 1950s."[11] In 2008 Alan Wolf noted that "if academics are not especially willing to give their advice to governments, governments are even less willing to seek it from academics."[12] This stance, following a litany of strategic, cultural, and information operations failures in Iraq and Afghanistan, would not hold, and Wolfe's observation—"if a military-industrial-academic complex once existed, by the start of the twenty-first century, it existed no longer"[13]—would prove short-lived in light of such miscarriages. Instead, by 2008 it had become increasingly clear to Pentagon decision-makers that a shift was necessary, that brute force was not enough to succeed in twenty-first-century conflicts, and that fresh perspectives and ideas were needed.

Whether or not the Minerva Initiative was an attempt to restore the 1950s, its creation came on the heels of embarrassing information operations failures in Iraq and Afghanistan. Indeed, "senior DOD leadership was quick to recognize the importance of systematizing the military's approach to coordinating action in the information sphere."[14] The battlespace had shifted in such a way that the Pentagon needed to move from an approach that heavily relied on kinetic action, to one that more robustly considered information "fire": addressing motivations, discrediting enemy actions, and looking specifically at the informational aspects of perception, message crafting, and message delivery.[15]

It was in this context—where "information environment shaping" was not only "unsuccessful, but barely moved the needle in one direction or the other"[16]—that Secretary Gates sought to "initiate changes in both the definition and application of information operations capabilities."[17] Gates launched the Minerva Initiative to buoy this effort, seeking to enhance cultural and social awareness, while simultaneously creating a funding pipeline to explore developing a knowledge-base to understand, build, and synchronize information capabilities. This was, as Craig Calhoun noted, "occasioned by the conviction that the nature of the wars the US military is called on to fight is changing, and so too the larger strategic context that will shape future conflicts." [18] Or, as Kristine Ringler noted, "No longer are military operations won by the most powerful physical force, but rather victory often goes to the smarter, information-dominant, culturally aware, net-centric force."[19]

A CLOSER LOOK: MINERVA & RHETORIC STUDIES

The Minerva Initiative's research priorities shift year to year and are determined by the Pentagon—that is, the military both sets the research agenda and frames the issues on its own terms and with its own language. From the perspective of those who study rhetoric, this itself is a shrewd maneuver because the Pentagon retains control over the ways in which potential projects are developed and proposed, the language deployed within those projects as they are conducted and written about, and situates the findings—or work product—of those projects in a way that is most useful to the military, rather than the broader development of knowledge for social good. Craig Calhoun has observed, "Regarding Minerva, and military funding of academic research more generally, questions turn on who sets the research agenda and who frames the issues. . . . This core issue remained: Minerva would establish priorities and topics for research . . . the DOD was setting the agenda."[20]

The DoD continues to set the agenda, with millions of dollars annually going to projects contextualized within a specifically, and carefully, crafted rhetorical frame. A review of Minerva's research priorities shows that there has been a consistent—and increasing—interest in issues implicating rhetorical knowledge. Bizzell and Herzberg note that rhetoric studies encompasses the following areas: "The practice of oratory [discourse or speech]; the study of strategies of effective oratory; the use of language, written or spoken [or electronic] to inform or persuade; the study of the persuasive effects of language; the study of the relation between language and knowledge; the classification and use of tropes and figures; and, of course, the use of empty promises and half-truths as a form of propaganda."[21] Rhetoric studies, then, may be viewed from the military perspective in this way: "All too often stereotyped and disregarded as pure academia, rhetorical theory is at the very core of military analytical development."[22] If rhetorical theory is at the very core of military analytical development, then the Minerva Research Initiative has made the explicit move of requesting new perspectives, backed by academic research, on topics of interest that intersect with rhetoric studies. While the initiative routinely lists a broad array of priorities that align with obvious areas of interest, such as Chinese Military and Technology Studies and Military Cyber Defense, there has also been an unambiguous interest in areas that overlap with rhetoric studies.

For example, in 2012 the Minerva Initiative requested proposals on "information diffusion," "perceptions and impacts of government communications," "counter-messaging" and "counter-dialogues," and "social media as an influence on collective behavior."[23] In 2014 requests included research on "information dissemination," "dynamics of group decision-making" and influence, and studies on language usage in "hacking forums."[24] More recently, in 2017 the initiative shifted to request research on "how communities construct meaning," "influence operations," and information control "techniques" to create favorable decision outcomes.[25]

From the study of discursive networks and counter-dialogues to interest in social media influence, hacking forum language, and community-based meaning making and cultural identity, many of the Minerva Initiative's research priorities have mirrored the conversations going on within the realm of rhetoric studies. In many respects, these research priorities read like a hot topics list pulled together by scholars in rhetoric studies. To what end? This should not be surprising. As David Spurr noted in *The Rhetoric of Empire*, the institution of the imperial project "takes over as it takes cover," seeking to appropriate knowledge "while it also appropriates the means by which such acts of appropriation are to be understood."[26]

Therefore, we might read the Minerva Initiative priorities relating to information capabilities as a dual-edged act of appropriation and an enacted rhetorical strategy: by mirroring ongoing questions being asked in rhetoric studies, albeit under a different name and using different language, the Minerva Initiative appropriates the rhetorical knowledge of the academy in an attempt to weaponize it, while simultaneously appropriating the rhetorical toolkit that could draw that usage into question. It is in this that we might be able to see an attempt to mask—or at least, lessen the perceived impacts—of its motivations. As Spurr wrote, "the rhetoric of appropriation carries within it the transference and displacement of its own colonizing motives."[27] Such transference and displacement are readily identified in pledges from the Pentagon that the Minerva Initiative would pursue a policy of transparency, committing to "complete openness and rigid adherence to academic freedom and integrity."[28] The Pentagon has stated that the research funded by the Minerva Initiative is unclassified, developed a memorandum of understanding with the National Science Foundation to help manage research proposals, promised that transparency would be effectuated by posting project summaries for the public, and allowed researchers to publish their findings in academic publications. The reality remains that such efforts are red herrings, enacted rhetorical maneuvers designed to misdirect. After all, the fact that Minerva Initiative-funded research has, from proposal to publication, been framed by the Pentagon draws the very integrity of that research into question. Indeed, in June 2016 Peter Baker reported in the *Nation*, that "despite proclamations of transparency, many Minerva grants are classified."[29] And, notably, from year to year, the Minerva Initiative has repackaged requests for proposals in increasingly benign language. Over time, one notes that in reading the Broad Agency Announcements (BAA) and Funding Opportunity Announcements (FOA), that there has been a substantial reduction in detail. Notably, the increasing opaqueness has been accompanied by a move from the Defense Technical Information Center (DTIC) website to a new home on defense.gov, and with it, a severely reduced availability of information.[30]

In a 2012 defense of the Minerva Initiative, Ringler et al. observed: "Today's military, much like governments and businesses in modern society, is based on the operations research premise that astute information processing can produce the knowledge to inform multiple-criteria, multidimensional decision making to yield sufficient wisdom to ensure operational success."[31] In the attempt to "yield sufficient wisdom" the Minerva Initiative has, over the past decade, made more than $75 million available to researchers—a drop in the bucket in terms of Pentagon budget, but a hefty sum from the perspective of social scientists and humanists, who now exist in an environment where money is increasingly hard to come by. The Minerva Institute's priorities give us perspective into the areas deemed important. To fully understand the Minerva Institute, however, requires more than looking at its priorities—it necessarily requires us to examine the actual projects it has funded. As the adage goes: follow the money.

To date, there has not been a comprehensive analysis of Minerva Initiative-funded projects. At the time of writing, seventy-six university-based projects have received Minerva Institute funding—of those, eleven (or, 14 percent) clearly intersect in some way with rhetoric studies[32]:

At Georgia State University, a project explored the positive and negative themes of ISIS propaganda messages and tactics. Another conducted an analysis of the recirculation patterns of online propaganda.

A study out of the University of Exeter looked at the operating methodologies of information warfare by authoritarian states.

Researchers at the University of California–Davis explored how shocks to communication networks cascade into other networks.

Arizona State University researchers attempted to identify the hallmarks of "viral" information to develop measures for countering social influence. Another project created a database of Islamist narratives and studied how they were mobilized to influence.

A project out of Cornell University examined social contagion through "the digital traces of transmitted ideas" on social media platforms, based on an earlier Minerva Institute-funded project that looked at deception and misinformation in the context of discourse and social dynamics.

A University of Memphis study looked at the speeches of international actors to identify motives, threats, and predictive patterns of language.

University of Maryland researchers studied social networking in the context of radicalization and deradicalization.

Finally, a project out of the University of Virginia examined the intersections of influence, bargaining, and sensitivity in decision-making.

If, as Gary Mills asserted, rhetorical theory is at the very core of military analytical development, then it necessarily follows that the Pentagon hopes to use such research for the purposes of weaponizing rhetorical knowledge. In this chapter's introduction, I posited that from the vantage point of military decision-makers rhetoric is, indeed, another weapons system. A weapons system, in a practical sense, is a device, object, or method consisting of "one or more weapons and a means of delivery."[33] According to the Geneva Academy of International Humanitarian Law and Human Rights, a weapons system "can be used for purposes other than killing, injuring, disorienting, or threatening or person or inflicting damage on a physical object."[34] In this sense, rhetoric serves as the weapons system that, as method or device, consists of multiple approaches to information delivery and control. Indeed, the aforementioned projects all seek to leverage rhetorical knowledge for the purposes of conducting or deterring information warfare, controlling information flows on social networks, responding to shock events to communication networks, and using language analysis to make predictions. In other words, the intersection between rhetoric studies and the Minerva Institute's funded projects is clear: it opens up the possibility of weaponizing rhetoric for systemic use across "the bloodless battlefields of information and influence."[35]

Viewed through this lens, the Minerva Initiative—rather than a benign source of research funding—could be seen as a knowledge-acquisition program that, in part, seeks to develop weapons systems for the purposes of filling capability gaps in responding to the highlighted concerns of hyperconnectivity, disinformation, and disaffection. The Pentagon's weapons system development process rests on multipronged process: identifying capability gaps, identifying requirements, allocating resources to research capability gaps, and subsequent systems development.[36] If we take documents such as *At Our Own Peril* at face value, then the notion that military thinkers consider there to be a long-standing gap in information capabilities rests as a statement of need for the development of new rhetoric-based weapons systems. I pointedly note the use of the same language used in weapons system development. In this sense, the Minerva Initiative serves as a carefully developed resource allocation vehicle to research and find solutions to DOD-identified information capability gaps. Weaponizing rhetoric is their answer.

CONCLUSION

The Minerva Institute's funding has spanned the fields of communication, cultural studies, anthropology, political science, and computer science, among others; rhetoric studies, as a field, does not appear to have been implicated in Minerva Institute work (i.e., no researchers in rhetoric/composition appear to have yet received Minerva Institute funding). There are important and notable divergences between the work we do and the way similar questions are being weaponized by Minerva Institute-funded research. For instance, Liza Potts's work on the use of social media looks at participant networks across social media to improve disaster communication; Jim Ridolfo and Danielle DeVoss developed the concept of rhetorical velocity to increase understanding about information composition and re-composition; Bill Hart-Davidson and Ryan Omizo developed computational rhetorics tools, accompanied with questions about the ethics and role of computational rhetorics; Alexander Reid's study of discursive networks has drawn into question scholarly production and the reproduction of knowledge; Jennifer Sano-Franchini's examination of text-making practices has led us to think about ways in which cultural identities are sustained; and Brian McNely and Christa Teston explored the ethical dimensions of rhetorical action in networked spaces. While many of these projects overlap with the same, or similar questions, posed by the Minerva Research Initiative, they diverge in the sense that actual scholars who do rhetoric studies are deeply invested in the responsible use of rhetoric to build, sustain, and support social frameworks and communities, that is, we seek to make things better; the Pentagon asks the same questions for the purposes of weaponization.

This reality should trouble those of us who do rhetoric in the academy. Rhetorical scholarship, research, and inquiry—as produced from within the field—have garnered notice within military institutions, including the US Army War College.[37] It is ever more important that we understand and evaluate the ways in which our scholarship, whether funded via the Minerva Initiative or not, provides an inroad to weaponization. Scholars with stakes in the kinds of information capability that projects like the Minerva Initiative seek to develop position their work as an alternative to developing "hard" weapons or engaging in violent conflict. This, in many ways, aligns with the more traditional stance with regard to rhetorical work. Even so, while information capability development can be an alternative modality to violent conflict generally, such views neglect to acknowledge that militaries specifically exist to project power through violent means, and that the military functions within and propagates an environment defined by persistent rhetorical and physical violence. It seems naively optimistic to rest easy on the presumption that rhetorical knowledge cannot or will not be weaponized simply because academics have an orientation to use rhetorical knowledge nonviolently and as an alternative to conflict.

As the military continues to view rhetoric as a weapons system, rhetorical scholarship is both implicated and holds responsibility to draw into question the uses to which rhetorical knowledge is put. While the question of pursuing funding from programs like the Minerva Initiative represents a series of complex calculations on the part of researchers, it seems at least prudent to recommend caution in joining into symbiotic academic-military relations. Building productive, rather than destructive, rhetorical knowledge need not be dependent on military funding—the money that flows from the Pentagon into academia is not an act of philanthropic benevolence. If we are not careful, such rhetorical work can exacerbate or enact kinds of violence that we are not yet well prepared to deal with—that, in fact, should be a driving question for our field, and the time has never been more pressing than now. It is in this that I believe the existence of the Minerva Research Initiative and its attendant interest in information capabilities opens up a pressing area of inquiry for rhetoric scholars. As rhetorical knowledge moves from research to weapons systems development to deployment, we can play a critical role in not only identifying rhet ops but interrogating the implications of weaponized rhetoric as deployed abroad, and domestically. This is particularly the case now because, as Thomas Asher observed: "Like its Roman namesake, the Minerva Research Initiative conjoins wisdom with war in a moment when arguably our public policy is equipped with too little of one and is infused with too much of the other. The Minerva initiative offers the opportunity for the generation of wisdom out of catastrophe but also suggests the cultivation of a gloomy form of knowledge . . . which might encourage new catastrophic incursions."[38]

The question for those involved in Minerva Initiative–funded programs is to what extent rhetorical research can generate wisdom out of catastrophe, rather than cultivating a gloomy form of knowledge. I respect the hope that drives such work; but history, I think, should give us pause. Scholars of rhetoric are equipped to play an important role in examining not only the co-opting of rhetorical knowledge for military purposes and weaponization, but also to interrogate and illuminate the growing impact of military-based rhet ops across society writ large. Our work brings with it a responsibility to increase understanding of how the weaponization of rhetorical knowledge is impacting discourses, values, and ideas in ongoing struggles over culture, meaning, and identity in daily life.[39]

NOTES

1. Freier et al., *At Our Own Peril*, 59.
2. Freier et al., 4.
3. Freier et al., 43.
4. Department of Defense, Minerva Research Initiative, *Broad Agency Announcement*, 3
5. Ahmed, "Pentagon Preparing for Mass Civil Breakdown."
6. Petras, "Procuring Academics for Empire."

7. Giroux, "Politics of Higher Education," 109.
8. Giroux, 109.
9. Gusterson, "Project Minerva and the Militarization of Anthropology," 5.
10. Gusterson, 5.
11. Gusterson, 12.
12. Wolfe, "Academia (Kind Of) Goes to War," 40.
13. Wolfe, 42.
14. Collings and Rohozinskil, "Shifting Fire Information Effects," x.
15. Collings and Rohozinskil, 21
16. Lazzara, "Information Operations," 6.
17. Lazzara, iii.
18. Calhoun, "Social Science Research and Military Agendas," 1103.
19. Ringler et al., "USMA's Minerva Initiative," 29.
20. Calhoun, "Social Science Research and Military Agendas," 1102.
21. Bizzell and Herzberg, *Rhetorical Tradition*, 1.
22. Mills, "Role of Rhetorical Theory in Military Intelligence Analysis," 3.
23. Office of Naval Research, "2012 Broad Agency Announcement."
24. Office of Naval Research, "2014 Broad Agency Announcement."
25. Department of Defense, Minerva Research Initiative, "Funding Opportunity Announcement."
26. Spurr, *Rhetoric of Empire*, 28.
27. Spurr, 38.
28. Mervis, "DOD Funds New Views on Conflict," 576.
29. Baker, "Bad Intelligence."
30. At the time of writing, funded project information prior to 2014 is no longer available on the Minerva Initiative's website. The author reached out to Dr. Harold Hawkins, one of the initiative's program managers, to inquire about the lack of information available now compared to what had been previously available on DTIC (which is not cached and appears to have been wiped from public access). The author did not receive a response.
31. Ringler et al., "USMA's Minerva Initiative," 29.
32. Minerva Research Initiative, "Funded Projects."
33. Weapons Law Encyclopedia, "Weapons System."
34. Weapons Law Encyclopedia.
35. Freier, *At Our Own Peril*, 43.
36. Schwartz, "Defense Acquisitions," 3.
37. Mills, "Role of Rhetorical Theory Military Intelligence Analysis," 3.
38. Asher, "Making Sense of Minerva Controversy and the NSCC."
39. Giroux, "Politics of Higher Education and the Militarized Academy," 117.

REFERENCES

Ahmed, Nafeez. "Pentagon Preparing for Mass Civil Breakdown." *Guardian*, June 12, 2014.

Asher, Thomas. "Making Sense of Minerva Controversy and the NSCC." Unpublished paper, http://essays.ssrc.org/minerva/files/2008/10/asher.pdf.

Baker, Peter. "Bad Intelligence." *Nation*, June 16, 2016.

Bizzell, Patricia, and Bruce Herzberg, eds. *The Rhetorical Tradition: Readings from Classical Times to the Present*. Boston: Bedford Books, 1990.

Calhoun, Craig. "Social Science Research and Military Agendas: Safe Distance or Bridging a Troubling Divide?" *Perspectives on Politics* 8, no. 4 (December 2010): 1101–6.

Collings, Deidre, and RaFal Rohozinskil. "Shifting Fire Information Effects in Counterinsurgency and Stability Operations: A Workshop Report." US Army War College, n.d.

Department of Defense, Minerva Research Initiative. *Broad Agency Announcement W911NF-11-R-0011.* Durham, NC: US Army Research Office, 2011.

Department of Defense, Minerva Research Initiative. "Funding Opportunity Announcement #WHS-A.D.-FOA-17-01." Washington, DC: Acquisition Directorate, 2017.

Freier, Nathan, et al. *At Our Own Peril: DOD Risk Assessment in a Post-Primacy World.* Carlisle, PA: US Army War College, 2017.

Giroux, Henry. "The Politics of Higher Education and the Militarized Academy after 9/11." *Alif: Journal of Comparative Poetics* 29 (2009): 104–26.

Gusterson, Hugh. "Project Minerva and the Militarization of Anthropology." *Radical Teacher* 86 (Winter 2009): 4–16.

Lazzara, Frank. "Information Operations, Finding Success as Afghanistan Draws to a Close." Naval War College, May 2012.

Mervis, Jeffrey. "DOD Funds New Views on Conflict with its First Minerva Grants." *Science* 323, no. 5914 (January 2009): 576–77.

Minerva Research Initiative. "Funded Projects." www.minerva.defense.gov.

Mills, Gary. "The Role of Rhetorical Theory in Military Intelligence Analysis: A Soldier's Guide to Rhetorical Theory." Master's thesis, Air University, 2003.

Office of Naval Research. "2014 Broad Agency Announcement #14-013."

Office of Naval Research. "2012 Broad Agency Announcement #12-016."

Petras, James. "Guest Editorial: Procuring Academics for Empire: The Pentagon Minerva Research Initiative." *Dialectical Anthropology* 33 (2009): 1–4.

Ringler, Kristine, et al. "USMA's Minerva Initiative: Why is Understanding Culture Important for the Military?" *PHALANX* (2012): 29–32.

Schwartz, Moshe. "Defense Acquisitions: How DOD Acquires Weapons Systems and Recent Efforts to Reform the Process." Congressional Research Service Report. Washington, DC: Congressional Research Service, May 23, 2014.

Spurr, David. *The Rhetoric of Empire.* Durham, NC: Duke University Press, 1993.

Weapons Law Encyclopedia. "Weapons System." http://www.weaponslaw.org/glossary/weapons-system.

Wolfe, Alan. "Academia (Kind Of) Goes to War: Chomsky and His Children." *World Affairs* 170, no. 3 (Winter 2008): 38–47.

6

INSURGENT CIRCULATION, WEAPONIZED MEDIA

WAGING THE LATE SIXTIES WAR WITHIN

BRAD E. LUCAS

Capitalizing on the affordances of digital media, contemporary rhetorics of social change owe a considerable debt to the protest rhetorics in the sixties (ca. 1963–1974), an era that gave rise to the subfield of social movement rhetorics. In what historians now refer to as the dominant "declension narrative," the turn to violence in the late sixties marked a strategic decline as an array of militant actors diversified their tactics and took up direct action against the state. These operations occurred through open conflict with police and eventually arson and bombing campaigns in a concerted—albeit decentralized, distributed, and ideologically chaotic—effort to challenge the intertwined forces of US capitalism and imperialism on its own militaristic terms. Exhausting the affordances of sit-ins, marches, and peaceful assembly, sixties word wars turned to direct action, "armed propaganda," and diverse forms of violent action against the state as a multidimensional movement adapted to seventies domestic surveillance and counterinsurgency operations. Agents of social change turned to militancy not only to "bring the war home" on the domestic front but also to join liberation forces on a global scale with Third World allies resisting US military operations in eastern Asia, Africa, and throughout Central and South America.

For decades, the sixties declension narrative centered around the New Left and the Vietnam antiwar movement, cast in various ways along this common line: "In 1969 Students for a Democratic Society, whose 1962 Port Huron Statement had served as an idealistic manifesto for nonviolent radical change, split into rival (and increasingly irrelevant) leftist factions, and spawned the terrorist Weather Underground."[1] Unfortunately, this binary framework continues to dominate popular political, social, and cultural thinking, in which the battle lines were fairly clear: one side marked by club-wielding police and rifle-bearing national guardsmen and the other side marked by peaceful protestors demonstrating for civil rights and against the relentless bombing campaigns in Vietnam and Cambodia. In this account, when protestors declared war against the state and armed themselves with clubs, rifles, and bombs, many observers cast the sixties as an era in which a progressive revolution, the movement, had gone astray. Rather than a decline of traditional rhetorical performances because agents of change grew frustrated with the results, we can instead trace the progression of the movement weaponizing the media at its disposal and responding to heightened state violence with its own adaptations to, and of, violence.

As the historian Dan Berger explains, the declension narrative obscures the state's role in prompting the rise of radical militancy: "Without understanding the impact of state repression, radical movements don't make sense. . . . In its own words, the FBI was attempting to 'expose, disrupt, misdirect, discredit, or otherwise neutralize' political opposition, particularly among insurgent people of color."[2] Indeed, the era's most neglected stories are the rhetorical operations of the federal government against radical and militant groups whose networks were growing more intertwined—and whose critiques of systemic oppression circulated not just more widely, but in new modes adaptive to changing technologies. Rhetorical studies can benefit from more developed attention to these oppressive state operations, particularly when the state flouts the rule of law and exploits the affordances of new technologies to thwart challenges to its authority. We need to consider the ways that resistance groups adapt to and rise up to such extralegal challenges, particularly when the terms of struggle indicate shifting modes of rhetorical and technological engagement that remain obscured from public consideration—or simply dismissed through frames of violence and extremism. In this chapter, I trace how the combined efforts of anti-racist, -state, and -capitalist rhetorics of the late sixties became infused with violence, weaponizing media to enact rhetorical performances against the state that would, consequently, inform the decades of anti-state protest that followed. By highlighting the dynamics of rhetorical circulation in an era of heightening surveillance and violence, we can see clearer patterns of adaptive continuity—rather than decline—between the 1960s and 1970s and, more broadly, between eras of traditional and contemporary rhetorical practices.

The proliferation of social, cultural, and political change in the 1970s marks grassroots resistance to the dehumanizing effects of emergent digital technologies; those critics, in turn, would exploit those technologies against the very institutions that promoted them. Of course, these changes were gradual, and even the rudimentary features of early computing culture appeared in radical social action. For example, during the 1964 Free Speech Movement at the University of California, Berkeley, the burgeoning student movement highlighted the alienating effects of bureaucratization through the IBM Hollerith cards used to manage university records. Students wrote "Do not bend, fold, spindle, or mutilate me" on the cards and wore them on their clothes, and a small group had learned to hack computer operations by inserting their own punch cards into programming stacks to disrupt university systems.[3] Phil Lapsley also documents how "phone phreaks" around the country learned how to manipulate the telephone systems in the 1960s to create collaborative discussion spaces and make toll-free calls by whistling, playing musical tones, and developing "blue boxes" to control local and national telephone networks. On a larger level, what became self-referential as the Movement resisted the corporate state and developed their own alternative media operations, with a proliferation of newspapers, newsletters, pamphlets, and flyers not only to compete with the propagandizing effects of corporate mass media but also, and more importantly, to establish open-access spaces for political and cultural exchange. Thriving at a peak era in print culture when the tools of production became accessible and inexpensive, this rhetorical production and circulation not only served as a precursor for rhet ops but undoubtedly influenced the development of digital environments themselves.

The transitional years into digital culture, however, have been complex terrain reduced to the facile pivoting of the declension narrative. In his critique of US surveillance culture, Stephen Paul Miller focuses on the 1970s as a period "lost" in historical memory, without definition or narrative clarity, attributable to its position between epistemic eras, or long-developing eras of knowledge production. Miller posits the notion of "rippling epistemes," the transitional spaces between two epistemic eras: a span wherein "the mindsets of eras intertwine with one another and make each other possible. This ripple, or relational space between eras that occupies no fixed time, actually composes eras. Relations between eras *are* eras."[4] Epistemic periods are far different from chronological periods, and they are not as easily or clearly demarcated; in the transition period of rippling epistemes, there is always overlap and imbrication of ideas as one discursively defined era gives way to another. Miller breaks down the 1970s into microperiods of 1970–1971, 1972–1974, 1975–1977, and 1978–1979 to enable a relational analysis of cultural developments that "'read' like important distinctions within an unclearly connected story."[5] Through a relation analysis of cultural and rhetorical developments in the transition period of rippling epistemes we can more clearly examine what would otherwise be an unclearly connected narrative. Miller concludes from his work that "surveillance and self-surveillance were dominant traits, or tropes, of seventies culture,"[6] showing how the 1970s marks a period of transition from external surveillance to an internalization of that surveillance. As Yasha Levine explains, by 1972 the early internet was instrumental in this work, as the Advanced Research Projects Agency Network (ARPANET) "was used to help the CIA, the NSA, and the US Army spy on tens of thousands of antiwar and civil rights activists."[7] My analysis here focuses on those initial epistemic ripples, not as the "good sixties" declined into the "bad sixties," but as rhetorical circulation failed, changed, adapted, and distorted operations on all sides of a war spun out abroad and at home.

DEMOCRACY IN CIRCULATION: STUDENTS FOR A DEMOCRATIC SOCIETY

Organized resistance against the state deeply involves the circulation of rhetoric, the purposing and repurposing of texts and symbolic acts—all part of the purview of social movement rhetorics.[8] Social change comes about through the rhetorical circulation not only of texts but also a wider range of symbolic activity. Stemming from the work of Catherine Chaput and Laurie Gries, we can now benefit from the more dynamic models of rhetorical circulation rather than the staid model of "the rhetorical situation" put forth by Lloyd Bitzer, Richard Vatz, and others. In a crude formation, we might say that what circulates is the available means of persuasion—but it is much more than the movement of rhetoric. Instead, as Benjamin Lee and Edward LiPuma initially clarified, circulation is "a cultural process with its own forms of abstraction, evaluation, and constraint, which are created by the interactions between specific types of circulating forms and the interpretive communities built around them."[9] Attending to the full complexity of circulation also requires attention not only to distortions and power struggles but also to precedent in historical activity and medium. As Sean O'Rourke, Lester Olson, and others have argued, the circulation of some texts, and not others, shapes not only the affordances of public arguments, but also, as Mary E. Stuckey explains, their institutional dimensions: "by performing and circulating performances of institutions and social roles those institutions and roles are created."[10] The late 1960s shows us how the production and circulation of texts is disrupted by the epistemic ripples of the 1970s, both adapting to, co-opting, and weaponizing media during the rise of the high-surveillance state and the institutions that supported it. In particular, if we look closely at Students for a Democratic Society (SDS) as a high-growth network striving for its own institutional stature but collapsing in late 1969, we can see how traditional approaches to social movement rhetorics transformed to meet the challenge of a repressive government—and how both entities adapted to the practices of violence along the way.

The complex history of SDS is beyond the scope of this discussion, but I focus here on some key developments to highlight its role in the circulation of Movement rhetoric up until the late 1960s. Founded in 1960, the tenuously organized SDS grew in numbers nationwide largely due to opposition to the military and corporate presence on college campuses, and it later gave rise to a militant faction called Weatherman, which assumed control of SDS and carried out a rhetorically charged media-spectacle bombing campaign against government and corporate targets throughout the early 1970s. However, according to Kirkpatrick Sale—its most comprehensive historian—SDS had emerged out of a long-standing labor organization called the Student League for Industrial Democracy (SLID), and SDS had a unique mission: not to build SLID chapters devoted to local causes but instead to develop SDS chapters that would serve as campus hubs to develop networks of existing student organizations. More importantly, these campus chapters would be nationally coordinated, not necessarily controlled, to galvanize disparate efforts to enact systemic change and rally student power from coast to coast.[11] It would be a multi-issue party, motivated primarily to unite student activism of all types. In 1962 founding members Al Haber and Tom Hayden wrote collaboratively with over fifty members to develop the SDS manifesto, "The Port Huron Statement," which would be mimeographed and sent out to over twenty thousand readers by 1964, then produced and distributed as forty thousand booklets by 1966.[12] Along the way, SDS became a political organization with an ideology advocating insurgency, particularly in the universities, and widespread systemic change to fight poverty and racism.

In the spring of 1964, SDS issued a monthly *SDS Bulletin*, which offered a literature list of nearly one hundred titles, some used for SDS reading groups, and others even as required reading in college classes. As Sale notes, SDS was astounding in its rhetorical production and circulation: it became known as "the '*writingest*' organization around, and the prolificity is, considering the obstacles, amazing."[13] The surprising production capacity and market demand for SDS texts was not lost on its members, as a picture of a mimeograph machine adorned one of the walls in the national office, captioned with the simple phrase *Our Founder*[14]—ironic for its reverence to a machine yet revealing in identifying its locus of power. In many ways *Our Founder* was a logical extension of the "mimeograph revolution," an unprecedented outpouring of poetry books and magazines with origins in a World War II conscientious objectors' camp and a surge in the 1960s that caught the attention, and co-opting, of corporate publishing by 1970.[15] Given the organization's insistence on an annual rotating leadership, student status for membership, and growth beyond anything it could have anticipated, the SDS mimeograph machine may, indeed, have been one of its most stable and inspiring entities—and powerful weapons.

As the historian John McMillian argues, it is an apt metaphor for the underground presses of the sixties, and he pointedly argues that such publications were less motivated by precursor papers like the *Village Voice* than they were by SDS itself; that is, "[SDS] was the organization that set the template for underground newspapers that functioned as open forums, to which virtually anyone could contribute. . . . Before long, underground newspapers in every region of the country began playing a similar role."[16] Without a doubt, SDS was a major conduit and structural model not only for the circulation of Movement rhetoric throughout the country but also its invention, transformation, and threat to the state.

Of course, few of these newspapers were truly underground, with most of them circulating freely—and subject to scrutiny and tracking by local, state, and federal officials, particularly when predominantly white student groups allied themselves with black freedom struggles in the South and, later, in urban centers across the country. As US involvement in Vietnam escalated, SDS struggled to hold its mission as a multi-issue party, rather than an entity singularly focused on the war, yet mass media attention increasingly targeted SDS as the organizational epicenter of the antiwar movement.[17] By October 1965 a federal internal security committee and major media outlets labeled SDS a treasonous, Communist threat.[18] Internally, SDS still had little in the way of structure, policies, strategy, or communication with its members, but it was centrally identified with protests and activism on campuses across the country. Public opinion, shaped by mass media and reinforced by federal investigations, made out SDS to be more of an orchestrated threat than it truly was. The effort to give shape to the nation's restless youth would continue for the next several years, with especially dire consequences for those in leadership positions.

True to its roots, by 1966 SDS had relegated power and control to the local and regional sectors of SDS, rather than a singular leadership structure or constituting document.[19] Its publications reflected the sprawling networks of SDS connections, as the newsletter-style *SDS Bulletin* fell to the wayside and was replaced by the newspaper *New Left Notes*. At the same time, another newspaper was growing in circulation nationally, more so in urban centers than college campuses: the *Black Panther*, issued out of Oakland, California, where the Black Panther Party for Self-Defense was founded by Bobby Seale and Huey P. Newton in October 1966.[20] The Black Panthers play a crucial role in understanding the demise of SDS and are equally worth analysis in the rippling epistemes of the era.

By 1967, aiming for "revolutionary consciousness" was pervasive throughout the Movement, particularly so in SDS; women's rights had further complicated the debates over social justice. Moreover, a succession of large, national antiwar demonstrations had led many to conclude that nonviolent protest and marches were pointless and futile—especially because police and guard units stepped up their violent tactics, bringing tear gas and mace for the first time to campus protests.[21] The Black Panthers had made national headlines for demonstrating at the California capitol grounds with shotguns, and resistance to the draft increased as the casualties in Vietnam continued to climb.

After the surprisingly large turnout for the October 1967 antiwar demonstrations at the Pentagon, the federal government feared that it was underprepared for the threat and increased its surveillance and intelligence activities against the Movement, coordinating with local law enforcement in regular, and often brutal, crackdowns.[22] By 1968 alliances with black freedom struggles become even more prominent in SDS, most notably with the takeover of Columbia University buildings in opposition to the administration's incursion into Harlem. SDS capitalized on media coverage and not only began to expect violence but to internalize the militaristic discourse of a battle against the state. In the wake of the Columbia takeover, the Weatherman faction took shape as the pervasive discourse of SDS turned increasingly violent.[23] No longer merely a production tool, SDS weaponized the *Our Founder* mimeograph machine. In 1968, for example, writers in the SDS national office referred to its texts as "shotgun pamphlets" that would be distributed on the streets, textual weapons circulating for the revolution to come.[24] The violence between police and protestors at the National Democratic Convention in Chicago in October 1968, later described by the Walker Commission investigation as a "police riot," inspired the more militant factions to envision revolutionary changes that would undoubtedly involve violence along the way.

PROFESSIONAL, LIFELONG REVOLUTIONARIES

By October 1968, after the National Democratic Convention, SDS national secretary Bernadine Dohrn developed a proposal, co-written with John Jacobs and Jeff Jones, calling for a two-day national strike. Given the assassination of Martin Luther King Jr. and the incarceration of Black Panther Party founder Huey P. Newton (and scores of other Black Panthers across the country), it importantly speaks to the vulnerabilities of social movements whose leaders were identified as targets and whose organizations were susceptible to government sabotage, through what we later learned was the COINTELPRO operations of the FBI—the proposal states, "We should think in terms of what programs now will develop the seeds of revolution most broadly. Involving large numbers of people directly in decisive actions will make the difference between a movement which depends overly on its 'leaders,' and can be repressed easily, and one with resilience and depth which continues to multiply and grow under adverse conditions."[25] The themes circulating in SDS centered on extending durable networks beyond the college campuses, establishing coalitions with labor organizations and other revolutionary groups—particularly the Black Panthers, but more broadly any entity supporting the struggle of Third World peoples against US imperialism.

The SDS transformations that split SDS in June 1969 are important to understand the full significance of the clash between militant organizations and the state within the critical lens of its alliances with other militant groups, particularly the Black Panthers. Sixties scholars like Todd Gitlin, not insignificantly the SDS national president in 1963, reflect on the convention upheaval as an act of "organizational piracy," in which Weather "walked away with" control of SDS.[26] One group was allied with the Progressive Labor Party, an orthodox Marxist-proletarian faction that foregrounded class struggle. The other group was more militant, wanting direct action and hoping for a "revolutionary youth movement"—coupled with support for the Black Panthers—to fight a cultural revolution against all forms of imperialism. The latter group became Weatherman, named from its founding manifesto, "You Don't Need a Weatherman to Know Which Way the Wind Blows," published in June 1969—the collaboratively written product of an eleven-member committee established around the time of the Columbia University strikes.[27] At the forefront of the discussions was the idea of a professional, lifelong revolutionary SDS—not reliant on leaders, durable in its networks, and driven by direct-action strategies.

In addition, the move to covert operations after the convention reveals more than an effort to evade criminal prosecution; Weather's move underground and use of armed propaganda reflects a heightened awareness of—and response to—the threat posed by federal repression and surveillance. Mass production of authored texts, even with the weaponized mimeograph, would make SDS a more vulnerable target. Its departure from the print culture foundations of SDS toward orchestrating media spectacles marks the epistemic ripples that would continue well into the following decade.

DAYS OF RAGE TO UNDERGROUND

Through Weather's "action strategy," street fighting and staged spectacles were designed to radicalize white youth, particularly off college campuses, and to lead by example in fighting against daily oppressors: teachers, principals, bosses, and police officers. Weather carried out random vandalism and disrupted everyday settings ranging from coffee shops to public beaches and government buildings. They staged what they called "jailbreaks" by storming into public school buildings and trying to incite students into radical action and solidarity. Weather aimed to foment riots, vandalize government property, and draw law enforcement toward Weather and (as they would have it) away from the black community. Abandoning traditional protest dynamics, Weather staged public events as shocking spectacles that would draw mass media attention—in effect, using orchestrated violence to manipulate production and circulation of Movement ideas.

The most prominent of Weather actions, the Four Days of Rage in Chicago in October 1969, aimed to capitalize on the violent confrontations with police a year earlier at the Democratic National Convention. The Days of Rage drew only a crowd of hundreds, not the thousands it had anticipated, and what resulted were violent confrontations with the police and destruction of property. It was not only a complete renunciation of nonviolent strategy but an all-out embrace of physical, symbolic destruction (certainly a prototype for contemporary black bloc actions). By December 1969 the failure of and fallout from the Days of Rage prompted Weather leadership to go underground. It would make itself no longer visible, less easy to surveil, as it announced in Flint, Michigan, its plans to carry out the revolution as an absent presence, empowered by the very privilege and ubiquity of whiteness in the enemy state and its tools of oppression. Put another way, Weather used its whiteness as a counter-surveillance strategy: "White revolutionaries live behind enemy lines. We are everywhere: above, below, in front, behind, and within. While we possess none of the machinery of the state, it is always close at hand. Our ability because we are white to move within the structure of the state, to locate ourselves in and around all of its institutions, opens up explosive possibilities for undermining its power. Our strategy must take into account the ways in which this particular asset can be used to prove material support for the strategy of the black colony."[28] Weather had outlined a theory of armed struggle, noting a "growing sense of frustration" with public rhetoric and mass demonstrations as lacking an "overall strategy." The schism of the Movement, as they saw it, was toward either terrorism or apathy. People were either engaging in "nonstrategic terrorist activity" or were opting out of protest participation altogether. Weather's solution was instead a third course, one that would urge people to act but not to the extreme of terrorist violence that would generate fear among the general population; instead, targets would be limited to the state—highly visible displays designed for mass media coverage and public consumption. The mass actions and weaponized print media that had driven the Movement for years were, instead, merely a useful precursor for people to "understand the reality of revolutionary motion," asserting that "public violence is increasingly key. That is, planning, organizing, and carrying off public and visible violent action against the state."[29] In effect, in late 1969 Weather was striving toward a coalition in which a network of groups with varying agendas could be galvanized in armed struggle to dismantle the imperialist state. Rhetorical circulation for the Movement would henceforth be carried out by the very mechanisms that stood opposed to them: the corporate media and the government. Speeches, marches, mass gatherings and the like would be replaced by spectacles that could not be ignored, events framed by communiqués that would reinforce the "terms of the struggle" without getting mired in the ideological differences that had kept SDS and its coalitions divided. The newly configured Weather Underground Organization (WUO) worked as a clandestine organization, a dispersed network of militant cells that would bomb federal and other establishment buildings throughout the early 1970s.

ARMED PROPAGANDA AND NIXON'S END

Despite Franklyn S. Haiman's radical (but muted) supposition in 1967 that "even the 'rhetoric of the riot,' mindless and indiscriminate as it may be, has its positive function in contemporary America,"[30] the role of violence in rhetorical criticism has long been neglected. In terms of social movement rhetorics, violence is usually narrowly categorized as either catalytic instances, "triggering events," last-ditch efforts to inspire followers, or markers of a movement's termination, whether through suppression, incarceration, diffusion, and death.[31] In other words, our treatment of social movements tends to retreat from instances of violence as evidential failures of rhetoric, as sites where rhetoric ends or ceases to be productive. Extending the work of Heather Ashley Hayes, I contend that understanding late sixties surveillance-militancy requires that we consider "where violence and rhetoric circulate together" and "travel together and create new rhetorical situations and subjectivities."[32]

The Weatherman faction of SDS, like many militants of the time, spoke and wrote using the language of armed struggle and advocated guerilla warfare tactics—a rhetoric that was circulating globally as a challenge to Western imperialism and multiple liberation fronts fighting for independence from (post-)colonial oppression. Particularly inspiring to SDS members was the Tupamaros Movimiento de Liberación Nacional in Uruguay, which articulated a vision of armed propaganda as the tactic of "transmitting political messages through violence of a spectacular and symbolic, yet measured, nature . . .

to generate admiration and support for the perpetrator, rather than the fear inherent to terrorism."[33] Following the Tupamaros lead, the WUO targeted government and corporate buildings only after ensuring that they were unoccupied—or providing enough advance notice to evacuate personnel. Each incident of property destruction was tied to a communiqué that connected the act to the revolutionary struggle, a combination that the journalist Bryan Burrough calls "exploding press releases."[34] For example, its bombings targeted NYPD buildings, the Presidio in San Francisco, a Bank of America building in New York City, and eventually the Pentagon and US Capitol.[35] Along the way, in 1969 the Tupamaros version of nonviolent armed propaganda—spectacular displays—also circulated on a global scale and was imitated not only in the United States but also in Puerto Rico, Argentina, Japan, Italy, and Germany.

As Harold Jacobs notes, the Days of Rage "made Weatherman a national force. The media created a Weathermyth: Weatherman soon became known as the most militant and omnipresent of white revolutionary organizations."[36] The WUO functioned as a dispersed network of cells (based on what Che Guevara and Regis Debray called "foco" groups) that had legendary status not only through mass media attention but also by eluding the FBI. By February 1970 FBI director J. Edgar Hoover said the agency "considers the Weatherman as the most violent, persistent and pernicious of revolutionary groups."[37]

CONCLUSION

In rhetorical scholarship, Weatherman has largely been written off as a domestic terrorist organization.[38] What we know today is that the Weather operations may have been tactical failures, but the overall strategy resulted in a Weathermyth that was, in turn, materialized in the institutional structures of the federal government. Through its circulation as a revolutionary threat to the government, the WUO pushed the FBI and its supporters beyond the very laws they were charged to enforce. As Stephen Heidt has shown, the presidency is "a permeable space" for rhetorical circulation, and we can see—by extension—the FBI as a similarly permeable space for the collation of messages about threats, real and imagined, and the very material consequences of that circulation. As Arthur M. Eckstein has argued, based on thousands of newly released classified records, Richard Nixon and the FBI were so rattled by Weather that they actually materialized the Weathermyth—brought it into its bureaucratic systems—by changing their classification definitional criteria with "the lumping together of Weatherman actions with Weatherman-*type* actions."[39] That is, in 1970 the federal government attributed—documented, filed, and pursued—any and all militant, revolutionary, or Marxist activity directed against the state to Weather. Consequently, Eckstein concludes, "The war against Weatherman waged by an enraged and frightened Nixon helped lay the basis for the eventual Watergate scandal."[40] While fugitives, Weather members scaled back their armed propaganda in favor of weaponized print, carrying out a massive clandestine operation in 1975 by publishing over forty thousand copies of its book *Prairie Fire* and remained successfully free from government capture.[41] Years later, they would turn themselves in, free from prosecution given the illegal means used by Nixon's operatives to build any case against them.

The rippling epistemes of the 1970s remain difficult waters to navigate, not simply for the reductive narrative legacies of the sixties but for the challenges in recognizing a progression of media adaptations and acknowledging the transition from rhetorical situations to rhetorical circulation. Rhetorical studies has had an aversion to interrogating the violence of the late sixties, a period in which the promise of reasoned, civilized, democratic discourse gave way to a different set of logics and an array of new rhetorics that followed—perhaps to our discomfort—when that discourse failed to realize its aims. Of course, this shift has been underway for some time, with terroristic threats drummed into discursive tools and government surveillance as easily imagined as nefarious hackers coordinating efforts to undermine Western civilization. Rhetorical studies, for its part, still needs to do what Weather acknowledged early on: to "work out the role of all kinds of struggle . . . strategy has to be a dynamic thing; its internal elements and relationships will change as the struggle goes on."[42]

NOTES

1. Simon Hall outlines three trends—the conservative sixties, the global sixties, and the long sixties—challenging the "rise and fall" framework of the declension narrative. See Hall, "Framing the American 1960s," 6. Examples of the narrative include Aronowitz, Gitlin, Isserman, Miller, and Sale. See Evans, "Beyond Declension," for a useful discussion of the declension narrative with regard to feminist radicalism.

2. Berger, *Outlaws of America*, 8

3. Lubar, "'Do Not Fold, Spindle or Mutilate.'"

4. Miller, *Seventies Now*, 29; emphasis in original.

5. Miller, 28.

6. Miller, 2.

7. Levine, *Surveillance Valley*, 8.

8. See Cox and Foust, "Social Movement Rhetoric."

9. Lee and LiPuma, "Cultures of Circulation," 192.

10. Stuckey, "On Rhetorical Circulation," 609.

11. Sale, *SDS*, 24–25.

12. Sale, 69.

13. Sale, 125; emphasis in original.

14. Sale, 223; see Newfield, *Prophetic Minority*, 117–18.

15. Clay and Phillips, *Secret Location on the Lower East Side*, 14–16; Loewinsohn, "After the (Mimeograph) Revolution," 222–23.

16. John McMillian, *Smoking Typewriters*, 14.

17. Sale, *SDS*, 193.

18. Sale, 228.

19. Sale, 247–48, 309.

20. See Hilliard, *Black Panther.*

21. Sale, *SDS*, 335.

22. Sale, 406.

23. Sale, 441–47.

24. The extent of SDS mimeograph production and distribution is difficult to measure due to erratic record keeping by the national office. However, the high volume and broad range of mimeographed work is evident throughout the archival collection Students for a Democratic Society Records, 1958–1970 (fifty-six archival boxes) at the Wisconsin Historical Society Library and Archives, Madison, Wisconsin, one of the nation's largest repositories of materials related to Vietnam antiwar activity.

25. Quoted in Sale, *SDS*, 484.

26. Quoted in *Weather Underground.*

27. See Ashley et al., "You Don't Need a Weatherman," 3–9.

28. "Everyone Talks," 443.

29. "Everyone Talks," 444.

30. Haiman, "Rhetoric of the Streets," 19.

31. Stewart, Smith, and Denton Jr., *Persuasion and Social Movements*, 92–96, 320; Bowers et al., *Rhetoric of Agitation and Control*, 47–50.

32. Hayes, *Violent Subjects and Rhetorical Cartography*, 4–5.

33. Brum, "Revisiting Urban Guerrillas," 396.

34. Burrough, *Days of Rage*, 5.

35. Berger, *Outlaws of America*, 136–38.

36. Jacobs, *Way The Wind Blew*, 144.

37. Jacobs, 38.

38. Weather has appeared only on a few occasions in rhetorical scholarship. See Chesebro, Cragan, and McCullough, "Small Group Technique of the Radical Revolutionary"; Gustainis and Hahn, "While the Whole World Watched"; Foss, "Out From Underground"; Hoerl, "Death of Activism?"

39. Eckstein, *Bad Moon Rising*, 131; emphasis in original.

40. Eckstein, 257.

41. Eckstein, 212.

42. "Everyone Talks," 445–46.

REFERENCES

Aronowitz, Stanley. *The Death and Rebirth of American Radicalism*. London: Routledge, 1996.

Ashley, Karin, et al. "You Don't Need a Weatherman to Know Which Way the Wind Blows." *New Left Notes*, June 18, 1969, 3–9.

Atkinson, Joshua D., and Laura Cooley. "Narrative Capacity, Resistance Performance, and the 'Shape' of New Social Movement Networks." *Communication Studies* 61, no. 3 (2010): 321–38.

Berger, Dan. *Outlaws of America: The Weather Underground and the Politics of Solidarity*. Oakland: AK Press, 2006.

Bitzer, Lloyd F. "The Rhetorical Situation." *Philosophy and Rhetoric* 1, no. 1 (1968): 1–14.

Black, Jason Edward. "Native Authenticity, Rhetorical Circulation, and Neocolonial Decay: The Case of Chief Seattle's Controversial Speech." *Rhetoric & Public Affairs* 15, no. 4 (2012): 635–45.

Bowers, John W., Donovan J. Ochs, Richard J. Jensen, and David P. Schulz. *The Rhetoric of Agitation and Control*. 3rd ed. Long Grove, IL: Waveland Press, 2010.

Brum, Pablo. "Revisiting Urban Guerrillas: Armed Propaganda and the Insurgency of Uruguay's MLN-Tupamaros, 1969–70." *Studies in Conflict & Terrorism* 37, no. 5 (2014): 387–404.

Burrough, Bryan. *Days of Rage: America's Radical Underground, the FBI, and the Forgotten Age of Revolutionary Violence*. New York: Penguin, 2015.

Chaput, Catherine. "Rhetorical Circulation in Late Capitalism: Neoliberalism and the Overdetermination of Affective Energy." *Philosophy and Rhetoric* 43, no. 1 (2010): 1–25.

Chesebro, James W., John F. Cragan, and Patricia McCullough. "The Small Group Technique of the Radical Revolutionary: A Synthetic Study of Consciousness Raising." *Speech Monographs* 40, no. 2 (1973): 136–46.

Clay, Steven, and Rodney Phillips. *A Secret Location on the Lower East Side: Adventures in Writing, 1960–1980*. New York: New York Public Library, 1998.

Cox, Robert, and Christina R. Foust, "Social Movement Rhetoric." In *The SAGE Handbook of Rhetorical Studies*, edited by Andrea A. Lunsford, Kirt H. Wilson, and Rosa A. Eberly, 605–27. Thousand Oaks, CA: SAGE, 2009.

Eckstein, Arthur M. *Bad Moon Rising: How the Weather Underground Beat the FBI and Lost the Revolution*. New Haven, CT: Yale University Press, 2016.

Edbauer, Jenny. "Unframing Models of Public Distribution: From Rhetorical Situation to Rhetorical Ecologies." *Rhetoric Society Quarterly* 35, no. 4 (2005): 5–24.

Evans, Sara M. "Beyond Declension: Feminist Radicalism in the 1970s and 1980s." In *The World Sixties Made: Politics and Culture in Recent America*, edited by Van Gosse and Richard Moser, 52–66. Philadelphia: Temple University Press, 2003.

"Everyone Talks about the Weather . . ." *Weatherman*, edited by Harold Jacobs, 440–47. San Francisco, CA: Ramparts Press, 1970.

Foley, Megan. "Sound Bites: Rethinking the Circulation of Speech from Fragment to Fetish." *Rhetoric & Public Affairs* 15, no. 4 (2012): 613–22.

Foss, Karen A. "Out From Underground: The Discourse Of Emerging Fugitives." *Western Journal of Communication* 56, no. 2 (1992): 125–42.

Gitlin, Todd. *The Sixties: Years of Hope, Days of Rage*. Toronto: Bantam Books, 1987.

Gries Laurie. "Agential Matters: Tumbleweed, Women-Pens, Citizen-Hope, and Rhetorical Actancy." *Ecology, Writing, Theory, and New Media: Writing Ecology*, edited by Sidney Dobrin. London: Routledge, 2011.

Gustainis, J. Justin, and Dan F. Hahn. "While the Whole World Watched: Rhetorical Failures of Antiwar Protest." *Communication Quarterly* 36, no. 3 (1988): 203–16.

Haiman, Franklyn S. "The Rhetoric of the Streets: Some Legal and Ethical Considerations." *Quarterly Journal of Speech* 53, no. 2 (1967): 99–114.

Hall, Simon. "Framing the American 1960s: A Historiographical Review." *European Journal of American Culture* 31, no.1 (2012): 5–23.

Hayes, Heather Ashley. *Violent Subjects and Rhetorical Cartography in the Age of the Terror Wars*. New York: Palgrave Macmillan, 2016.

Heidt, Stephen. "The Presidency as Pastiche: Atomization, Circulation, And Rhetorical Instability." *Rhetoric & Public Affairs* 15, no. 4 (2012): 623–33.

Hilliard, David, ed. *The Black Panther: Intercommunal News Service*. New York: Atria Books, 2007.

Hoerl, Kristen Elizabeth. "The Death of Activism? Popular Memories of 1960s Protest." PhD diss., University of Texas at Austin, 2005.

Inabinet, Brandon. "Democratic Circulation: Jacksonian Lithographs in U.S. Public Discourse." *Rhetoric & Public Affairs* 15, no. 4 (2012): 659–66.

Isserman, Maurice. *If I Had a Hammer: The Death of the Old Left and the Birth of the New Left*. New York: Basic Books, 1987.

Jacobs, Harold, ed. *Weatherman*. San Francisco: Ramparts Press, 1970.

Jacobs, Ron. *The Way The Wind Blew: A History Of The Weather Underground*. London: Verso, 1997.

Lee, Benjamin, and Edward LiPuma, "Cultures of Circulation: The Imaginations of Modernity." *Public Culture* 14 (2002): 191–213.

Lee, Choonib. "Women's Liberation and Sixties Armed Resistance." *Journal for the Study of Radicalism* 11, no. 1 (2017): 25–52.

Levine, Yasha. *Surveillance Valley: The Rise of the Military-Digital Complex*. New York: PublicAffairs, 2018.

Loewinsohn, Ron. "Reviews: After the (Mimeograph) Revolution." *TriQuarterly* 18 (1970): 221–36.

Lubar Steven. "'Do Not Fold, Spindle or Mutilate': A Cultural History of the Punch Card." *Journal of American Culture* 15 (1992): 43–55.

Miller, Stephen Paul. *The Seventies Now: Culture as Surveillance*. Durham, NC: Duke University Press, 1999.

McMillian, John. *Smoking Typewriters: The Sixties Underground Press and the Rise of Alternative Media in America*. New York: Oxford University Press, 2011.

Newfield, Jack. *A Prophetic Minority*. New York: New American Library, 1966.

Olson, Lester. "Pictorial Representations of British America Resisting Rape: Rhetorical Re-Circulation of a Print Series Portraying the Boston Port Bill of 1774." *Rhetoric & Public Affairs* 12 (2009): 1–36.

O'Rourke Sean Patrick. "Circulation and Noncirculation of Photographic Texts in the Civil Rights Movement: A Case Study of the Rhetoric of Control." *Rhetoric & Public Affairs* 15, no. 4 (2012): 685–94.

Sale, Kirkpatrick. *SDS*. New York: Random House, 1973.

Stewart, Charles J., Craig Allen Smith, and Robert E. Denton Jr. *Persuasion and Social Movements*. 6th ed. Long Grove, IL: Waveland Press, 2012.

Stuckey, Mary E. "On Rhetorical Circulation." *Rhetoric & Public Affairs* 15, no. 4 (2012): 609–12.

Vatz, Richard. "The Myth of the Rhetorical Situation." *Philosophy and Rhetoric* 6, no. 3 (1973): 154–57.

The Weather Underground. Directed by Sam Green and Bill Siegel. New York: Free History Project, 2002. DVD.

7

GAMERGATE

UNDERSTANDING THE TACTICS OF ONLINE KNOWLEDGE DISRUPTORS

MICHAEL TRICE

In May 2016 Russian agents managed to stage competing rallies in front of an Islamic center in downtown Houston, Texas. According to data released by Congress, the Russian agents accomplished this feat by advertising the initial protest and counterprotest on Facebook, relying solely upon existing cultural animosity between the two protest groups to actualize both sides of the event.[1] While the counter-protestors would claim it was the original protestors that drew them to the rally, and not the Russian Facebook ads, such claims are immaterial to the fact that the Russian agents were able to activate the original protestors—who would then activate the counterprotesters—into a physical confrontation in downtown Houston.[2] The event put to rest the slow fading myth that what happens online is in any way disconnected from action in the physical world. It also marked a complete reversal of Henry Jenkin's and David Thorburn's onetime position that the might of traditional mass media could hold in check the polarization of online media.[3]

The response from Congress around disinformation in the 2016 presidential election has focused almost exclusively upon Russia and other foreign actors. Some, like Senator Angus King, have called for social media companies to attribute news sources that are foreign in origin as such.[4] Other senators, like Kamala Harris, have suggested mandating a digital ombudsman for social media platforms to uncover foreign disinformation.[5] While such policies might narrowly address the specific strategies of Russian agents in the 2016 election, they lack a full reckoning with the scope of disinformation within social media and suggest a lack of appreciation for the root causes of disinformation online—one situated firmly within the ethos of the platforms currently favored for online deliberation and arising from the genre activity systems available to online activists, both foreign and domestic.

Within this chapter, I will explore the tactics of GamerGate, an online movement whose largest influence was felt in 2014 and 2015, to explain what I call the *dissentivist* ethic driving much of the current deliberative environment online, and an ethic that played directly into Russia's hands in 2016. By *dissentivist*, I refer to a community ethic driven first and foremost by disrupting consensus as a means of strategic activism. Dissentivists target areas of conversation, knowledge bases, and the production of knowledge for disruption as their central goal and utilize activities and genres that support this disruption of consensus. Importantly, *dissentivists* do not seem to seek to form new, lasting definitions and broad consensus in the wake of their disruption—the goal is to undermine knowledge workers and the institutions that support knowledge work without concern for what comes next outside of the community. That said, community-building may remain important to these groups, with the community firmly entrenched in an ethos of antagonistic action with some community of knowledge: games journalists, mainstream media, climate scientists, or even a national body politic.

Claiming that such an ethos is possible arises from two traditions: one in the study of online governance and the other from the rhetoric of technical platforms. The idea that platforms might promote an ethic has a history in both. One of the clearest articulations of this belief in platform governance as ethic is Jonathan Zittrain's description of *netizenship*.[6] Zittrain describes netizenship as the act of belonging to a project community as opposed to the individual use of the net as a communication tool.[7] Wikipedia was Zittrain's project of choice in 2008 and his primary source of praise for Wikipedia as an example of netizenship rested in what he described as its "system of self-governance that has many indicia of the rule of law without heavy reliance upon outside authority or boundary."[8]

While Zittrain's fondness for Wikipedia's ability to resemble the rule of law without regulation of government oversight is clear, those who promote a more regulated civic space for deliberative platforms also share some of his views about the ability of platforms to create core values. Coleman and Blumler, in hypothesizing a civic commons run as a BBC-like independent but publicly funded online space, state that the value of such a platform exists in its ability to hold public officials accountable and in its ability to ensure civil behavior amongst its members.[9] This joint accountability ethos between citizen and state represented a democratic ideal for Coleman and Blumler, one obtainable through proper platform design and governance.

Scholars interested in the connection between rhetoric and technology have made similar observations about ethos and technical platforms. William Hart-Davidson et al. connected the design and workflows of content management systems to the ethos of the community using them.[10] Spinuzzi also connected workplace activities and genres to the possibility of generating civic participation within labor environments.[11] Potts has also discussed the ways in which social media participants come together to turn data into knowledge outside of traditional structures, suggesting a possibility that the right participant experience could expand and encourage reliable knowledge work in disaster situations.[12]

Yet much of this work focuses upon communities that actively wish to create reliable knowledge. What has been left underexplored are those communities and activists actively seeking to disrupt knowledge bases and the deliberative process itself. In other words, what happens when a deep understanding of platform rhetorics creates an intentionally destructive ethos to the knowledge-making process itself? A closer look at how GamerGate operated opens a door into the kind of work that goes beyond asking how we can stop what happened in 2016. Instead, it offers us a chance to understand how social media platforms invite an ethic of knowledge disruption, so that we can begin to address the culture of dissent for its own sake.

GAMERGATE: DEFINING A DISSENTIVIST MOVEMENT

In 2014 a relatively small online community galvanized tens of thousands of online accounts as a mob-like counter-resistance against institutional new media with the self-proclaimed purpose of increasing accountability within that media.[13] The rallying cry of GamerGate would become one of "ethics in gaming journalism," even though the movement began as a direct response to sordid rumors originating from the angry ex-partner of a relatively unknown indie game designer.[14] In addition, the movement would regularly focus its attention on personalities, both celebrities and lesser-known journalists, culture critics, and artists.[15] The attempt to rebrand GamerGate from a mob of anonymous accounts spreading salacious rumors to one championing journalistic accountability would include attracting celebrities and pundits to the cause; the igniting of a highly politicized culture war around games; and it would provide an early test run for some of the more radical players in the 2016 presidential election, particularly Breitbart and Milo Yiannopoulos.[16] The movement would also involve a low accountability governance that would allow GamerGate to operate in parallel as a salacious rumor mill and as a populist outcry for a certain class of consumers feeding off grievances related to feminism, political correctness, and the media. These two sides would allow GamerGate to regularly serve as an attack upon journalism as a form of knowledge making while creating a vehicle for spreading rumors as community vetted information.

It would also provide a blueprint for how skillful online practitioners could repurpose online services from social networks (Twitter, Facebook) to code repositories (GitHub) to wikis (Wikipedia) to fora (4chan, Reddit) to YouTube into theaters of conflict with the specific purpose of disrupting knowledge workers, including journalists, scholars, culture critics, and even Wikipedians.[17] Importantly, GamerGate did not serve as a challenge to what we might call traditional media, it sought to undermine the frontline (and most vulnerable spaces) of knowledge by targeting gaming websites, Wikipedia, and social media communities. It is this strategy of disrupting consensus and knowledge in generative and digital knowledge-making communities that continues to make GamerGate relevant, particularly in light of similar tactics that have been exposed by foreign agents as it relates to the 2016 presidential election and beyond. This new activism of dissenting knowledge work, or dissentivists, represents one of the most significant new dangers to online communication because it champions an ethos of conspiracy and paranoia that makes consensus impossible, even within the activist community itself.

To properly understand GamerGate, a number of points require exploration. First, it is a platform of disruption beyond any one digital space. Second, that the central agreement governing GamerGate is an underlying ethos built around adversarial interaction with knowledge workers. Third, those behind GamerGate view knowledge work's disruption as an ideological goal unto itself.

It is also worth noting that GamerGate as discussed within this chapter largely no longer exists. Most of its activist energy moved to other objectives in 2016. Yiannopoulos quite publicly moved into alt right activism supporting President Trump's election. Even the subreddit home for GamerGate now has rules about not using the community as a personal army and largely forbids many of the calls to action that marked the form of disinformation discussed within this chapter. That said, the GamerGate playbook remains openly available and the areas discussed within this chapter are obtainable as of this writing. Just as importantly, the tactics discussed here have been embraced by other groups and still prove effective in generating dissent. For example, the QAnon movement that arose after the initial drafting of this chapter.

VISUALIZING THE GENRE ECOLOGY OF GAMERGATE

As stated before, GamerGate should not be viewed as something singularly of 4chan, YouTube, Reddit, or Twitter. Each of these platforms serves as a key foundation for the GamerGate community and movement, but none fully define nor contain GamerGate. Rather than demonstrating a disconnect between ethic and technological platform, however, this variance highlights how GamerGate became informed by a variety of technological platforms and infused each space with its dissent-based values. GamerGate offers a prime example of networked activism utilizing multiple digital genres to maximize its goals. The hub of this ethic is best viewed not from any of the social media platforms but from the spaces where GamerGate documented its ethic: code repositories and Reddit's r/KotakuInAction.

In fact, GamerGate can be visualized as a classic technical communication genre ecology, a mediated network of genres working to achieve a related activity.[18] Consider the basic relationship of sites used by GamerGate in figure 7.1. GamerGate located its operational documents on chan boards and GitHub. It utilized IRC (Internet Relay Chat) groups to organize synchronous action. It activated communities on Twitter for audience engagement and Reddit for internal community building—in other words, Twitter allowed GamerGate to engage with a non-GamerGate audience and Reddit allowed an intraorganizational communication space that was more acceptable to a wider community than a chan board. YouTube videos were also central to GamerGate's content stream, with a YouTube video shared by the actor Adam Baldwin leading to the coining of the GamerGate name as a Twitter hashtag. Like many chan conspiracies, YouTube videos would provide the secondary sources that drove GamerGate and vetted its primary rumors into community knowledge. Eventually, a handful of Facebook pages would become active, but they would see far less activity than sites that promoted anonymity. As will be discussed later, anonymity—and particularly the concern of having a member's true identity known—was a central fear and driving ethical canon of GamerGate.

Beyond this, GamerGate started its own wiki to collect sources and build a community consensus around events that defied the popular consensus the group could not alter in newspapers or Wikipedia. It also utilized image sites like Imgur to share community memes and talking points. Pages like archive.is were used to shared content from blacklisted media sites, so that GamerGate could send content without driving traffic to any site that had produced content deemed critical or offensive to the community. This tendency to blacklist any site that offered a critical opinion to the point of stealing content and denying traffic was a pillar of how the network functioned. The archived links could be stored in lists on Reddit, GitHub, or the wiki and then shared on Twitter so that any conversation about an article did not produce traffic for that article's publisher and writer. In the end, GamerGate could be mapped as a central communication network of Reddit, Twitter, Facebook, 4chan, and YouTube with a number of peripheral archival and production spaces that fed into the central communication network (figure 7.1).

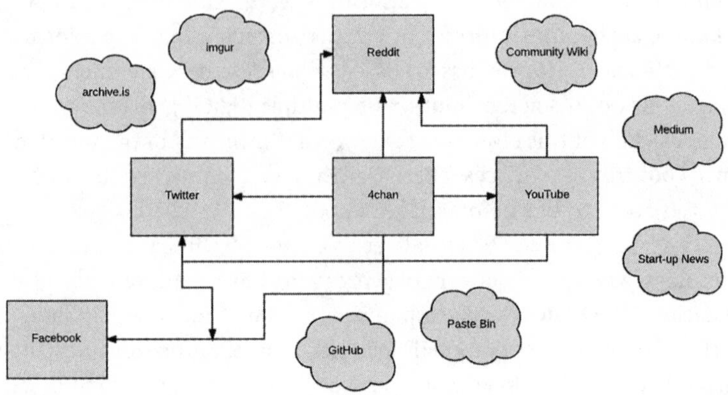

FIGURE 7.1. GamerGate as Genre Ecology. A map of the initial spaces of communication used by GamerGate.

However, the network as originally designed, did not last. As the controversy over GamerGate grew, sites like GitHub and 4chan banned the group. Rather than leaving holes in the ecology, GamerGate replaced these sites with 8chan and an open-source GitLab community that GamerGate called GitGud, as shown in figure 7.2. While some members of GamerGate would grate against the rules of Twitter and Reddit, the need for an active audience prevented attempts to move the community completely to platforms like Voat and Gab, which would become far more popular with the far right due to laxer rules on hate speech.

The ability of GamerGate to adapt demonstrates a number of important issues to consider in how resilient a network ecology can become online. In almost all cases, if a group understands the purpose of a platform and how it relates to the rest of the network, it can be replaced. The only exception to this rule rests in the spaces defined by enormous existing audiences: YouTube, Reddit, Twitter, and Facebook. Since the community cannot replace the built-in audiences of these spaces, they become the only spaces where the network ecology could be reasonably constrained. Any other activity offers only a minor technical challenge to duplicate and then plug into the assemblage. It is this combination of technical and rhetorical competency that makes groups like GamerGate so effective at survival, volume, and reaching new audiences.

What GamerGate included and excluded within its network helps determine its focus activity as much as looking at its content might. For example, GamerGate attempted a strong beachhead of Wikipedia's GamerGate Con-

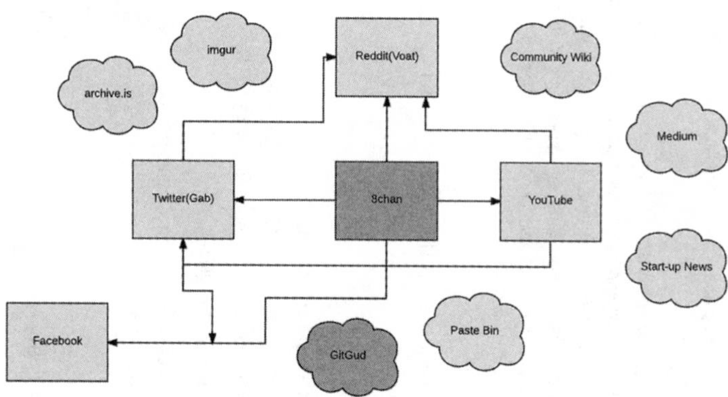

FIGURE 7.2. GamerGate Adapts. A map of the spaces of communication used by GamerGate after platforms began to ban the group.

troversy page early in the event. As figure 7.3 shows, by September 2014, only a month after the hashtag was coined, GamerGate was arguing about bias in the Wikipedia article. GamerGate activists would continue to attempt to argue that news sources covering the movement were biased while also attempting to incorporate their preferred community sources (figure 7.4), which would include YouTube videos, websites built by GamerGate, and even tweets and comments. A critical part of the debate in the Wikipedia article—and one reason that GamerGate would eventually promote its on wiki instead of the Wikipedia entry—was that Wikipedia had a clearly articulate rule about the need for secondary sources and that such secondary sources be reliable. GamerGate needed, and fought hard to use, less reliable community sources and primary sources. When they could not do so on Wikipedia, they built their own knowledge bases in GitGud, the GamerGate.me wiki, Deep Freeze, and on Reddit. This act summarizes the purpose of the GamerGate network as a communicative act: to push against the vetting of traditional knowledge bases from news sites, culture publishers, and even Wikipedia in favor of information vetted primarily by the GamerGate community. It also highlights a victory for Zittrain's netizen ethos, as Wikipedia's rules and community were one of the digital spaces to reject GamerGate's disruption without banning the movement completely from the site.

However, Wikipedia's victory did little to slow GamerGate, as it enacted new spaces to store its personal accounts. The importance of personalized and participatory documentation within the genre ecology of the gaming community has been previously highlighted by Julia Mason.[19] Mason points out not (talk) 09:12, 8 September 2014 (UTC)

1. This article seems biased to me due to the bulk of the sources presenting only one side of the whole story. Since GamerGate is mostly a debate between many "public" video game journalists and anonymous internet users, the bias towards one side of the argument is predictable. I don't know of the proper way to fix this issue, Wikipedia's rules on reliable sources are usually a good thing to ensure high quality. But in this case it is only causing one voice, that of anonymous posters to be completely ignored in favor of well connected video game journalists, who anonymous claim to be corrupt in the first place. This is my first time editing so I am sorry if I mess up on the proper format. (talk) 21:31, 15 September 2014 (UTC)

   : We have had this issue you describe with most "scandals" regarding video games, which are typically covered in a homogeneous way by the press, which are limited by commercial concerns and thus tend to adopt quite risk-free approaches. I believe the solution may involve accepting as reliable sources the opinions of self-published experts, in order to expand the variety of opinions and significant viewpoints from what the press can provide. It seems that this possibility is gaining consensus below; though their use needs to be limited to material that doesn't involve information about living persons. In this article, this means that we can use those to include opinions on their perspective of what the #gamergate tag is about, but not about how it has affected particular persons. (talk) 09:32, 17 September 2014 (UTC)

FIGURE 7.3. Wikipedia Discussion about GamerGate Page, Part 1. A discussion of the bias GamerGate saw in the Wikipedia article due to the sources used.

This is the first video that kicked the GamerGate events off. https://www.youtube.com/watch?v=Equc1QnQ9rw Is it about harassment? Also http://attackongaming.com/gaming-talk/reddit-mod-outs-reddit-for-censorship-during-gamergate/ http://www.forbes.com/sites/erikkain/2014/09/04/gamergate-a-closer-look-at-the-controversy-sweeping-video-games/ . Are these unrealiable sources in your opinion? (talk) 19:38, 8 September 2014 (UTC)

YouTube and AttackOnGaming are, yes, obviously unreliable sources. (talk) 19:49, 8 September 2014 (UTC)

To be clear, if a site you considered an RS were to make the claims in the Youtube video, and cite the Youtube video as evidence, would that pass muster? If not, can you explain how the evidence for Anita Sarkeesian's harassment is any stronger than that? Or is Twitter @femfreq now considered an RS? (talk) 13:34, 11 September 2014 (UTC)

FIGURE 7.4. Wikipedia Discussion about GamerGate Page, Part 2. A second discussion illustrating GamerGate's attempts to widen Wikipedia's rules on reliable sources to allow community-generated content.

1. If you already have a Twitter account that you intend to use, go to step 8. Otherwise, keep reading.
2. Make a cock.li/Gmail throwaway email address if you don't want your new Twitter account to be linked to your main email address.
3. Create your new Twitter account, using your new email address if appropriate. Also make sure to choose a Twitter username not associated with any of your other accounts, to reduce doxxing risks.
4. Choose a self-representative account name and write a self-representative description for your account, but make sure not to give away details that can get you doxxed.
5. Choose a profile picture/photo and a cover picture/photo not associated with any of your other accounts, to reduce doxxing risks.
6. Make a testing tweet.
7. Make a few tweets proclaiming your newness.
8. Make a few tweets about **#GamerGate**, spread the links in this file and this one.
9. (If you are not a white cis-scum male) make a few tweets about **#NotYourShield**.
10. Increase your visibility by following people: Search the **#GamerGate** tag and follow people you like. Remember, you're legit new, so at least some should follow you back.
11. FOLLOW THE PEOPLE WHO ARE FOLLOWING THESE PEOPLE. Chances are some of these are your fellow anons, so with luck we can increase our follow counts.
12. Seach the hashtag, Image: favorite-icon favorite and Image: retweet-icon retweet **#GamerGate**-supporting tweets. Get your fellow anons to the top.
13. If you get stuck with zero followers, reply to someone, chime in that you agree with them. But don't argue on this step. Let them do that if they want to do that.

FIGURE 7.5. GitGud Excerpt for GamerGate's Twitter Instructions. This figure lists the thirteen steps the GamerGate operational documents provided for new Twitter users to join GamerGate.

only the importance of documentation in shaping the gaming experience for a community but also in its potential to move from player to professional. This idea that engaging in genre activities can help professionalize gamers plays a central role in Mason's argument that video game genre ecologies can serve as pedagogical models and opportunities for teaching technical communication. GamerGate serves as a dystopic extension of Mason's argument, as the documentation of the movement's ethos and activities helped turn the group's use of Twitter, Reddit, and email into a form of organized labor directed at disrupting knowledge and replacing that knowledge with GamerGate's version of reality. In the end, GamerGate attempted to follow the same path from amateur gamer to professional gamer that Mason observes in her work, but they applied it to rumor and propaganda.

GAMERGATE REJECTED CONSENSUS MAKING AS A VALUE

While GamerGate started its operational life on 4chan, it quickly duplicated much of its instructional material on GitHub. As stated earlier, when GitHub revoked access to the GamerGate community, they seamlessly made use of a similar repository system named GitGud created from the GitLab open-source project. This ability to replicate communication spaces would happen frequently. Currently, GitGud itself is largely abandoned in favor of GamerGate's home on Reddit: r/KotakuInAction. However, this shift to Reddit highlights how the operationalize phase of GamerGate has long passed in favor of a new and ongoing community phase.

Going back to the days of the operational phase, the use of code repositories offered a number of advantages for GamerGate. It meant new recruits no longer needed to be exposed to a chan board, as they were easily directed from Twitter, YouTube, Facebook, or Reddit to the repository. It also allowed for a more stable document base, since chan postings required regular replacement and updating. Now all operational data could be edited and controlled by the group in a single, reliable location that appealed to much larger and more moderate (compared to chan culture) audience.

It included:

Instructions for using Twitter
A running list of boycotted websites, charities, and professionals
A list of what websites, charities, and professionals to support
Current happenings (events that GamerGate activist should focus upon)
Current operations—a list of the groups many crowdsourced actions against media outlets GamerGate disliked.

FIGURE 7.6. Icons of GamerGate from knowyourmeme.com. GamerGate created numerous images that promoted celebrities it found supportive.

In figure 7.5 the thirteen-step process for creating a GamerGate Twitter account is specified. The process offers excellent insight into the values of GamerGate as a community. Anonymity is first and foremost among the concerns of these instructions. The documentation walks through creating a throwaway Gmail account. It repeatedly connects anonymity to concerns about doxxing (having personal information revealed). The doxxing concern guides the selection of email, image, and account name. These instructions build paranoia into every aspect of identity. These identity concerns also happen to ensure that duplicate accounts and bot accounts are indistinguishable from the average GamerGate activist.

Once an activist creates an account, the concern is locking the person into the community quickly through hashtags, retweets, and favorites. And, of course, participants must share the GamerGate community approved links. GamerGate's use of Twitter involved two important forms of broadcast, and sharing the GamerGate-approved knowledge base was the first crucial step.

The second important step on Twitter involved engaging verified accounts. GamerGate learned a crucial lesson when Adam Baldwin coined the word *GamerGate*: verified accounts also verify information into knowledge. Zeynep Tufekci outlined years ago that activist movements on Twitter often center around microcelebrities, who become the hub of the movement.[20] However, GamerGate took this idea to its next logical step by both using actual celebri-

Websites	Journalists
Polygon	**Current Staff:** Chris Grant, Editor-in-Chief; Justin McElroy, Managing Editor; Brian Crecente, News Editor; Arthur Gies, Reviews Editor; Griffin McElroy, Senior Editorial Producer; Phil Kollar, Deputy Reviews Editor; Matt Leone, Deputy Features Editor; Michael McWhertor, Deputy News Editor; Danielle Riendeau, Senior Reviewer; Charlie Hall, Features Writer; Emily Gera, Senior Reporter; Samit Sarkar, Reporter; Megan Farokhmanesh, Reporter; Dave Tach, Reporter; Colin Campbell, Senior Reporter; Ben Kuchera, Senior Editor - Opinion; Owen Good, Senior Reporter
Kotaku	**Current Staff:** Stephen Totilo, Editor-in-Chief; Tina Amini, Deputy Editor; Kirk Hamilton, Features Editor; Brian Ashcraft, Senior Contributing Editor - Japan; Luke Plunkett, Contributing Editor - Oceania; Jason Schreier, News Editor; Michael Fahey, Senior Reporter; Patrick Klepek, Senior Reporter; Evan Narcisse, Reporter; Patricia Hernandez, Reporter; Yannick LeJacq, Reporter; Nathan Grayson, Reporter; Leigh Alexander, Contributing Columnist; Tim Rogers, Contributing Columnist
VG247	**Current Staff:** Patrick Garratt, Founder and Publisher; Matt Martin, Editor; Dave Cook, Deputy Editor; Stephany Nunneley, Global News Editor (US); Brenna Hillier, News Editor (Australia); Sam Clay, Video Editor / **Former Staff:** Nathan Grayson, Contributor (US); Stace Harman, Contributor (UK); Martin Taylor, Designer
Rock, Paper, Shotgun	**Current Staff:** Graham Smith, Managing Editor; Alec Meer, Senior Editor; Jim Rossignol, Editor; John Walker, Senior Editor; Adam Smith, Reviews Editor; Alice O'Connor, News Editor; Philippa Warr, Contributor; Cara Ellison, Contributor / **Former Staff:** Kieron Gillen, Editor; Lewie Procter; Cassandra Khaw; Quintin Smith, Contributing Editor; Nathan Grayson, Contributor
Offworld	**Current Staff:** Leigh Alexander, Editor-in-Chief; Laura Hudson, Senior Editor / **Former Staff:** Brandon Boyer, Founder
Boing Boing	**Current Staff:** Mark Frauenfelder, Founder / Editor; Cory Doctorow, Editor; David Pescovitz, Editor; Xeni Jardin, Editor; Rob Beschizza, Managing Editor; Jason Weisberger, Publisher / **Former Staff:** Brandon Boyer, Founder (*Offworld*)

FIGURE 7.7. Shills in a Barrel. GamerGate collected Twitter addresses of verified journalist accounts it targeted, naming them shills in a barrel.

ties as hubs for its information and by turning the verified accounts of journalists and pundits into hubs for the hashtag. Those who GamerGate considered supportive (and certainly not all such figures fully embraced the community) were lionized and turned into literal icons, as figure 7.6 shows. These images were stored in multiple places, including GitGud, for ease of sharing on Twitter and elsewhere.

While chan boards birthed GamerGate and GitGud served as its central operational space, Twitter allowed GamerGate to become a phenomenon. Twitter not only offered access to celebrities, pundits, and YouTubers that the activists could rally around for increased exposure—it also provided direct access to the writers and culture critics that GamerGate targeted. Twitter holds enormous appeal to journalists and writers for its ability to allow them to spread their work, engage with sources, and respond to readers; however, it also made these figures easy targets due to their verified identities. While

GamerGate championed anonymity among its members, it understood that supporting and attacking public identities significantly increased the range and volume of its network. In fact, as figure 7.7 shows, one GamerGate document collected direct links to dozens of journalists on Twitter.

DISSENTIVISTS SEE DISRUPTION AS VALUE AND POLICY

What should hopefully be clear by now is that GitGud served as the playbook for GamerGate. All the core spaces connected back to GitGud and GitGud provided all the walkthroughs for how GamerGate activists could and should advance the cause. It offered an incredibly coherent understanding for how each genre in the ecology worked and how to handle variant audiences across them. In many ways, GitGud articulates the rhetorical anchor that stabilized GamerGate's use of a platforms as something specifically of and for GamerGate. This included GamerGate's objectives and achievements as well.

GamerGate's list of operations was diverse in tactics, but the goals were straightforward: attack media companies and cultural opponents. These tactics involved blacklisting sites, organizing email campaigns against advertisers (Operation Disrespectful Nod), making Freedom of Information Act requests (Operation Argus), and even teaching argumentation tactics to its participants (Operation Vulcan). The operations were punitive in nature and never deliberative in regard to the media or journalists themselves. In fact, GamerGate rejected the concept of a deliberative outcome in its own documentation.

When it came to goals, GamerGate stated in no uncertain terms:

> No objectives, no goals, no demands, no philosophies, no lists.
> (1) It screws up the framing of the issue by forcing us to focus on specific issues.
> (2) The corrupt journos will adhere to the letter of the list and not the spirit. They will find a way to weasel around them.
> (3) The second nobody is looking, they'll go back to being dishonest.
> (4) This idea was put forth by a well-meaning PR person, not someone experienced in consumer activity. PR is the journo's game. Not ours.
> (5) It divides us into the goals we each specifically want and we don't all want the same things. What appeases you will not appease another, etc.
> (6) Demands are things that terrorists make. We are a consumer revolt. We are not violent. We are not underhanded. We are not a political movement.
> (7) Philosophies are for philosophers, not consumer revolts. We don't need philosophy to obtain the moral high ground, the opposition has already given it to us. We have no benefit in philosophies.
> (8) Goals are for games, not a consumer revolt.

> (9) Objectives are for military operations, not a consumer revolt.
> (10) Lists are for nerds.
> (11) It is true that it may increase our numbers (in an absolute sense, but we're still divided over the goals) because people have specific things to champion. However, this will bring us fence-sitters and those of weak will and not people that will do the work of writing emails and investigation of corruption. If they aren't invested on the merits, they aren't invested and thus are not helpful.
> (12) We do not need clear end points. If people are discouraged by a perceived lack of progress, take a break. This is an extended and long-term approach and you must take breaks. If you need specific goals for yourself, participate two or three days a week. Phrase it in those terms. Creating goals is not necessary.
> (13) It does not help people get into this. What does help people get into this is a more coherent and concise set of facts that they can evaluate and come to their own conclusions.
> (14) Numbers are not an argument. Facts create numbers. Numbers don't necessarily create facts.
> (15) Phrasing these goals incorrectly will put them as lines in the sand. We cannot change them once they're satisfied. We cannot move goalposts like they do.[21]

GamerGate outright rejected the concept of consensus in numerous ways: journalists would agree to their terms and then back out (2), consensus within the community was impossible (5), and (most tellingly) achievable goals within the group are secondary to group labor (12). There was never any chance of victory unless that victory came with the retirement of every journalist and the bankruptcy of every site.

GamerGate successfully made the argument to its members that attacking ideological targets in perpetuity was superior to articulating a single achievable outcome. And for over a year, that line held. GamerGate's core value was the act of dissent and dissent without the possibility of affecting agreed upon policy change.

NAMING THE DISSENTIVISTS

It is important not to confuse GamerGate's lack of ability to form cross-community consensus with a lack of community. Community was vital for GamerGate, and this need for community is why some form of ethic had to emerge. That said, GamerGate began with a deep-level resentment that gaming sites failed to cover claims of cheating by one partner against another—a clear violation of traditional journalism norms that weigh newsworthiness against the possibility to do harm.

When GamerGate forged an identity around that issue, it chose a purpose that must be cast as a desire to lower standards for what counted as journalism and evidence. That same issue played out within the Wikipedia page. This attempt to lower journalistic standards under a claim of ethics in journalism became the central activity of the communicative network that is GamerGate. The desire to see opponents attacked with whatever form of accusation exists became the driving force of the community. The same way it did for both sets of protestors in Houston, Texas. The goal of GamerGate was to disrupt the perception and practice of knowledge making in journalism under the guise of claiming to address ethics in journalism. By juxtaposing an emotionally satisfying means of vetting information (gossip and lore) against the unresponsive but vetted knowledge making of professional journalism, GamerGate managed to completely undermine the methodology of published knowledge within a sizable audience.

Additionally, what GamerGate made visible is that tools for participatory disinformation have never been easier to access nor more viable in application. Complex assemblages can generate, store, and spread alternative media vetted by nothing so much as a community's need to believe in the worst of their ideological opponent. More concerning, the owners of most of the tools have little power to prevent these activities if the group has sufficient technical and rhetorical skill. GamerGate made use of more than a dozen services for very specialized applications, but other than Facebook, Twitter, Reddit, and YouTube any of them could have been replaced. Those that could not be replaced are the dominant platforms most likely to reject their role as a publisher or arbiter of content.

In this new land of disinformation, the audience remains king—where can they be reached and how easily? This makes mapping the systems of disinformation vital so that scholars, policymakers, corporations, and citizens can understand where both the technical and rhetorical weak points rest in the spread and consumption of disinformation. It also places significant weight upon those of us who deal in expert knowledge and methodology to examine these new methods of knowledge making so they can be understood, named, and addressed as needed. We must acknowledge that Zittrain's dream of a netizen ethos are now set firmly against a rising dissentivist ethos whose interest is not the rule of law, but how best to shape paranoia and conspiracy as a weapon against their political and cultural foes.

NOTES

1. Albright, "Russian Facebook Page Organized a Protest in Texas."
2. Arriaga, "Counterprotesters Say White Supremacists Drew Them to Rally."

3. Jenkins and Thorburn, *Democracy and New Media*.

4. “Sen. Angus King on Tech Companies and Russia.”

5. “Sen. Kamala Harris on Social Media and Russian Propaganda.”

6. Zittrain, *Future of the Internet*, 142–43.

7. Zittrain, 142.

8. Zittrain, 143.

9. Coleman and Blumler, *Internet and Democratic Citizenship*.

10. Hart-Davidson, Bernhardt, McLeod, Rife, and Grabill, “Coming to Content Management.”

11. Spinuzzi, *Tracing Genres through Organizations*.

12. Potts, *Social Media in Disaster Response*.

13. Mortensen, “Anger, Fear, and Games,” 5.

14. Mortensen, 3.

15. Mortensen, 2–6.

16. Mortensen, 4.

17. Flöck, Laniado, Stadthaus, and Acosta, “Towards Better Visual Tools.”

18. Spinuzzi and Zachry, “Genre Ecologies.”

19. Mason, “Video Games as Technical Communication Ecology.”

20. Tufekci, “Not This One.”

21. GitGud, GamerGate, Goals and Demands Philosophy, https://gitgud.io/gamergate/gamergateop/blob/master/Notices-and-Pastas/Goals-Demands-Philosophies-Objectives-Lists.md.

REFERENCES

Albright, Claire. “A Russian Facebook Page Organized a Protest in Texas: A Different Russian Page Launched the Counterprotest.” *Texas Tribune*, November 1, 2017. https://www.texastribune.org/2017/11/01/russian-facebook-page-organized-protest-texas-different-russian-page-l/.

Arriaga, Alex. “Counterprotesters Say White Supremacists, Not Russian Facebook Ads, Drew Them to Rally.” *Texas Tribune*, November 6, 2017. https://www.texastribune.org/2017/11/06/existing-racism-made-houston-residents-susceptible-fall-russia-created/.

Coleman, Stephen, and Jay G. Blumler. *The Internet and Democratic Citizenship: Theory, Practice and Policy*. Cambridge: Cambridge University Press, 2009.

Flöck, Fabian, David Laniado, Felix Stadthaus, and Maribel Acosta. “Towards Better Visual Tools for Exploring Wikipedia Article Development—The Use Case of ‘Gamergate Controversy.’” In *Proceedings of the Ninth International AAAI Conference on Web and Social Media*. Palo Alto, CA: AAAI Press, 2015.

Hart-Davidson, William, Grace Bernhardt, Michael McLeod, Martine Rife, and Jeffrey T. Grabill. “Coming to Content Management: Inventing Infrastructure for Organizational Knowledge Work.” *Technical Communication Quarterly* 17, no. 1 (2007): 10–34.

Jenkins, Henry, and David Thorburn. *Democracy and New Media*. Cambridge, MA: MIT Press, 2003.

Mason, Julia. “Video Games as Technical Communication Ecology.” *Technical Communication Quarterly* 22, no. 3 (2013): 219–36.

Mortensen, Torill Elvira. “Anger, Fear, and Games: The Long Event of #GamerGate.” *Games and Culture* (2016). https://journals.sagepub.com/doi/10.1177/1555412016640408.

Potts, Liza. *Social Media in Disaster Response: How Experience Architects Can Build for Participation*. London: Routledge, 2013.

"Sen. Angus King on Tech Companies and Russia." NPR, November 1, 2017. https://www.npr.org/2017/11/01/561310544/sen-angus-king-on-tech-companies-and-russia.

"Sen. Kamala Harris on Social Media and Russian Propaganda." NPR, November 2, 2017. https://www.npr.org/2017/11/02/561505689/sen-kamala-harris-on-social-media-and-russian-propaganda.

Spinuzzi, Clay, and Mark Zachry. "Genre Ecologies: An Open-System Approach to Understanding and Constructing Documentation." *ACM Journal of Computer Documentation (JCD)* 24, no. 3 (2000): 169–81.

Spinuzzi, Clay. *Tracing Genres through Organizations: A Sociocultural Approach to Information Design*. Vol. 1. Cambridge, MA: MIT Press, 2003.

Tufekci, Zeynep. "'Not This One': Social Movements, the Attention Economy, and Microcelebrity Networked Activism." *American Behavioral Scientist* 57, no. 7 (2013): 848–70.

Zittrain, Jonathan. *The Future of the Internet—and How to Stop It*. New Haven, CT: Yale University Press, 2008.

PART II

DIGITAL PRACTICES

8

ISIS VERSUS THE UNITED STATES

RHETORICAL BATTLE IN THE MIDDLE EAST

WILLIAM M. MARCELLINO AND MADELINE MAGNUSON

ASYMMETRICAL WARFIGHTING: ISIS AND RHETORIC

The Islamic State in Iraq and Syria's (ISIS) sophisticated use of social media in recruiting and fundraising makes clear the central position of rhetorical production in contemporary warfare. Global communication technology is no longer a state monopoly, and nonstate actors such as ISIS are able to connect with and potentially influence persons across the globe.

Unlike conventional warfare, where the material power of Western states like the United States grants an asymmetrical advantage, in rhetorical warfare the United States is potentially at a profound disadvantage. The ability to engage in rhetorical information operations—Rhet Ops—is intimately tied to cultural understanding of the audience, and the US-led efforts to engage in rhetorical operations have been prone to cultural mirroring—for example, speaking to an Afghan audience using American discourse practices.[1] In this chapter, we look at a specific example of Rhet Ops—the struggle between the Islamic State of Iraq and Syria (ISIS) and the United States —where both state and nonstate actors engage in a cross-cultural rhetorical battle.[2] While ISIS has recently experienced large-scale battlefield losses, we feel the lessons from the rise of ISIS are of ongoing relevance. Many in the West have ignored the rhetorical power and sophistication ISIS has displayed, using the barbarity and fundmamemtalism of ISIS as a basis to dismiss the group's appeal.[3] We believe this is a mistake, and that it is imperative to take ISIS seriously as a rhetorical foe, worthy of study, and that the lessons learned from such study will have ongoing relevance in future Rhet Ops.

One possible way to frame this rhetorical battle being fought in the Middle East is as a dialogue—albeit a hostile dialogue at times—between a Western democracy and a putative neo-Kharijite movement exemplified by ISIS. [4] We feel this is a more accurate and nuanced model than popular ideas of "Islam versus the West" because it acknowledges the diversity in the Islamic world and the agency on display in the many Islamic states that are peacefully engaged with the West.

In our analysis, we compare the rhetorical strategies of ISIS and the United States, and do so at two linguistic levels:

Lexical: The *aboutness* dimension of both entities' rhetoric, made visible by detection of statistically meaningful keywords and collocations.

Lexicogrammatical: The *stance* dimension of each entity's rhetoric, visible by detection of statistically meaningful variations in style.

We use machine-based approaches in this analysis, combining methods from corpus linguistics and digital rhetorics. Machine-based approaches offer particular affordances that human serial reading and analysis cannot match in terms of reliability and scalability.

Machine reading of text data lacks the contextual meaning making of human reading, but has a reliability that human analysis cannot match. While not sophisticated, machine analysis of text is not biased or variable in attention the way human reading can be. Because expert human labor is a scarce, expensive resource, and even given the resources to conduct large-scale human labor analysis, the aforementioned concerns over reliability and validity increase with scale. To be able to make generalizable claims about language use, corpus approaches with very large data sets require scalable, machine-based approaches.[5]

We do point out, however, that while we use machine-based text analysis methods, the interpretation of the results still includes humans in the loop. While machine-based approaches can give us very reliable, valid descriptions of large corpora, machines cannot make meaning. Thus, while we can push a button to get a list of overly present keywords in a text corpus, it is up to human analysts to contextually interpret what those words mean, how to group them usefully, how to compare them with keywords from another corpus, and so on. Similarly, we can push buttons to detect linguistic latencies through exploratory factor analysis (EFA), but no computer can tell us how those factors function.

In the rest of this chapter, we will describe our data sets, corpus methods applied to both sets, present analytical findings, and discuss their implications.

DATA: US GOVERNMENT AND ISIS PUBLIC SPEECH

For this analysis, we created two text corpora: (1) an English corpus of US government talk about ISIS, and (2) an Arabic corpus of general ISIS public talk.

US PUBLIC SPEECH

The US public speech corpus is from US government talk about ISIS (we used ISIS and ISIL as search terms) from the White House, State Department, and Department of Defense from between 2009 and 2017, totaling 134,551 words across 71 documents.[6] We excluded press briefings and short news briefs (anything less than a page in length), and made a judgment to exclude documents that were flagged with the search terms *ISIS* or *ISIL* because of an incidental mention. We included longer articles, speeches, and policy documents that were substantively about ISIS, the US military relative to anti-ISIS operations, and diplomatic efforts with coalition partners against ISIS. When public speeches included press questions, we excluded text from reporters.

ISIS PUBLIC SPEECH

The ISIS corpus is composed of sixty-one documents, totaling 229,813 words. Document types included speech transcripts from top-level IS leaders and spokesmen, announcements of martyrdoms, daily news round-ups, and official statements, all between 2014 and 2017. Sources included internet news sites, pro-ISIS hashtags/pro-ISIS user tweets, sites that support and spread news about ISIS, and blogs that collate ISIS publications.[7]

COMPARATIVE CORPORA: THE FROWN CORPUS AND ARABIC PRE-PLANNED DISCOURSE

Both of the text analysis methods we used are inherently comparative. Keyness testing works by comparing found frequencies of words against an expected baseline count. For example, we might compare a large corpus of hobby articles against baseline for English in general (e.g., the FROWN Corpus of Contemporary English)[8] and look for words that appear significantly more often in the hobby corpus than the baseline. If words like *daisy*, *rose*, and *chrysanthemum* are showing up in much greater frequency than is usual in English, it is a signal that the hobby corpus is about flowers or gardening.

The choice of what baseline corpus to use in Keyness testing is not automatic. Using the FROWN Corpus, which is all preplanned discourse even when oral (such as radio addresses) as a baseline for a corpus of conversational speech, would highlight differences between planned discourse and spontaneous speech, deemphasizing topic differences. However, in this case, the FROWN Corpus is likely a good choice as a baseline for the kind of preplanned presidential, diplomatic, and military discourse in the US corpus. For the ISIS corpus, we created a preplanned Arabic discourse baseline of 138,000 words, collected from Arabic-language sources such as Al Jazeera, Al Arabiya, and CNN Arabic, from 2015 to 2017.

We also used these corpora for stance comparison. Ordinarily in stance comparison for data in the same language we would directly compare corpora to look for rhetorical differences, but we cannot directly compare an English and Arabic corpus. Instead we tested the US and ISIS corpora for differences in stance as against the FROWN and Arabic preplanned discourse corpora, respectively.

Our choices about comparative corpora affect what our analysis shows, because we have chosen specific backgrounds to act as a contrast. We can imagine other comparative corpora—for example, a more focused US government foreign policy corpus, or an Arabic corpus of broad Islamist speech that would highlight what is distinctive about the Salafi-Jihadist speech of ISIS.[9] Therefore, our analysis is preliminary, and we plan to use both more data and different contrasts to try and gain new and more fine-grained insights.

METHODS: KEYNESS TESTING AND STANCE COMPARISON

For our analysis, we used software developed at the RAND Corporation. RAND-Lex is a scalable text analysis suite that brings together text analytics methods from variety of disciplines—corpus linguistics, digital rhetorics, and computer science—as well as supervised and unsupervised machine learning algorithms. RAND-Lex is being applied to a range of public policy problems, including counterviolent extremism, counterterrorism, and counter-Russian propaganda, and for this analysis we used the keyness testing and stance comparison functions of RAND-Lex.[10]

KEYNESS TESTING

Keyness testing answers the question "what is a text collection primarily *about*" by comparing word frequencies in the collection against expected frequencies.[11] Expected frequencies come from a purposefully chosen baseline text collection (the FROWN Corpus of Contemporary English in this case). The degree of overpresence for a word is measured through Dunning's Log-Likelihood (LL), a confidence measure that the word is indeed key.[12] In this analysis, we used a frequency minimum of fifty occurrences to exclude very infrequent words.

STANCE COMPARISON: EXPLORATORY FACTOR ANALYSIS

Stance in this sense refers to the stylistic choices speakers make, as they represent the world in ways that reflect their rhetorical purposes—for example, choices about hedging language and modal use to construct an epistemic stance.[13] These style choices happen at the level of lexicogrammar, and corpus-driven approaches are increasingly being used to analyze stance for insight into rhetorical purposes.[14] RAND-Lex's stance analysis uses phrasal dictionaries developed by the rhetorical scholars David Kaufer and Suguru Ishizaki at Carnegie Mellon University.[15] The dictionaries have been useful across a range of applications, including linguistic forensics,[16] text classification tasks,[17] and cross-cultural English as a Second Language (ESL) instruction.[18]

The value of these dictionaries is in their precision and dynamic grain size. Unlike sentiment thumb-up or thumb-down sentiment analysis, the Carnegie Mellon stance dictionaries we used have a large a taxonomy of—that is, future- and past-oriented language—certainty and hedging language, positive and a variety of negative affect (sadness, fear, remorse, apology, anger, and general negativity) and so on, for a total of 119 representational categories. This allows for the detection of a broad range of functional and rhetorical meaning. This is further enhanced by a dynamic grain size, where longer strings of words trump smaller strings. For example, the word *egg* is coded as an observable object, whereas *egg on* is coded as negative social interactions.

While the English dictionary we used is relatively long-standing and has been used fruitfully in a variety of applications, the Arabic dictionary we used is exploratory, and has not been validated. It was built in imitation of the English dictionary, using the same taxonomy, but whether that taxonomy is as useful in Arabic language work as in English has not been established. So while the results here and our broader use of the Arabic dictionary seems to have face validity, we wish to make clear that there is a difference in the level of confidence associated.

ANALYTICAL FINDINGS: WARTALK AND EPIDEICTIC ARGUMENT

We found that at the lexical level, both sides were fairly similar, with both engaging in talk about military operations, places, and actors. One lexical difference between the two collections was a small subtopic of religion words in the ISIS keywords. We had expected a more pronounced difference along secular/religious division between the two sides, where the United States discursively framed the issue as geopolitical and ISIS as a religious issue. Instead we found more alikeness than difference. The majority of keywords from both corpora could be grouped into three parallel subtopics: *actors* (e.g., national forces, non-state actors, leaders), *operations* (e.g., battle reporting, military terminology, operational goals), and *geography* (e.g., cities, countries, regions).

Research at Stanford's Literary Lab suggests that genre "like buildings, possess distinctive features at every possible scale of analysis: mortar, bricks, and architecture . . . the mortar . . . of Most Frequent Words, the bricks of . . . lexico-grammatical categories, and the architecture of themes and episodes that readers recognize."[19] This lexical parallelism between the two collections may reflect a kind of pragmatic entailment similar to genre entailments, in that both sides are speaking about active armed conflict.

ABOUTNESS SUMMARY: WARTALK

Tables 8.1–8.3 show US keywords, grouped in three tables for actors, operations, and geography, while tables 8.4–8.7 show the ISIS keywords. The US tables include the top fifty keywords ranked by LL scores, from the most to the least key, along with frequency numbers for each word.[20]

One group of keywords is about actors in the conflict: Iraqi and Syrian forces, ministers, terrorists, US and coalition forces. Another group of words is about military operations: operations, campaigns and strategy; what the United States and coalition "will" do, fighters, partners and terrorists, and so on. The last group is the geography of the conflict: cities and countries; global, foreign and homeland places.

ABOUTNESS SUMMARY: ISIS KEYWORDS

The ISIS keyword tables include thirty-seven keywords, and in addition to LL scores and frequency, include a translation for the word.[21] Like the US corpus, there is an actor, operations, and geography group, but also a small, three-word religious word group as well. The IS actor keywords are filled with religiously tinged terms for IS's enemies. For example, *Rafidhi/Rawafidh*, *Nusayri*, *apostate*, etc., are all religiously tinged ways to refer derogatorily to enemies (members of Shia, Alawite, and Sunni sects of Islam, respectively). *Awakening* (plural) is a reference to Sunni anti-ISIS (a la Anbar Awakening) groups, not the event of the Awakening. The ISIS operations terms are generally tactical and tangible (*killed*, *explosive*, *attack*, etc.) as opposed to the US ones that seem more strategic and abstract (*strategy*, *efforts*, and *support*). The ISIS geography terms (*village*, *Rawa*, *sites*) seem more local than the US, global and nation-state oriented lexicalization. ISIS, on the other hand, tends to deemphasize nationality in favor of Pan-Islamic legitimacy.

TABLE 8.1. US KEYWORDS: ACTORS

Keyword	Log Likelihood	Frequency
Isil	2977.0	689
Isis	2478.6	577
Forces	1800.7	548
Coalition	1747.3	437
Iraqi	1540.0	399
Security	1080.2	368
Fighters	872.6	219
Partners	847.9	237
Terrorist	752.2	222
ISIL's	730.2	169
United	639.3	375
Military	587.0	278
Syrian	541.4	135
Ground	408.1	189
Terrorists	387.5	112
Iraqis	378.1	90
States	374.6	312
Secretary	330.7	144
Civilians	307.0	82
Force	286.9	168
Minister	268.6	115
Da'esh	263.6	61
Communities	258.4	95

TABLE 8.2. US KEYWORDS: MILITARY OPERATIONS

Keyword	Log Likelihood	Frequency
Support	563.4	297
Fight	525.1	208
Continue	500.3	215
Defeat	499.1	148
Efforts	428.2	198
Will	403.8	653
Effort	371.7	179
Attacks	363.7	122
Threat	403.4	152
Humanitarian	389.5	103
Terrorism	344.7	104
Operations	335.8	143
Against	318.1	308
Campaign	314.1	170
Strategy	266.9	115
Stabilization	252.8	70
Strikes	251.4	81
Liberated	250.2	66

TABLE 8.3. US KEYWORDS: GEOGRAPHY

Keyword	Log Likelihood	Frequency
Iraq	563.4	609
Syria	525.1	496
Mosul	500.3	157
Raqqa	499.1	134
Countries	428.2	219
Global	403.8	135
Foreign	371.7	196
Homeland	363.7	80
Region	403.4	135
Territory	250.2	104

TABLE 8.4. ISIS KEYWORDS: ACTORS

Keyword	Translation	Log Likelihood	Frequency
جنود	Soldiers	838.8	1571
الدولة	The state	461.5	1232
المرتدين	The apostates	221.3	296
الرافضي	The Rafidhi (derogatory for Shia)	174.1	341
الصحوات	The Awakening (plural)	172.6	207
النبا	Al-Naba (IS magazine, the *Harvest*)	159.3	180
مرتدا	Apostate	138.0	156
الإسلامية	The Islamic	133.1	356
الروافض	The Rawafidh (derogatory for Shia)	129.7	236
مرتدي	Apostate	119.5	213
الجيش	The army	116.1	839
المجاهدين	The mujahideen	114.7	221
المجاهدون	The mujahideen	106.4	153
لجنود	For soldiers	105.4	158
صحوات	Awakening (plural)	102.9	155
الخلافة	The caliphate	97.6	529
المرتد	The apostate	84.2	120
KKP	PKK (in English letters)	87.6	99
الطاغوت	The tyrant	76.5	133

TABLE 8.5. ISIS KEYWORDS: OPERATIONS

Keyword	Translation	Log Likelihood	Frequency
هجوما	Attack	146.7	201
العدد	The number	121.8	211
ناسفة	Explosive	108.2	352
الخفيفة	Light (as in weaponry)	89.4	144
تدمري	Destructive	77.8	88
اثر	Effect	77.5	144
ومقتل	And those killed	75.8	127
مقتل	Those killed	74.6	442

TABLE 8.6. ISIS KEYWORDS: GEOGRAPHY

Keyword	Translation	Log Likelihood	Frequency
مدينة	City/Medina	160.0	727
منطقة	Region	147.5	972
مواقع	Sites	142.9	336
قرية	Village	108.1	266
غرب	West	90.5	240
رواه	Rawa (Iraqi town)	83.9	113
مواقعهم	Their sites	82.3	93
مدينة	City/Medina	160.0	727

TABLE 8.7. ISIS KEYWORDS: RELIGION

Keyword	Translation	Log Likelihood	Frequency
الله	God	926.9	3225
الردة	Apostasy	203.9	289
تعالى	Almighty	78.0	167

STANCE COMPARISON: MARSHALLING VALUES FOR WAR

The parallelism we found at the lexical level seems to break down at the level of stance and style. Exploratory factor analysis showed each side has argument patterns embedded in their discourse: repeated covariance of stance markers (both words and phrases) to accomplish some kind of pragmatic end. We used EFA to find covariance of stance features.[22] Imagine, for example, a genre pattern like *thank-you* notes: directly addressing the gift giver (*I* and *you* words), expressing positive emotion (*thank-you*, *really enjoyed*), and future talk (*will wear, will use*). Such a consistent pattern of language covariance can be used to identify rhetorical strategies, argument tactics, and register/genre patterns. Factor analysis found two factors each for the English and Arabic collections, using a total of 13 of the 121 stance categories the dictionaries code for—we describe those thirteen in more detail below.

US RHETORICAL STANCE: AGAINST THE ENEMY, AND FOR THE TROOPS

We found two factors that distinguished the US text collection from general US English preplanned talk. The two US factors are epideictic: vituperative speech condemning ISIS as a force for evil and chaos, and encomium delivered at US bases praising and thanking US troops.

Factor 1: Against the Enemy

Fear
Negative Values
NEGATIVE RELATIONSHIPS
Negative Emotion

The international community has made progress in degrading **terrorist** safe havens. In particular, the US-led coalition to counter ISIL has made significant strides in reducing ISIL's control of territory in Iraq and Syria, as well as the finances and foreign **terrorist** fighters available to it. At the same time, continued instability in key regions of the world, along with **weak** or nonexistent governance, sectarian **conflict**, porous borders, and widespread online presence provide **terrorist** groups like ISIL the opportunity to expand their influence, *terrorize* civilians, attract and mobilize new recruits, and *threaten* partner countries. In the face of increased military pressure, ISIL, Al Qaeda, and both groups' branches and adherents have pursued mass-casualty ATTACKS against symbolic targets and public spaces. **Terrorist attacks** in Bamako, Beirut, Brussels, Jakarta, Paris, and elsewhere demonstrate that these groups remain resilient and continue to target innocent civilians. We contend that ISIL ATTACKED Brussels on March 22, in an effort to assert a narrative of victory in the face of steady losses of territory in Iraq and Syria and generate persistent violence and *fear in* the West.

Factor 2: For the Troops

Reason Forward
Inclusiveness
IMMEDIACY
Acknowledgement

So I'm here today more than anything else to say thank you for your service. *Thank you* for your courage. And as the proud father of a United States Marine, let me also just take a Moment to give THESE soldiers a chance to say *thanks to* all the family members who are **with us** here today who make it possible for the men and women of **our** Guard and Reserve to serve. (Applause.) The truth is your loved ones enlist, but it's families who serve. And I know that well. So I just want to express again my *appreciation* for everyone who keeps the home fires burning. When you're sent overseas, as some in THIS unit are AS WE SPEAK, it's the families that take care of things at home and give you the peace of mind to be able to step forward and serve our country

ISIS RHETORICAL STANCE: WINNING THE FIGHT, AND RELIGIOUS VALUES FOR TODAY

The two ISIS factors include both battle reporting, and religious storytelling—the former a kind of forensic argument using logos, to argue for the puissance of ISIS, and the latter an exhortatory call to live according to religious values.

ISIS Factor 1: News updates on the fight against the "Rafidhi" enemy (i.e., Iran and its Iraqi and Syrian allies)

Spatial Relations communicate locations of skirmishes and battles (near the base, west, regions, inside).

Negative Values brand the enemy, using terms like *apostates*, *Crusaders*, and *Rafidhi* or *Rawafidh*. These last two words are derogatory terms for Shia that ISIS uses as a demeaning shorthand for the Shia-dominated security forces of Iran, Iraq, and the Assad regime.

Causation and Consequence communicate battlefield causes and effects, usually detailing the successful results of ISIS soldiers' attacks on the enemy.

Disclosure here comes only via the phrase *which is what exploded*, and so functionally closely resembles the causation and consequence language categories.

<u>Spatial Relations</u>
Public Vices
Causation
Consequence
<u>Disclosure</u>

مقتل ۱۰ روافض وتدمين ۳ دبابات 72 وفي السياق ذاته، صالت مجموعة منجنود الدولة الاسلامية الجمعة (٦ محرم)، عل عدة ثكنات للجيش الرافضي جنوب غربي الشرقاط، مما ادى الى مقتل عدد من عنا صبره. واوضح المكتب الاعلامي لولاية دجلة ان جنود الخلافة اقتحموا ثكنات الروافض واشتبكوا معهم بالاسلحة الخفيفة والمتوسطة، مما تسبب بمقتل ۸ مرتدين واصابة عدد اخر. الى جانب ذلك، تسلل ۲ من جنود الخلافة الى ثكنات للجيش الرافضي قرب قاعدة القيارة، وزرعوا عبوة ناسفة فياحدى الثكنات ويجروها عل عناصر الرافضة اثناء دخولهم الى الثكنة، مما اسفر عن مقتل وجرح عدد منهم.

Translation: Ten Rawfidh were killed and three T-72-tanks were destroyed, and in the same context, on Friday, (6th of Muharram), a group of Islamic State soldiers assaulted some barracks belonging to the *Rafidhi* army, <u>south</u>west of Sharqat, **which is what led to** the deaths of a number of us.[23] And the Media Office of Dijlah province explained that the soldiers of the Caliphate stormed the barracks of *the Rawafidh* and clashed <u>with them</u> using light and medium weapons, ***causing*** the deaths of eight apostates and wounding some others. In addition, two of the soldiers of the Caliphate infiltrated the barracks of *the Rafidhi* army <u>near</u> Al-Qayara Base, and planted an explosive device in one of <u>the barracks</u>; they pulled it on some of *the Rafidhi* elements as they entered the barracks, <u>*which is what exploded*</u>, killing and injuring a number of them.

ISIS Factor 2: Religious Reasoning and Storytelling

This factor uses the language of immediacy (e.g., *right now, just then*) and specifiers (*this*, *in particular*) in the context of religious storytelling. Specifying in this factor works through frequent use of *this* (هذه and هذا) and *these*. In Arabic, immediacy terms are somewhat difficult to distinguish from specifiers, shown here as *that which* (الذي) and *for this* (لهذ). More unique immediacy terms highlighted here include *it is time* (حان الوقت), *that* (ذلك), *now* (الان), and *it is upon us* (علينا).

This religious reasoning is a key source of ISIS's rhetorical power, as characterized by Salazar: "the caliphate's high oratory, its uncompromising dialectic, its scriptural demands, and the epic hailing of its heroes and martyrs."[24] By using language with immediacy-infused words like *these, that which*, and *now*), while sharing stories of religious heroism, ISIS may discursively be suggesting these precepts to the present day, suggesting how a virtuous person should live, and reinforcing its own virtue:

<u>Specifiers</u>
Immediacy

لكان الزمان هذا ،بالجماعة عليه الله انعم ثم ،حياته كانت هكذا

:الله رحمه ،نضرة ابو وقال ،((قلباخوانك في والحقيقة المعرفة هذه يثبت ومما هولاء جهاد اعمالهم افضل من

الصالحات تتم بنعمته الذي لله والحمد كان))

Translation: "This is how his life was, and then God blessed him with the community. At ***this*** time, it was one of the best of acts of jihad of ***these*** people. And that proves ***this*** knowledge and truth in the heart of your brothers. And Abu Nadra, may God have mercy on him, said: (Thanks to God, <u>whose</u> grace is good)."

فجعل سفيان يقول] :الانفال .٢٦؛ :انعم الله علينافي كذا، انعم الله علينا في كذا، وهذه النعمة <u>التي</u> يتنعم

بها الان تستوجب عليه ان شاء الله تعالى.

Translation: "And so Sufyan said: [Al-Anfal: 26]; God has showered blessings ***upon us*** in this way, God has showered blessings ***upon us*** in this way, and this goodness <u>which</u> he has blessed is now blessed, God willing."

فبعد سنوات من العمل يف مكة الذي تركز عىل توحيد الله وترسيخه يف النفوس، واعالن الرباء من املرشكني
وفعالهم التي اخرجتهم عن التوحيد، حان الوقت ه لله عز وجل

Translation: "After years of working in Mecca, in which he concentrated on the unity of God and establishing him in the soul, and providing for benefits of people and their actions <u>that</u> took them out of monotheism, ***it is the time*** for God Almighty."

We note that our interpretation of the second factor is tentative. While the strings that are coded in stance comparison are unique (a word or phrase cannot for example be both in the specifier and immediacy categories), unique strings from both categories have overlap in component words. In essence, in Arabic, the line between specifying and immediacy may be finer than in English.

MARSHALLING SUPPORT THROUGH DISTINCT KINDS OF RHET OPS

In both corpora, we can see the United States and ISIS engaged in rhetorical operations, legitimizing themselves and their efforts, while discursively attacking their enemies. Even though there is significant diversity in corpus authors, the kinds of settings and genres, and spans of years of production, at the aggregate level there are both strong aboutness and stance patterns in the text that seem to serve pragmatic ends. Both the United States and ISIS talk about generally similar topics, and this likely reflects the entailments of public speech while at war. Similarly, both sides deploy values arguments, mostly in epideictic argument, but also a kind of forensic battle reporting to demonstrate success and relevance.

We think it is plausible that both sides have a good sense as native speakers and members to effectively engage domestic audiences. It makes sense that US government speakers should praise the troops or condemn ISIS, and it seems understandable that a Jihadi-Salafist group like ISIS would report their battlefield success and extol Salafi (old-time) religious values. But these differences could be instructive. To the degree that the United States wishes to contest violent extremism in the Islamic world, reaching out to Arabic-speaking audiences, US rhet ops need to be informed by what groups like ISIS are doing discursively.

STUDY IMPLICATIONS

We have shown how both ISIS and US government officials make use of sophisticated rhetorical strategies for representing their interpretation of the conflict. ISIS, for example, uses battle reporting to validate their effectiveness, and hortatory arguments to encourage membership and adherence; whereas the United States valorizes military members and condemns its enemy, and by extension validates the war effort. We have also shown how these rhetorical strategies are machine detectable, and that human/machine methods can be fruitful for understanding how and why these different approaches work for different audiences. Two implications for future US efforts spring from our analysis, both short-term and long-term.

An immediate implication for US policymakers interested in combatting international terrorism and extremism is to discard volume/productivity models in favor of models for rhetorical struggle that conceptualize effects. For example, the joint task force opposing ISIS should reconsider volume-oriented measures of effectiveness: reducing the total amount of rhetorical activity.[25] In place of measuring the volume of ISIS rhetoric, we should attend to its relevance to the target audience and effectiveness. Of course this implication is broader than any specific group like ISIS: anywhere that the United States wants to engage in rhetorical operations, military and public diplomacy practicioners need to be able to usefully assess rhetorical effectiveness.

A second implication is the need to continue to develop and integrate operationally relevant text analysis methods to support tradecraft—that is, to supplement human approaches to understanding rhetorical conflict with machine-supported means that can reliably find deep patterns at scale. There is an asymmetry between the amount of talk reflecting rhetorical struggle across the globe, and the linguistic and cultural resources available to the United States and its allies. From terrorist groups to state-sponsored disinformation, there is an enormous volume and variety of languages and settings for antisocial rhetorical efforts that undermine global human safety and dignity. Even if there were endless supplies of culturally sensitive native speakers available to conduct rhet ops against malevolent actors and regimes, as we have noted, there are limitations to human-only analysis. It is therefore imperative that the United States develop a robust capability to conduct rhet ops.

The US Global Engagement Center (GEC), with its "lead, synchronize, and coordinate efforts of the Federal Government to recognize, understand, expose, and counter foreign state and non-state propaganda and disinformation efforts aimed at undermining United States national security interests," is a logical place of insertion for such an effort. [26] In turn, this robust capacity to conduct rhet ops could be operationalized within the US Commbatant Commands in regionally localized ways.

NOTES

1. Marcellino, "Revisioning Strategic Communication."

2. ISIS has also been referred to as ISIL, IS, and DAESH. For simplicity's sake, we have chosen to use ISIS throughout this chapter.

3. Salazar, "A Caliphate of Culture?"

4. A term from early Islamic history meaning "defectors" or "those who left the group," the Kharijites originally referred to an Islamic group that rebelled against the fourth caliph, 'Ali ibn Abi Talib. Extreme Kharijites believed that even self-professed Muslims who committed serious sins were apostates deserving of capital punishment. Modern-day figures in Salafism (a conservative reform movement defined by an attempt to emulate the earliest followers of Islam) brand ISIS members as Kharijites in order to delegitimize them. This allusion highlights ISIS members' tendencies to excommunicate other self-professed Muslims who disagree with them as apostates.

5. Biber, Conrad, and Reppen, *Corpus Linguistics*; McEnery, Xiao, and Tono, *Corpus-Based Language Studies.*

6. All text came from the US Department of State website, https://www.state.gov; the Obama Administration White House archive, https://obamawhitehouse.archives.gov; the US Department of Defense website, http://www.defense.gov; and centcom.mil.

7. Including the blog الدولة الإسلامية باقية بإذن الله, http://al-dawla-ba9iya.blogspot.fr/; and Jihadology, http://jihadology.net/; and JustPast.it., https://justpaste.it/.

8. The FROWN Corpus is a million-word representative corpus of English, commonly used in English language corpus linguistics. See VARIENG: Research Unit for the Study of Variation, Contacts and Change in English, Freiburg-Brown Corpus of American English (FROWN), http://www.helsinki.fi/varieng/CoRD/corpora/FROWN/.

9. Islamist in the sense of advocating for Islam as central to law and public life. See the Brookings Institute brief by Shadi Hamid and Rashid Dar, "Islamism, Salafism, and Jihadism: A Primer," July 15, 2016, https://www.brookings.edu/blog/markaz/2016/07/15/islamism-salafism-and-jihadism-a-primer/.

10. Bodine-Baron, Helmus, Magnuson, and Winkelman, *Examining ISIS Support and Opposition Networks*; Helmus et al., *Russian Social Media Influence*, 2018; Marcellino, Cragin, Mendelsohn, Cady, Magnuson, and Reedy, "Measuring the Popular Resonance of Daesh's Propoganda," 4.

11. Scott, "PC Analysis of Key Words—and Key Key Words"; Baker, Gabrielatos, Khosravinik, Krzyżanowski, McEnery, and Wodak, "A Useful Methodological Synergy?"

12. Biber, Connor, and Upton, with Anthony, and Gladkov, "Rhetorical Appeals in Fundraising."

13. Marcellino, "Talk Like a Marine."

14. Auría, "Stance and Academic Promotionalism," 112.

15. David Kaufer, Suguru Ishizaki, and Carnegie Mellon University Department of English, DocuScope: Computer-Aided Rhetorical Analysis, https://www.cmu.edu/dietrich/english/research/docuscope.html. For a good example application of the DocuScope dictionaries to a contested rhetorical example, see Al-Malki, Kaufer, Ishizaki, and Dreher, *Arab Women in Arab News.*

16. Airoldi, Anderson, Fienberg, and Skinner, "Who Wrote Ronald Reagan's Radio Addresses?" Airoldi, Anderson, Fienberg, and Skinner, "Whose Ideas? Whose Words?"

17. Collins, *Variations in Written English*; Hope and Witmore, "Hundredth Psalm to the Tune of 'Green Sleeves.'"

18. Yongmei, Kaufer, and Ishizaki, "Genre and Instinct."

19. Allison, Heuser, Jockers, Moretti, and Witmore, *Quantitative Formalism.*

20. Log likelihood scores over are statistically significant (99.9th percentile; 0.1 percent level; $p < 0.001$). LL scores between 100 and 1000 indicates high levels of keyness—highly pointed talk, while LL >1000 are fundamentally what a text collection is about. For example, a collection of talk about the NFL football team the New England Patriots might have sport-related keywords in the double digits, keyword LL scores from prominent names like Belichick and Brady in the hundreds, and words from what the collection is fundamentally about (*New*, *England*, and *Patriots*) would likely score over a thousand.

21. The ISIS corpus had many misspellings/spelling variants, and our software cannot distinguish that *awesome* and *aw3some* are the same word. Hence variant spellings, which do not occur in the baseline corpus, can have an artificially high LL score despite being very infrequent (and were almost always duplicative of top keywords). We discarded these, hence the thirty-seven legitimate keywords for this corpus.

22. Marcellino and Matthews, *RAND-Lex User's Guide.* Factor loading for significance in this test was ≥ .04.

23. Note how the speaker, while acknowledging ISIS casualties, topicalizes (and thus shifts focus to) opponent losses.

24. Salazar, "Caliphate of Culture?"

25. See, for example, Inherent Resolve (@CJTFOIR), "في تشرين الثاني ، كانت الوسائل الاعلامية لدعاية داعش أقل بنسبة ٨٨٪ مما كانت عليه في ذروتها في عام 2015," Twitter, January 27, 2018, 12:55 a.m., https://twitter.com/CJTFOIR/status/957175113337704453.

26. US Department of State, Under Secretary for Public Diplomacy and Public Affairs, "Global Engagement Center," https://www.state.gov/r/gec/.

REFERENCES

Airoldi, E. M., A. G. Anderson, S. E. Fienberg, and K. K. Skinner. "Who Wrote Ronald Reagan's Radio Addresses?" *Bayesian Analysis*, no. 2 (2006): 289–320.

Airoldi, E. M., A. G. Anderson, S. E. Fienberg, and K. K. Skinner. "Whose Ideas? Whose Words? Authorship of the Ronald Reagan Radio Addresses." *Political Science & Politics*, no. 40 (2007): 501–6.

Allison, Sarah Danielle, Ryan Heuser, Matthew Lee Jockers, Franco Moretti, and Michael Witmore. *Quantitative Formalism: An Experiment.* Stanford, CA: Stanford Literary Lab, 2011.

Al-Malki, Amal, David Kaufer, Suguru Ishizaki, and Kira Dreher. *Arab Women in Arab News: Old Stereotypes and New Media.* London: A&C Black, 2012.

Auría, Maria Carmen Pérez-Llantada. "Stance and Academic Promotionalism: A Cross-Disciplinary Comparison in the Soft Sciences." *Atlantis* 30, no. 1 (2008): 129–45.

Baker, Paul, Costas Gabrielatos, Majid Khosravinik, Michał Krzyżanowski, Tony McEnery, and Ruth Wodak. "A Useful Methodological Synergy? Combining Critical Discourse Analysis and Corpus Linguistics to Examine Discourses of Refugees and Asylum Seekers in the UK Press." *Discourse & Society* 19, no. 3 (2008): 273–306.

Biber, Douglas, Susan Conrad, and Randi Reppen. *Corpus Linguistics: Investigating Language Structure and Use.* Cambridge: Cambridge University Press, 1998.

Biber, D., U. Connor, and A. Upton, with M. Anthony, and K. Gladkov. "Rhetorical Appeals in Fundraising." In *Discourse on the Move: Using Corpus Analysis to Describe Discourse Struc-*

ture, edited by D. Biber, U. Connor, and A. Upton, 121–51. Amsterdam: John Benjamin, 2007.

Bodine-Baron, Elizabeth, Todd C. Helmus, Madeline Magnuson, and Zev Winkelman. *Examining ISIS Support and Opposition Networks on Twitter.* Santa Monica, CA: RAND Corporation, 2016.

Collins, J. *Variations in Written English.* Washington, DC: US Department of the Air Force, 2003.

Helmus, Todd C., et al. *Russian Social Media Influence: Understanding Russian Propaganda in Eastern Europe.* Santa Monica, CA: RAND Corporation, 2018.

Hope J., and M. Witmore, "The Hundredth Psalm to the Tune of 'Green Sleeves': Digital Approaches Shakespeare's Language of Genre." *Shakespeare Quarterly*, no. 61 (2010).

Marcellino, William M. "Talk like a Marine: USMC Linguistic Acculturation and Civil–Military Argument." *Discourse Studies* 16, no. 3 (2014): 385–405.

Marcellino, William M. "Revisioning Strategic Communication Through Rhetoric and Discourse Analysis." *Joint Force Quarterly* 76, no. 1 (2015): 52–57.

Marcellino, William, and Luke Matthews. *RAND-Lex User's Guide: Text Analytics Software Suite.* Santa Monica, CA: RAND Corporation, 2015.

Marcellino, William M., Kim Cragin, Joshua Mendelsohn, Andrew Micahel Cady, Madeline Magnuson, and Kathleen Reedy. "Measuring the Popular Resonance of Daesh's Propaganda." *Journal of Strategic Security* 10, no. 1 (2017): 4.

McEnery, Tony, Richard Xiao, and Yukio Tono. *Corpus-Based Language Studies: An Advanced Resource Book.* Abingdon, UK: Taylor & Francis, 2006.

Miller, Ryan T., and Silvia Pessoa. "Corpus-Driven Study of Information Systems Project Reports." In *Learner Corpus Research: New Perspectives and Applications* edited by Vaclav Brezina and Lynne Flowerdew, 112–33. London: Bloomsbury, 2018.

Salazar, Philippe-Jospeph. "A Caliphate of Culture?: ISIS's Rhetorical Power." *Philosophy & Rhetoric* 49, no. 3 (2016): 343–54.

Scott, M. "PC Analysis of Key Words—and Key Key Words." *System* 25, no. 2 (1997): 233–45.

Yongmei, Hu, David Kaufer, and Suguru Ishizaki. "Genre and Instinct." In *Computing with Instinct: Rediscovering Artificial Intelligence*, ed. Yang Cai, 58–81. Berlin: Springer, 2011.

9

STORMWATCH

MACHINE LEARNING APPROACHES TO UNDERSTANDING WHITE SUPREMACY ONLINE

RYAN OMIZO

According a 2015 report from the Southern Poverty Law Center (SPLC), the visibility of radical, anti-government "patriot" groups in the United States have declined because participants in such groups face public exposure. However, while anti-government organizations may be abandoning their public fronts, anti-government and radical right-wing activities have continued as many groups have moved online to recruit members and share information.[1] One of the more notable of these online sites is Stormfront.org, the oldest white nationalist discussion forum founded by the former Ku Klux Klan member Don Black, in 1995.[2] Another SPLC report identifies Stormfront as the "murder capital of the internet."[3] Between 1995 and 2000 Stormfront members committed one hundred murders, including the murder of Wade Michael Page, who shot and killed six people at a Sikh temple in Oak Tree, Wisconsin, in 2012.[4] Perversely, because Stormfront generates revenue through ads and donations, the increased media coverage of these Stormfront connections has driven traffic to the site, thereby allowing Stormfront to financially profit on the spectacle of these hate crimes.[5] As of 2016, Alexa ranked Stormfront.org as the 7,675th most popular site in the United States and the 22,029th most popular site globally. Between October and December 2016, Stormfront's world rank has increased 7,474 places.[6]

As an all-purpose platform for white supremacy online, Stormfront features an array of discussion forum topics that include general news, health and fitness, "science and technology," "ideology and philosophy," and tips for "white dating."[7] Stormfront also offers forum threads in which members discuss technical specifications of guns and ammunition, share information about military tactics, martial arts training, internet security, and community organizing strategies.[8] Stormfront serves as more than just a venue to share white supremacist sentiments—it also functions as a site for the teaching and learning of potentially dangerous technical content, filtered through racist, anti-leftist, and anti-government lenses. While it is unknown whether the white supremacist terrorists profiled by Beirich have employed specific technical information circulated on Stormfront in attacks,[9] there is reason to believe that such discussion topics are fueling armed provocations by white supremacists.[10] A controversial 2009 report commissioned by the Department of Homeland Security argued that American right-wing extremists represent persistent threats that could have increased with the election of Barack Obama (although no acts of violence were found to be imminent) and that this threat might be increased because of the presence of internet technologies that enable members to share information about weapons and tactics.[11] Small-cell and lone-wolf attacks are viewed as increasing problems due to the decentralized nature of attack planning and difficulties posed in attempting to identify violent individuals before attacks have taken place. A 2017 report by the Department of Homeland Security and the Federal Bureau of Investigation renewed these warning, writing, "Although plot derived mass-casualty violence remains possible, we judge it more likely that violence will continue to be spontaneous and involve targets of opportunity. Despite a lack of shooting attacks in 2016, firearms likely will continue to pose the greatest threat of lethal violence by WSEs due to their availability and ease of use."[12] Thus, while the technical firearms content distributed through Stormfront may yet come to directly guide white supremacist terrorism, it does inform the rhetorical ecologies in which Stormfront adherents negotiate their positions as combatants against peoples of color, Jews, Muslims, women, LBTGQ groups, and the federal government within the white supremacist communities.

This chapter seeks to understand how the teaching and learning space of Stormfront functions through the lens of facilitation—a branch of pedagogy that is often applied in informal learning environments such as online discussion forums.[13] To analyze facilitated instruction of technical firearms content on Stormfront, I will utilize both close readings of Stormfront discussion forum posts and a support vector machine learning web application called the Faciloscope.[14]

The Faciloscope is a three-category classifier that has been designed to track the linguistic behavior of participants in online discussion forums at the sentence level. When processing natural language text, the Faciloscope tokenizes that text into sentence units and then labels each sentence as one of three, high-valued facilitation moves: staging, evoking, and inviting. Tracking the deployment of these facilitation moves within Stormfront discussion forum threads serves two purposes. First, identifying how Stormfront members are interacting rhetorically can glean insights into how technical training is delivered, received, and elaborated upon on Stormfront, which, in turn, will provide us with intelligence about how white supremacists mobilize around key nodes of knowledge. Second, the use of machine-learning applications to automatically analyze and distill topical and rhetorical information points to new ways in which anti-racist activists such as the SPLC can monitor the online activities of dangerous white supremacists. This last point is crucial because as Daniels points out in her discussion of the rise of the alt-right,[15] algorithmically-driven social media platforms allow white supremacists to broadcast their hate with greater reach and enable white supremacists rhetors to infiltrate more "mainstream" discussions through tactics such as appropriating Pepe the Frog in their meme warfare efforts.[16] More problematic is the function of the internet as an archive of hate. Noble presents the infamous case of Dylan Roof, who murdered nine African Americans in Charleston, South Carolina in 2015.[17] Before the mass shooting, Roof used Google to research racist ideas such as "black-on-white crime" and was pointed to white supremacist sites such as the Council of Conservative Citizens, possibly fueling his radicalization. According to Noble's research, such sites were/can be highly positioned on the Google search results page because of the search engine's lack of content curation and emphasis on advertising as opposed to knowledge curation. Noble writes: "[Search engines] oversimplify complex phenomena. They obscure any struggle over understanding, and they can mask history. Search results can reframe our thinking and deny us the ability to engage deeply with essential information and knowledge we need, knowledge that has traditionally been learned through teachers, books, history, and experience. Search results, in the context of commercial advertising companies, lay the ground work, as I have discussed throughout this book, for implicit bias: bias that is buttressed by advertising profits."[18] Within this paradigm, the facilitation of the technical content—the promotion and recording of any conversation on sites such as Stormfront—contributes to the creation of resources for racists. For malicious racists, Stormfront discussion forum threads are already framed as answers to their Googled questions.

WHITE SUPREMACY ONLINE

As Daniels notes in her critical study of cyber-racism,[19] white supremacists have long viewed the internet as an inexpensive and anonymizing tool for disseminating their message, recruiting, and linking splintered white supremacist groups around the world, fostering a "translocal white identity."[20] This translocal white identity, as Back writes, revives configurations of white colonial power in Western Europe and in former colonies such as Australia, Canada, and the

United States, and unites these disparate identities under the banner of a "white lineage" that transcends time and place due to networked capacities of the internet. Internet spaces, especially online communities such as Stormfront (directly cited by Back), allows white supremacists to project their idealized white selves into virtual worlds of their own delusions and connect with others.[21]

A significant characteristic of online white supremacy sites is the use of discussion forums. A content analysis by Schafer identifies the ability for white supremacists to converse with like-minded individuals online as key to the growth of white supremacy online.[22] Daniels references the use of interactive discussion forums as instrumental in Stormfront's rise to prominence.[23] According to Daniels, Stormfront's early leveraging of online communication technologies set it apart from its peers, which used the internet as a means to disseminate remediated print media such as brochures and pamphlets. Stormfront also employs moderators to facilitate conversations.[24] Daniels describes the case of Jamie Kelso, a Stormfront moderator who would pose "softball" questions to lurking members in the hopes of eliciting more public participation. Kelso also introduced the use of emoticons to allow members to further express their personalities and affectual response.

THE FACILOSCOPE

The Faciloscope is a web application that uses supervised support vector machine learning to classify sentences from natural language texts[25] according to one of three rhetorical moves: staging, inviting, and evoking.[26] Rhetorical moves here refer to discrete actions rhetors perform as components of larger rhetorical strategies, which are tailored to the genre conventions of that communicative situation.[27]

The Faciloscope classifier has been trained to label three rhetorical moves:

Staging: A move that is aimed toward making a statement that introduces an idea, concept, or example in order to frame discussion or understanding. For example:

"I found this information in National Geographic."

Inviting: A move that explicitly guides the development of discussion or an idea through direct requests. These are often questions. For example:

"What type of birds are people drawing?"

Evoking: A move that explicitly attempts to create connections among participants and/or maintain social relationships. For example:

"Thank you all for joining our live blogging of the debate!"

These rhetorical moves derived from coding schemes used in a previous but related facilitation study[28]—specifically, two facilitation training resources—a coding instructions tool for analyzing informal learning online and a "category specific facilitation tool" designed to help discussion leaders foster conversation.[29] The Faciloscope codebook represents a contraction of the coding scheme found in the facilitation cheat sheet, distilling what expert facilitators participating in the related study deemed significant for successful facilitation. Staging, evoking, and inviting moves are considered the constituents of sound facilitation strategies and can, in the hands of expert facilitators, be used to guide conversations as they unfold in ways that optimize participation and learning.

DATA

Data for this chapter comprises 354 posts (March 10, 2008–August 18, 2014) from the Stormfront discussion forum thread "Reloading for the AR" ("Reloading")"[30] and 115 posts (March 20, 2008–March 25, 2017) from the thread "Have a Rifle? Now Learn How to Shoot It!" ("Have a Rifle"),[31] which originated in the "Self-Defense, Martial Arts & Preparedness" parent forum on March 10, 2008.[32] In terms of activity with the "Self-Defense, Martial Arts & Preparedness" forum, "Reloading" is sixteenth in reply counts and has 129,964 views. However, among non-"sticky" and poll threads, "Reloading" is the fifth in replies and seventh in views. "Have a Rifle" is a "sticky post" and appears as the fourth ranked thread on the "Self-Defense, Martial Arts & Preparedness" forum. "Have a Rifle" has received 65,693 views.

ANALYSIS

Analysis for "Reloading" will follow two trajectories.[33] First, I will conduct a close reading analysis of "Reloading" in order to provide insights into the types of communication being deployed throughout this asynchronous and open-ended discussion. Second, I will complement this close reading with a facilitation move analysis courtesy of the Faciloscope. This Faciloscope-driven analysis will provide quantitative information about how facilitation moves are used and how they are arranged in the texts. I will discuss how the type of work accomplished by the Faciloscope can be redirected in opposition to the white supremacists' screes found in sites such as Stormfront by proposing a novel method for augmented monitoring of online discourse. These two strains of diagnosis can also be productively construed as an analysis of content and behavior, in which the close reading of the technical instructions and responses traces what is being written and the Faciloscope traces the types of rhetorical actions that are being undertaken by interactants via the lens of three high-value facilitation moves.

The exigency of "Reloading" is to provide advice on how to best reload AR-15–style rifles. The thread starter, 14words_of_truth, initiates discussion by promising to provide helpful, clarifying information about reloading AR-15 rifles to address current gaps in and speciousness of online resources. The post then performs common racist rhetoric that argues for the "white man's" technical mastery over firearms and the inferiority of African Americans and Jews in this specific regard; asserts that prowess in reloading AR-15 rifles will insure longevity of well-trained white men over other races and is a mark of moral superiority; and, lastly, asks for community feedback on the prudence of disseminating such crucial tactical information in open forums (people other than white supremacists could be reading it). This post provides little technical information about reloading spent AR-15 shells, so much of the work of this post is directed at melding white supremacist identity with the mastery of firearms. Firearms in this post represent manifestation of a white, gnosis power—one only truly accessible to white men:

> Firearms are strictly White Man's Technology.
> The Shooting Sports are strictly White Men's Sports.
> Reloading is a White Man's pastime.

This conflation of technological and racial superiority has been observed before in the work of Katz, who argues that the moral justification for the Holocaust cited by Hitler and Nazis depended on a "technological imperative."[34] This "technological imperative" relied on the belief that technological power derives from the scientific and objective truth of the technology and its expediency. For Katz, this technological ethos that is beholden only to its own fulfillment of expediency can inspire a bankrupted morality that, in turn, authorizes evils such as the Holocaust. In the technical memo drafted for the Final Solution—used as an exemplar of Nazi techno-rationality—Katz highlights the tendency for the memo writer, Just, to focus reader attention on the technical details for the improvements of "special vehicles" while eliding the fact that these recommendations are being offered to facilitate genocide. By emphasizing technical problems and technical solutions, the Nazi bureaucracy could avoid acknowledging the humanity of Jews and make the Final Solution a reality.[35]

Technical information about firearms reloading conform to a rhetorical pattern akin to the "open instructional sets" discussed by Selber.[36] Open instructional sets designate technical information such as online help and user manuals that are authored, edited, and maintained by communities of practitioners that may involve experts of various levels. Open instructional sets contrast with "self-contained instructional sets," which include official and unalterable guides created by product owners and/or subject area experts. Self-contained instructional sets are for users to read, not write or edit.[37] Selber further argues that open instructional sets are "bottom-up" enterprises and reflects the "organic Web." Consistent with the community-driven practices of open instructional sets and the discontinuous nature of the conversation, "Reloading" features a range of different rhetorical frames for technical content. Similar to the first post by 14words_of_truth, some posts in "Reloading" relay personal experiences with and evaluations of firearms. For example: "Link is good. I thank you, and so does my Lyman Turret! I have shot alot [*sic*] of Hornady A-MAX, and to be honest I think Sierra makes better stuff. For bulk reloading, though, you can't beat the prices on that link. A guy at the range told me that his .308 rifle likes the Sierra 110 gr. Spritzer bullets better than anything else. I do plan on testing some 110 gr. bullets later, but still testing some 150 gr. right now."

Other posts offer procedural information about reloading assault rifle ammunition:

> This is the method I came up with for powder charge testing.
> Charge weights are one tenth of a grain apart.
> Each charge weight is a group of three.
> The first cartridge of the each group is marked for identification. I use a magic marker to identify the first bullet in each group of three.
> A note card fits in my ammo box, so I mark the charge weights on that.
> Then I mark my targets with the charge weights.
> After that, all you have to do is shoot the ammo and evaluate the results.
> Later I will verify the results by loading several rounds of a charge weight that worked well on testing and make certain that it really does work that well, if it does then it is time to load up a lot of ammo!

The aforementioned mode of instruction offered—emphasizing step-by-step or how-to explanations of munitions handling, technical concepts, tool use, and personal experiences—appears prominently in "Reloading." Key to both the procedural and the evaluative nature of "Reloading" is the association with the *I* subject. Technical advice is anchored by hands-on testing and practice. Product reviews are anchored by first-hand accounts.

"Have a Rifle" engages in a different form of facilitation: resource sharing. The initial post functions as a word-of-mouth advertisement for Appleseed rifle classes, an organization that purports to train participants in marksmanship while celebrating America's colonizing past.[38] Thus, "Have a Rifle" is a thread attempting to bridge online participation with face-to-fact, brick-and-mortar participation (although several posters emphasize the need to cloak white supremacists affiliations if attending public events such as Appleseed clinics).

TABLE 9.1. DESCRIPTIVE STATISTICS FOR "RELOADING FOR THE AR" AND "HAVE A RIFLE?"

	Word #	Sentence #	Staging %	Evoking %	Inviting %
"Reloading for the AR"	63,386	2,968	85.21	9	5.8
"Have a Rifle?"	11,131	638	70.6	15.8	13.5

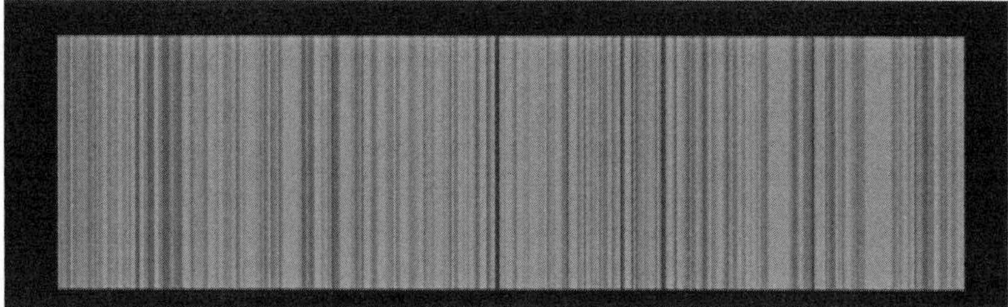

FIGURE 9.1. Bands Visualization of "Reloading for the AR" Facilitation Moves

FIGURE 9.2. Bands Visualization of "Have a Rifle?" Facilitation Moves

The Faciloscope classification scheme allows us to conduct an automated move analysis of Stormfront discussion forums. This move analysis can provide insights into the underlying generic conventions of the forum, suggesting what move is expected to be made or tolerated and when to sustain the sharing and teaching of technical content. In this section, I will discuss the results of the Faciloscope's facilitation move analysis; then, I will propose a novel method for using the Faciloscope for tracking Stormfront's content.

The visualizations depicted in figures 9.1 and 9.2 are outputs of the Faciloscope's web application for "Reloading" and "Have a Rifle." In the Faciloscope app, staging moves are green, inviting moves are purple, and evoking moves are blue. In the grayscale representation of the bands visualization, the lightest gray represents staging moves, the middling gray bands indicate inviting moves, and the darkest bands indicate evoking moves. The width of these bands indicates the length of each facilitation move segment in terms of character count. In the app, this "bands" visualization is interactive, allowing users to scrub and zoom through the bands and view the associated sections of the original text and discern how specific facilitation moves operate in context with other moves.[39]

Staging moves predominate in both "Reloading" and "Have a Rifle," which is to be expected in almost any online discussion texts. Because Staging moves establish the grounds of interactions, they appear more frequently than an inviting move that is only made intelligible because of antecedent staging moves. Examples of staging moves from "Reloading" include sequential descriptions of actions such as following:

> I will be reloading .50 Beowulf, 300 Win Mag, .30-'06 and 308 Winchester.
> It will work with all of these.

At the same time, racist characterizations are also classified as staging moves by the Faciloscope. The white racial frame in which 14words_of_truth anchors the discussion of AR-15 reloading processes cited earlier are all staging moves as defined by the coding rubric, illustrating how the rhetorical norming of racist ideologies is occurring within "Reloading"—claims about the superiority of whites versus other racial groups are not adjudicated—they are simply facts in this white supremacist universe.

That said, comparing the facilitation move distribution between "Reloading" and "Have a Rifle," we find notable differences between the prevalence of each move category. "Reloading" contains far less evoking and inviting moves than "Have a Rifle" and far more staging moves. When we consider the use of facilitation moves as rhetorical behaviors, the lack of inviting moves in "Reloading" becomes telling because Inviting moves indicate participation. The results of the Faciloscope suggest that "Reloading" is less interactive than "Have a Rifle," even though it is longer and more enduring. This seeming misalignment between the threads persistent and the lack of explicit interactions through Inviting moves can be explained by the fact that "Reloading" mostly consists of posts by the thread starter, 14words_of_truth, and his personal experiences and experiments. The count of staging moves reflects the streaming monologue of technical information accreting within the thread over time much like how a developer's blog might contain running reports and updates. We might dismiss "Reloading" as the ravings of a gun-obsessed racist—another "lone wolf." Two things belie this notion. First, while the content of "Reloading" is univocal, the thread has garnered 129,964 views. While not manifestly participatory, the thread has been viewed by large audiences. Second, an examination of the most recent posts to the thread reveals that participation is not arrested and could be increasing. Inviting and evoking moves are occurring at the tail end of the thread (see figure 9.1), suggesting that the topic still has the potential to foment interaction years after its inception. This raises the possibility of a mode of online instruction that relies more upon building a critical mass of technical information than interaction. This mode offers readers exacting, dense, and frequently updated information, creating a record of firearms instruction that can be indexed by human and nonhuman agents.[40] This contrasts with "Have a Rifle," which features more inviting and evoking moves that reflect questions about similar rifle training courses, additional gun advice, and phatic acts of thanking and affirmation. We can attribute some of these rhetorical behaviors by the nature of "Have a Rifle." Because the thread is connected to concrete, public events, the information and experience is more broadly applicable/accessible to Stormfront members as opposed to 14words_of_truth's reloading work, which is solitary in nature.[41] People asking for more details (e.g., "Any Groups in San Diego, Ca [*sic*] that i can practice or train with????") or solicitations of solidarity around the topic of marksmanship (e.g., "If anyone lives in orange, seminole, lake county, FL [*sic*] and wants to learn to shoot or shoot for fun let me know") would be expected. Consequently, where "Reloading" builds a critical mass due to its painstaking accumulation, we can argue that "Have a Rifle" invites more immediate participation because it is designed around resource sharing and social networking.

CONCLUSIONS

This chapter offers two main takeaways about (1) the rhetoric of technical instruction on Stormfront, and (2) future directions for automated content monitoring. On this first point, we can say that Stormfront makes use of what Selber calls "open instructional" sets for the framing of firearms education. "Reloading" demonstrates that highly visible threads can involve persistent postings of personal experiences by single members that employ denotative elements (staging moves) in favor of interactive elements. "Have a Rifle" demonstrates how resource sharing, especially when it relates to offline activities generates higher interactivity from more members through question posing and affect-driven statements (e.g., expressions of thanks). In terms of informal teaching and learning, the application of the Faciloscope on "Reloading" and "Have a Rifle" reveal two related pedagogical strategies of note. With its higher incidence and regular distribution of inviting and evoking moves, "Have a Rifle" operates as a more open-ended call to arms (literally), emphasizing community building through the linking of online and offline experiences with riflery. In this sense, "Have a Rifle" displays rhetorical behaviors typical of topic driven online forums like the informal learning website ScienceBuzz (whose work inspired and informs the Faciloscope's machine training).[42] The full title of the discussion thread—"Have a Rifle? Now Learn How to Shoot It!"—begins with inviting and evoking moves that attract user attention through the use of questioning and then spurs action by both challenging readers' sense of gun competence and promising novel information for those who participate in the thread. This prompting strategy resembles the Science-Buzz thread "Got the Cure? What to Do about Hiccups"—a thread with 187 comments revolving around the subject of hiccups cures.[43] "Reload" evidences a different pedagogical strategy—one that Noble's analysis of the Dylan Roof case renders more disturbing and one that should be familiar to many writing teachers—the "sage on the stage" or "transmittal model" of teaching and learning.[44] 14words_of_truth dominates the thread, holding court with (ostensible) demonstrations of firearms knowledge and racist ideologies consistent with the mission of Stormfront. While the "sage-on-the-stage" model of pedagogy has given way to process-oriented or project-based approaches in the rhetoric and composition and professional writing classrooms, the case of Stormfront as an educational and rhetorical resource for budding white nationalist extremists demands a reappraisal of this mode of instruction. Sites such as Stormfront offer readers durable resources that can be shared or returned to over and over, mitigating the lossy transmission of information that affects lecture-based classroom instruction.[45] Moreover, the univocal quality of "Reloading" may facilitate the transmission of content because it provides a unified and extensive source of information that may be more appealing to readers than fragmented yields of Google searches. In terms of potential monitoring techniques, the Faciloscope's reduction of rhetorical behaviors to three codes, though blunt, can offer analysts rapid, automated results about the engagement level of open threads, which can then inform strategic decisions. For example, given the univocal quality first intimated by the Faciloscope's global analysis of "Reloading," a watchdog group may decide that "Reloading" is a slow-developing thread that does not merit active monitoring. At the same time, eruptions of the evoking or inviting moves in such a stage-y thread may signal renewed interest. "Have a Rifle" may warrant more monitoring because of its higher level of activity and its connection with offline sites and activities.

NOTES

1. Potok, "Hate and Antigovernment 'Patriot' Groups Down."

2. See Southern Poverty Law Center, "Don Black's Stormfront Turns 20"; Associated Press, "World's Oldest Neo-Nazi Website Stormfront Shut Down"; Backover, "Hate Sets up Shop on Internet"; Schafer, "Spinning the Web of Hate."

3. Beirich, "White Homicide Worldwide."

4. See Beirich, "White Homicide Worldwide"; Elias, "Sikh Temple Killer Wade Michael Page Radicalized in Army"; "Sikh Temple Shooting Suspect Wade Michael Page Was White Supremacist."

5. Beirich, "White Homicide Worldwide."

6. "Stormfront.org Traffic Statistics," 2016.

7. Stormfront.org.

8. "Militia, Military Guerilla Warfare and Survival."

9. Beirich, "White Homicide Worldwide."

10. Yablon, "Guns Are Now the Weapon of Choice."

11. US Department of Homeland Security, 8.

12. FBI and US Department of Homeland Security, "White Supremacist Extremism Poses Persistent Threat." See Winter, "FBI and DHS Warned of Growing Threat" for the original foreignpolicy.com release of the Joint Intelligence Bulletin.

13. See Eraut, "Informal Learning in the Workplace," 246; Gutwill and Allen, "Facilitating Family Group Inquiry"; Marsick and Watkins, "Informal and Incidental Learning."

14. Omizo, Nguyen, Clark, Hart-Davidson, McDuffie, and Ridolfo, "You Can Read the Comments Section Again."

15. Daniels, "Algorithmic Rise of the 'Alt-Right.'"

16. Daniels.

17. Noble, *Algorithms of Oppression*, sec. 3, Kindle.

18. Noble, loc. 1891, Kindle.

19. Daniels, *Cyber Racism*, 9.

20. See Schafer, "Spinning the Web of Hate"; Gerstenfeld, Grant, and Chiang, "Hate Online."

21. Back, "Aryans Reading Adorno."

22. Schafer, "Spinning the Web of Hate."

23. Daniels, *Cyber Racism*.

24. Daniels, 103–10.

25. The Faciloscope relies upon the Natural Language Toolkit (Bird, Klein, and Loper) and Scikit-learn (Pedragosa et al.,) python packages for its natural language processing and machine learning protocols. It also relies upon text normalization scripts from Perkins, *Python Text Processing.*

26. Omizo, Nguyen, Clark, Hart-Davidson, McDuffie, and Ridolfo, "You Can Read the Comments Section Again."

27. Swales and Najjar, "Writing of Research Article Introductions."

28. See Grabill and Pigg, "Messy Rhetoric"; Sackey, Nguyen, and Grabill, "Constructing Learning Spaces"; Sackey and Flower, "Facilitation Annotated Bibliography."

29. Ellenbogen, Fleming, Grabill, and Livingston, "Studying Web 2 Experiences"; "Category Specific Facilitation Tool."

30. "Reloading for the AR."

31. "Have a Rifle?"

32. "Self-Defense, Martial Arts, & Preparedness."

33. "Reloading for the AR."

34. Katz, "Ethic of Expediency," 265.

35. See also Katz, "Aristotle's Rhetoric, Hitler's Program."

36. Selber, "Rhetoric of Electronic Instruction Sets," 107–110.

37. Selber, 100, 109.

38. Project Appleseed, "American Spirit is Alive and Well."

39. Furnas, "Generalized Fisheye Views."

40. Noble, *Algorithms of Oppression*.

41. For more research on Stormfront's offline, activist behaviors, see Hara and Estrada, "Hate and Peace in a Connected World."

42. Science Museum of Minnesota, "ScienceBuzz."

43. Science Museum of Minnesota, "Got the Cure?"

44. See King, "From Sage on the Stage," 30; Du, Rosson, and Carroll, "Communication Patterns for a Classroom Public Digital Backchannel."

45. On the topic of "vigilance decrement" that can be glossed as the moment in which students grow weary and inattentive to lectures, see Young, Robinson, and Alberts, "Students Pay Attention!" 42–43.

REFERENCES

Anthony, Laurence, and George V. Lashkia. "Mover: A Machine Learning Tool to Assist in the Reading and Writing of Technical Papers." *IEEE Transactions on Professional Communication* 46, no. 3 (2003): 185–93.

Associated Press. "World's Oldest Neo-Nazi Website Stormfront Shut Down." *Telegraph* (UK), August 29, 2017. http://www.telegraph.co.uk/technology/2017/08/29/worlds-oldest-neo-nazi-website-stormfront-shut/.

Back, Les. "Aryans Reading Adorno: Cyber-Culture and Twenty-First-Century Racism." *Ethnic and Racial Studies* 25, no. 4 (2002): 628–51.

Backover, Andrew. "Hate Sets Up Shop on Internet." *Denver Post*, November 8, 1999. http://extras.denverpost.com/enduser/digital/digital1108c.htm.

Beirich, Heidi. "White Homicide Worldwide: Stormfront, the Leading White Supremacist Web Forum, Has Another Distinction—Murder Capital of the Internet." Special Report, Southern Poverty Law Center, Montgomery, AL, 2014.

Bird, Steven, Ewan Klein, and Edward Loper. *Natural Language Processing with Python: Analyzing Text with the Natural Language Toolkit*. Sebastopol, CA: O'Reilly Media, 2009.

"Category Specific Facilitation Tool." http://facilitation.matrix.msu.edu/files/5713/8548/5077/Facilitation_tool_for_facilitators_v2.pdf.

Cortes, Corinna, and Vladimir Vapnik. "Support-Vector Networks." *Machine Learning* 20, no. 3 (1995): 273–97.

Cotos, Elena, Sarah Huffman, and Stephanie Link. "Furthering and Applying Move/Step Constructs: Technology-Driven Marshalling of Swalesian Genre Theory for EAP Pedagogy." *Journal of English for Academic Purposes* 19 (2015): 52–72.

Daniels, Jessie. "The Algorithmic Rise of the 'Alt-Right.'" *Contexts* 17, no. 1 (2018): 60–65.

Daniels, Jessie. *Cyber Racism: White Supremacy Online and the New Attack on Civil Rights*. Lanham, MD: Rowman & Littlefield, 2009.

Du, Honglu, Mary Beth Rosson, and John M. Carroll. "Communication Patterns for a Classroom Public Digital Backchannel." In *Proceedings of the 30th ACM International Conference on Design of Communication*, edited by Clay Spinuzzi and Mark Zachry, 127–136, New York: ACM, 2012.

Elias, Marilyn. "Sikh Temple Killer Wade Michael Page Radicalized in Army." Southern Poverty Law Center, November 11, 2012. https://www.splcenter.org/fighting-hate/intelligence-report/2012/sikh-temple-killer-wade-michael-page-radicalized-army.

Ellenbogen, Kirsten, Elizabeth Fleming, Jeff Grabill, and Troy Livingston. "Studying Web 2 Experiences: An Open Source Session." Visitor Studies Association, July 26, 2012. http://facilitation.matrix.msu.edu/files/6613/8548/5076/codinginstructions_facilitate.pdf.

Eraut, Michael. "Informal Learning in the Workplace." *Studies in Continuing Education* 26, no. 2 (2004): 247–73.

FBI and US Department of Homeland Security, "White Supremacist Extremism Poses Persistent Threat". FBI and Homeland Security, May 10, 2017. https://foreignpolicy.com/2017/08/14/fbi-and-dhs-warned-of-growing-threat-from-white-supremacists-months-ago/.

Furnas, George W. "Generalized Fisheye Views." *ACM* 17, no. 4 (1986).

Gerstenfeld, Phyllis B., Diana R. Grant, and Chau-Pu Chiang. "Hate Online: A Content Analysis of Extremist Internet Sites." *Analyses of Social Issues and Public Policy* 3, no. 1 (2003): 29–44.

Grabill, Jeffrey T., and Stacey Pigg. "Messy Rhetoric: Identity Performance as Rhetorical Agency in Online Public Forums." *Rhetoric Society Quarterly* 42, no. 2 (2012): 99–119.

Gutwill, Joshua P., and Sue Allen. "Facilitating Family Group Inquiry at Science Museum Exhibits." *Science Education* 94, no. 4 (2010): 710–42.

Hara, Noriko, and Zilia Estrada. "Hate and Peace in a Connected World: Comparing MoveOn and Stormfront." *First Monday* 8, no. 12 (2012).

"Have a Rifle? Now Learn How to Shoot It!" Stormfront, n.d. https://www.stormfront.org/forum/t470989/.

Katz, Steven B. "Aristotle's Rhetoric, Hitler's Program, and the Ideological Problem of Praxis, Power, and Professional Discourse." *Journal of Business and Technical Communication* 7, no. 1 (1993): 37–62.

Katz, Steven B. "The Ethic of Expediency: Classical Rhetoric, Technology, and the Holocaust." *College English* 54, no. 3 (1992): 255–75.

King, Alison. "From Sage on the Stage to Guide on the Side." *College Teaching* 41, no. 1 (1993): 30–35.

Larson, Brian, William Hart-Davidson, Kenneth C. Walker, Douglas M. Walls, and Ryan Omizo. "Use What You Choose: Applying Computational Methods to Genre Studies in Technical Communication." In *Proceedings of the 34th ACM International Conference on the Design of Communication*, edited by Douglas Walls, Michael Trice, and Sarah Gunning. New York: ACM, 2016.

Lenz, Ryan, and Mark Potok. "AGE OF THE WOLF: A Study of the Rise of Lone Wolf and Leaderless Resistance Terrorism." Special Report, Southern Poverty Law Center, Montgomery, AL, 2015.

Levin, Brian. "Cyberhate: A Legal and Historical Analysis of Extremists' Use of Computer Networks in America." *American Behavioral Scientist* 45, no. 6 (2002): 958–88.

Marsick, Victoria J., and Karen E. Watkins. "Informal and Incidental Learning." *New Directions for Adult and Continuing Education* 2001, no. 89 (2001): 25–34.

Montopoli, Brian. "DHS Report Warns of Right Wing Extremists." CBS News, April 14, 2009. https://www.cbsnews.com/news/dhs-report-warns-of-right-wing-extremists/.

"Militia, Military Guerilla Warfare and Survival." Stormfront.org.

Noble, Safiya Umoja. *Algorithms of Oppression: How Search Engines Reinforce Racism*. New York: NYU Press, 2018. Kindle.

Omizo, Ryan, M. T. Nguyen, I. Clark, W. Hart-Davidson, K. McDuffie, and J. Ridolfo. "You Can Read the Comments Section Again: The Faciloscope App and Automated Rhetorical Analysis." *DHCommons Journal* 2 (2017). http://dhcommons.org/journal/2016/you-can-read-comments-section-again-faciloscope-app-and-automated-rhetorical-analysis.

Pedregosa, F., et al. "Scikit-Learn: Machine Learning in Python." *Journal of Machine Learning Research* 12 (2011): 2825–30.

Perkins, Jacob. *Python Text Processing with NLTK 2.0 Cookbook*. Birmingham, UK: Packt Publishing, 2010.

Potok, Mark. "Hate and Antigovernment 'Patriot' Groups Down as Activism Shifts to Cyberspace." Southern Poverty Law Center, March 13, 2015. https://www.splcenter.org/hatewatch/2015/03/13/hate-and-antigovernment-'patriot'-groups-down-activism-shifts-cyberspace.

Project Appleseed. "The American Spirit is Alive and Well." https://appleseedinfo.org/.

"Reloading for the AR." Stormfront, n.d. https://www.stormfront.org/forum/t468155/?s=eacc04070d5d593d81ad8b83c1e270c7.

Sackey, Donnie, and Letitia Flower. "Facilitation Annotated Bibliography." 2014. http://facilitation.matrix.msu.edu/index.php/resources/.

Sackey, Donnie Johnson, Minh-Tam Nguyen, and Jeffery T. Grabill. "Constructing Learning Spaces: What We Can Learn from Studies of Informal Learning Online." *Computers and Composition* 35 (2015): 112–24.

Schafer, Joseph A. "Spinning the Web of Hate: Web-Based Hate Propagation by Extremist Organizations." *Journal of Criminal Justice and Popular Culture* 9, no. 2 (2002): 69–88.

Schulberg, Jessica, Dana Liebelson, and Tommy Craggs. "The Neo-Nazis Are Back Online." Huffington Post, October 4, 2017. https://www.huffingtonpost.com/entry/nazis-are-back-online_us_59d40719e4b06226e3f46941.

Science Museum of Minnesota. "ScienceBuzz." N.d. http://www.sciencebuzz.org/.

Science Museum of Minnesota. "Got the Cure? What to Do about Hiccups." August 24, 2006. http://www.sciencebuzz.org/blog/got-cure-what-do-about-hiccups#comment-1014427.

Selber, Stuart A. "A Rhetoric of Electronic Instruction Sets." *Technical Communication Quarterly* 19, no. 2 (2010): 95–117.

"Self-Defense, Martial Arts, & Preparedness." Stormfront, n.d. https://www.stormfront.org/forum/f35/.

"Sikh Temple Shooting Suspect Wade Michael Page Was White Supremacist." CBS News, August 6, 2012. https://www.cbsnews.com/news/sikh-temple-shooting-suspect-wade-michael-page-was-white-supremacist/.

Skalicky, Stephen. "Was This Analysis Helpful? A Genre Analysis of the Amazon.com Discourse Community and its 'Most Helpful' Product Reviews." *Discourse, Context & Media* 2, no. 2 (2013): 84–93.

Southern Poverty Law Center. "Don Black's Stormfront Turns 20." March 27, 2015. https://www.splcenter.org/hatewatch/2015/03/27/don-blacks-stormfront-turns-20.

Southern Poverty Law Center. "Lone Wolf Report." February 11, 2015. https://www.splcenter.org/20150211/lone-wolf-report#summary.

Stormfront.org. https://www.stormfront.org/forum/index.php/.

"Stormfront.org Traffic Statistics." 2016. http://www.alexa.com/siteinfo/stormfront.org.

Swales, John, and Hazem Najjar. "The Writing of Research Article Introductions." *Written Communication* 4, no. 2 (1987): 175–91.

US Department of Homeland Security. "(U//FOUO) Rightwing Extremism: Current Economic and Political Climate Fueling Resurgence in Radicalization and Recruitment." April 7, 2009. https://fas.org/irp/eprint/rightwing.pdf.

Winter, Jana. "FBI and DHS Warned of Growing Threat from White Supremacists Months Ago." *Foreign Policy*, August 14, 2017. http://foreignpolicy.com/2017/08/14/fbi-and-dhs-warned-of-growing-threat-from-white-supremacists-months-ago/.

Wu, Jien-Chen, Yu-Chia Chang, Hsien-Chin Liou, and Jason S. Chang. "Computational Analysis of Move Structures in Academic Abstracts." In *Proceedings of the COLING/ACL on Interactive Presentation Sessions*, 41–44. Association for Computational Linguistics, 2006.

Yablon, Alex. "Guns Are Now the Weapon of Choice for Violent White Supremacists." *Trace*, June 20, 2015. https://www.thetrace.org/2015/06/guns-are-now-the-weapon-of-choice-for-violent-white-supremacists/.

Young, Mark S., Stephanie Robinson, and Phil Alberts. "Students Pay Attention! Combating the Vigilance Decrement to Improve Learning during Lectures." *Active Learning in Higher Education* 10, no. 1 (2009): 41–55.

10

DARK INTERACTIONS

INTERFACES AND OBJECT ARRAYS AS SURVEILLANCE IN DIGITAL RHETORIC

JOHN GALLAGHER

Interactive online interfaces possess intelligence-gathering implications because they encourage users to monitor themselves. Rather than developing intrusive ways to monitor users, intelligence organizations can deploy interfaces as surveillance tools because they encourage users to report their own data and user-generated content. This type of data is a key distinction between contemporary social media surveillance and a more general vision of online surveillance that accounts for algorithms, website analytics, or government tracking.[1]

Through interactive interfaces, users participate in their own panoptic surveillance, both in terms of known features that enable data collection/monitoring, as well as more subtle, hidden features.[2] Interactive interfaces consequently play a role in advanced information-gathering techniques for the twenty-first century, techniques that involve structuring and analyzing the production of self-motivated rhetorical discourse. Intelligence operatives can build targeted profiles from user-generated content, which can then be used to monitor/track users and communities. For instance, in the 2016 US presidential election, Russian operatives produced targeted Facebook advertising, propaganda, and disinformation to influence the outcome.[3] Interfaces such as Facebook's are therefore not only concerns for designers of user experience but also for operatives involved in monitoring user-generated content. The overall aim of this chapter, then, is to show a link between web design and intelligence-gathering applications.

The rest of this chapter has five parts. First, I expand the notion of interactive interfaces toward object arrays in order to capture the full life cycle of information entered into websites. Here, I provide screenshots of the ways social media interfaces coerce users to participate in their own surveillance.

Second, I discuss the way object arrays normalize and scale into massive databases. I extend Alice Marwick's work about everyday surveillance, connecting it to information-gathering applications. I argue that self-reported data and user-generated content can be turned into surveillance databases, predictably in light of Foucauldian self-discipline and panopticism. I turn to the concept of *dark interactions*, a neologism that focuses on the reverse of Harry Brignull's dark patterns—that is, the idea that websites may implement design trickery to elicit secure data from users. I define *dark interactions* as straightforward front-end interactions that nevertheless may coalesce on the back end of a website in possibly deleterious ways, depending on the normalized interface and scale. To buttress my argument, I turn to two data visualizations of 450,000 comments from the *New York Times*. These visualizations use self-reported data from commenters. Third, I demonstrate that self-reported data and user-generated content have intelligence applications that may intersect with rhetorical studies. Here, I lay out four ways that online terrorist networks can be monitored or how they are monitored.[4] Fourth, activists or non-state actors may flip monitoring of user-generated content to their advantage. To demonstrate this possibility, I examine the 2016 Facebook movement wherein users checked-in to the Standing Rock Indian Reservation, a social media event meant to combat police surveillance of user-generated content. The digital check-in event was part of a larger movement involving the protest of the Dakota Access Pipeline. The Facebook check-in case study demonstrates savvy use of object arrays while showing the possible importance of user-generated content for intelligence gathering purposes. I conclude by reiterating the role of interfaces for surveillance and intelligence campaigns. Operationalizing interactive designs with the goal of rhetorical manipulation, what I call *dark interactions*, may play a significant role in social media intelligence operations. Dark interactions create habits and incentives for users to provide their data, which intelligence operatives can then observe and track. Future scholarship about intelligence operations and digital rhetoric ought then to connect design with surveillance, notably by studying application programming interfaces (APIs).

INTERFACES AND OBJECT ARRAYS

Interactive and participatory interfaces buttress twenty-first-century social media communication. These rhetorical designs enable precise user monitoring because users provide the information themselves. Website interfaces record prescribed types of user-input provided directly by people—not simply browser behaviors.[5] Interfaces enable, encourage, and coerce users to provide

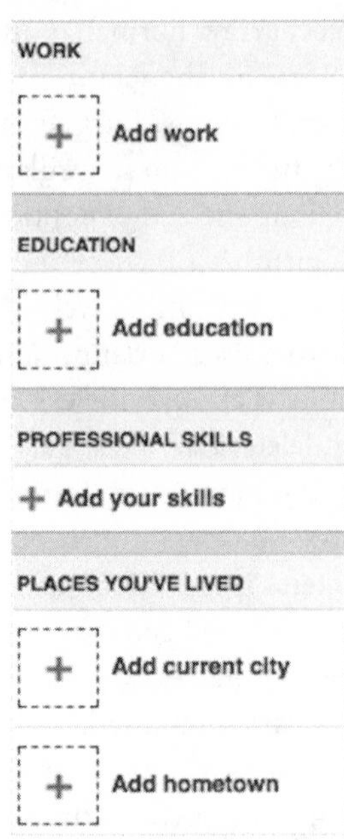

FIGURE 10.1. A sample of empty state fields of a user profile on Facebook

information about themselves on a recurring basis. Through this encouragement, these interfaces create the building blocks for present and future platforms to enable intelligence operations that may track users online as well as physical movements, habits, and moods.

Interfaces are part of a larger ecosystem of object arrays in that they represent more than interfaces in which users enter information. Object arrays, I believe, help to capture the full lifespan or lifeworld of information that is entered into the interface (the object) and then transmuted/transduced into an array for different purposes than the initial input information. *Arrays*, a term I draw from the language of JavaScript, helps describe the process by which individual data is labeled into a specific value in order to be standardized. In turn, these interactions are recorded, fed into massive ("big data") databases, and analyzed using sophisticated algorithms. Put less formally, object arrays describe the interface, input information, the way that information moves into a database, and how it is analyzed once it becomes part of a database.

Tracing how the lifespan of information from Facebook's template can be turned into advertising helps to illustrate my argument about object arrays. Facebook asks and reminds users to fill out their profiles. Figure 10.1 habitualizes active data production—that is, data that users produce themselves.

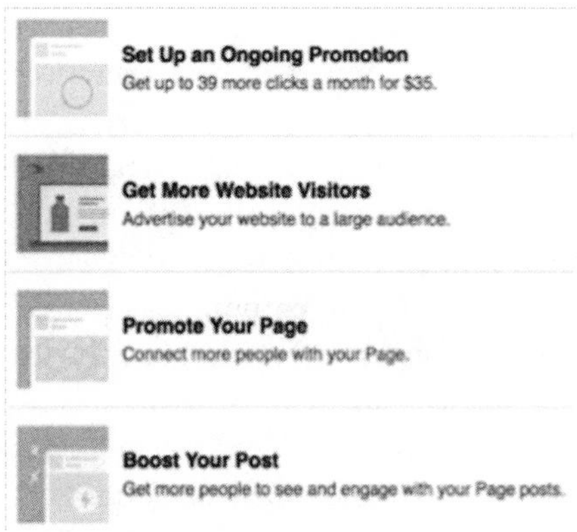

FIGURE 10.2. Screenshot of promoting a page on Facebook

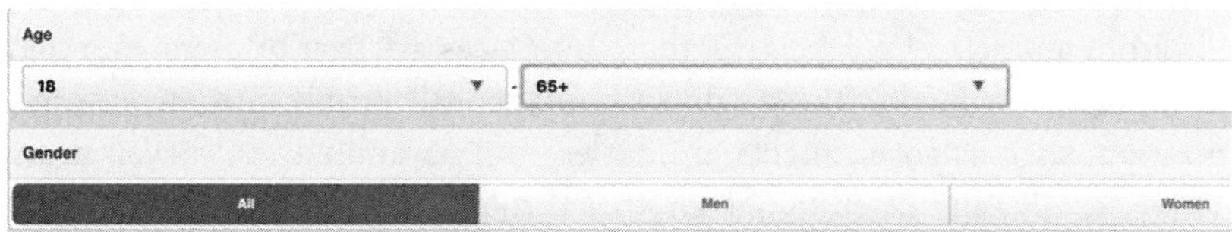

FIGURE 10.3. Screenshot of targeting users based on their input age and genders

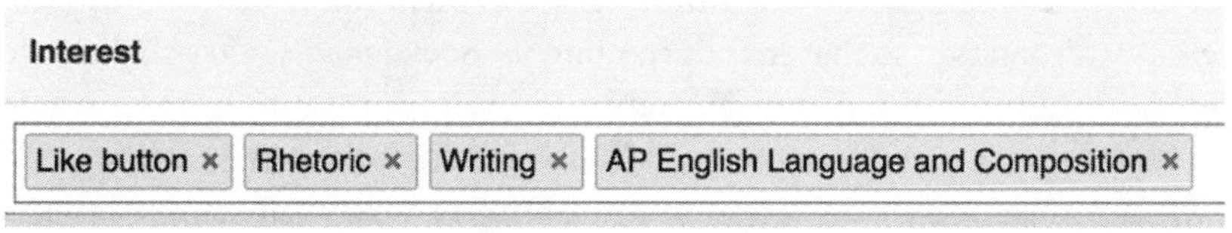

FIGURE 10.4. Screenshot of targeting user profiles based on their input interests

This interface field prompts and then documents a general record of users' online behavior. These empty interfaces, known as empty state pages in design theory, continuously ask users to fill out information. This prodding habitualizes the production of information that can in turn be processed into a commodity.

After naturalizing users to produce data about themselves, the information collected from these interfaces is placed into an array that will be able to sort and sell this information to interested parties, thereby enabling monitoring. This tracking is especially salient if users keep this profile information publicly accessible—something many users do not realize is the default with social media giants like Facebook. Even if users keep their settings private, intelligence operatives can target users if those operatives pose as advertisers or marketers.

As the life cycles of information continue, input data is manipulated into targetable databases. When users enter this information, social media platforms are able to target users with advertisements based on this input information. For instance, everyday users or corporations can create their own Facebook businesses and target users with advertisements based on a variety of factors, including age, gender, and interests (see figures 10.2–10.4). By creating targeted advertising with its proprietary ecosystem, Facebook has dramatically increased its ability to track users' behaviors (and its own economic value). State and non-state actors can target users, like the Russian disinformation campaign I mentioned in the introduction, based on information provided by targeted Facebook advertising. Targeted advertising, made possible by object arrays, becomes part of intelligence gathering campaigns and operations.

From a practical perspective, these interfaces are part of users' everyday communicative habits. These habits simultaneously enable intelligence organization, such as governments, militaries, and paramilitaries, surveil users. To write, talk, and listen to one another through these interfaces and object arrays, as we do through social media platforms and circuits, means our own communicative acts function as surveillance.

Take a concrete example: updating social networking sites with educational information. As users, we naturally desire to fill in these interfaces with accurate information so that friends can find us. Social media, after all, helps to connect users across time and geography. If this information is not accurate or extant, then we cannot connect with those high school or college friends with whom we have lost touch. Yet, by filling out these educational fields, we enable platforms, and the organizations that subpoena information from these platforms, to track us. Our desire to connect and socialize is the motivation for participating in online twenty-first-century surveillance.

NORMALIZING AND SCALING SELF-SURVEILLANCE OF EVERYDAY LIFE

Interfaces and object arrays facilitate *social surveillance*, a concept from communication scholars I extend to intelligence purposes but with two important features: they normalize social surveillance and scale it up.[6] Rather than sifting through unstructured data on endless databases, intelligence operatives can use social media databases to monitor and target users on the internet. This argument extends Alice Marwick's "The Public Domain: Social Surveillance in Everyday Life," whose work I draw upon when discussing social surveillance. I draw on Marwick's work because it explicitly draws out implications of interface and object arrays. I will provide visual examples of social surveillance for possible intelligence purposes.

Interfaces and their object arrays are engineered through their designs to create social surveillance. Social media companies entice users to police themselves via user designs. By way of Joinson and Tokunaga, Marwick uses the term *social surveillance* to capture the way social media sites allow users to see what "friends, family, and acquaintances are 'up to.'"[7] Marwick points out the informal nature of social surveillance that differs from common media depictions of surveillance. Marwick writes: "In addition to analyzing these traditional modes of surveillance, academics have begun to unpack the on-going eavesdropping, investigation, gossip and inquiry that constitutes information gathering by people about their peers. These practices are facilitated and extended by the digitization of social information normalized by social media."[8] Applying Marwick's aforementioned perspective about gossip and eavesdropping extends analysis of the Facebook interface (see, for example, figure 10.1).

These interfaces normalize giving away one's personal information as part of the expectation of social media platforms. What Marwick describes as social surveillance is normalized through online interfaces. Filling in a profile, updating a status, and inputting personal information all fall under social surveillance engineered through empty state pages. Users report their data, surveilling each other and themselves, because they are trained to do so through social decorum and expectation that arise from coercive interface design. Already deployed for user-to-user gossip and user tracking, people realize—and generally accept—that their information will be viewed by others. Colloquially, this is the entire purpose of social media: to see what people are doing.

While the connection between social media profiles and monitoring applications is apparent on an individual level, reorienting social surveillance at scale assists my argument with respect to intelligence applications. When viewed at scale, we can better see the way that individuals who broadcast social status, attention, and personal details to an audience are participating in a possible intelligence operation.[9] Figures 10.5 and 10.6 illustrate my meaning here. Figure 10.5 depicts the empty state page of the *New York Times* commenting function. Note the location field in the upper central area. While this field does not require commenters to fill out accurate information, it prompts users to provide their location. Figure 10.6, which was produced collaboratively, show the self-reported comment location distribution. In my view, these figures demonstrate the way that self-reported data in interface

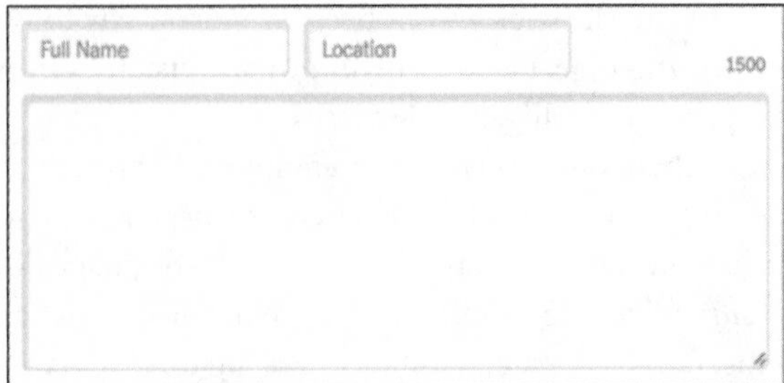

FIGURE 10.5. The empty state page of the *New York Times* comment function

fields can be tracked, collated, and visualized for surveillance purposes.[10] Figure 10.6 could be applied to tracking users who participate in democratic discussions, possibly for the purposes of controlling or quashing such discussion. It is plausible that this data visualization (figure 10.6) does not guarantee that self-reported data is going to be used to such ends or even that the data is accurate. The visuals instead demonstrate the possibility of such ends; the information can be rendered into visual images imbued as instruments of power.[11]

Broadly, this interface and visualization demonstrate what I will call *dark interactions*. Dark interactions takes its inspiration from the website Dark Patterns (founded by Harry Bringull), which documents website interfaces that try to trick users into supplying private or protected information, as well as coerce users into a particular action.[12] As a companion idea, *dark interactions* is my term to describe the way regular information—for example, information that users do not think about protecting or consider private, transitions into databases (with applications for intelligence operatives). These visuals enable the connection between interface design, object arrays, and databases. Depending on context, dark interactions may be productive while others are detrimental.

DARK INTERACTIONS AND COMBATING ONLINE TERRORISM

In this section, I argue that dark interactions enable combating cyber warfare if deployed for intelligence purposes. Dark interactions allow monitoring of online terrorist networks based on the self-reported information of those networks. Combating this type of cyber warfare is possible even if the platforms, such as Twitter, have no investment in stopping such aggression, likely due to economic reasons.[13] Four aspects about the rise of dark interactions illustrate a connection to intelligence operations.

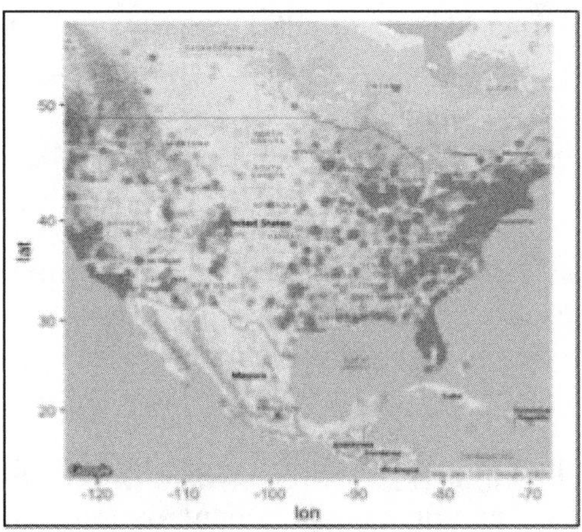

FIGURE 10.6. US self-reported distribution of commenter location

First, intelligence organizations and operatives can track users through the information they provide to register with that platform. Because everyday users typically do not create their own website, they rely on social media corporations or content management systems for their profiles. These entities typically, with a few notable exceptions such as the now-defunct social network Imzy, require access to users' personal information—for example, phone numbers, contacts, and browsing information. Intelligence organizations and operatives can request or buy this information in order to track terrorist cells. Second, intelligence organizations can track input information, such as geolocation tags, profile information, and platform-specific trends, to combat the spread of terrorists and hate group rhetoric. Third, intelligence operatives can use object arrays, via APIs, to infiltrate or join a terrorist organization by adding themselves to a geolocation tag, joining a hashtag discussion, or filling out a social media profile with inaccurate information (as terrorists themselves can do). Viewing location-based tags, for instance, may help operatives to develop relationships with friends of terrorists and convince those friends to report preemptively on violent activities. Fourth, considering design as an intelligence operation means that design can function as intelligence outreach. In these ways, dark interactions can function to help intelligence organizations with building relationships. For instance, in a time of need, intelligence organizations could ask social media platforms to introduce new functionalities and interface fields that help users to communicate emergencies.

While these ideas are conceptual in nature, they form a philosophical approach useful for combating an obscured sense of how interfaces and object arrays coalesce from individuated data into large-scale databases. Understanding empty fields as having surveillance and intelligence-gathering applications means that design spaces might be framed as spaces wherein users enter information freely but still guided for intelligence-gathering purposes. The various fields of Facebook's interface, such as the status update, reactions, work, and education, are places where surveillance is designed and integrated into users' habits. However, the intelligence-gathering purposes behind interfaces comes to fruition if the information provided by users is accurate. In this sense, data collected from dark interactions can be challenged if such data are viewed rhetorically.

RESISTING INTELLIGENCE GATHERING IN THE CASE OF THE DAKOTA ACCESS PIPELINE

People can challenge intelligence uses of dark interactions, sometimes for public, democratic protest. By doing so, these protesters might see the empty fields of interfaces and possible databases as savvy spaces of possible collection action. In the same way that an intelligence organization might see web design as a possible surveillance technique, users might view challenging this approach to web design if the fields of interfaces are seen as rhetorical. If users approach dark interactions with the same philosophy mentioned in the previous section, then manipulating information input into these interfaces offers us strategies for civic protest and engagement in the online public sphere.

To demonstrate this possibility, then, this section discusses the social media event that occurred in the fall of 2016 that involved people checking-in on their Facebook profiles to support protesters of the Dakota Access Pipeline. Before I analyze this case study in terms of interfaces, I first offer context. The Dakota Access Pipeline (DAPL) is an oil pipeline that stretches from oilfields in northwestern North Dakota all the way to Patoka, Illinois. The pipeline was originally scheduled to run through several non–Native American towns but was rerouted through these sacred lands due to concerns over possible oil spills. The DAPL route was redirected to pass directly through several Native American reservations.

In the fall of 2016, a protest of the DAPL developed in Morton County, North Dakota, from members of the Standing Rock Indian Reservation who had grave concerns over possible water contamination and violation of sacred burial grounds. As protests grew in the physical world, so did online protests—the protests drew support from around the United States, both offline and online. The hashtag #NoDAPL (No Dakota Access Pipeline) trended around Twitter in the fall. The hashtag continues to make reappearances

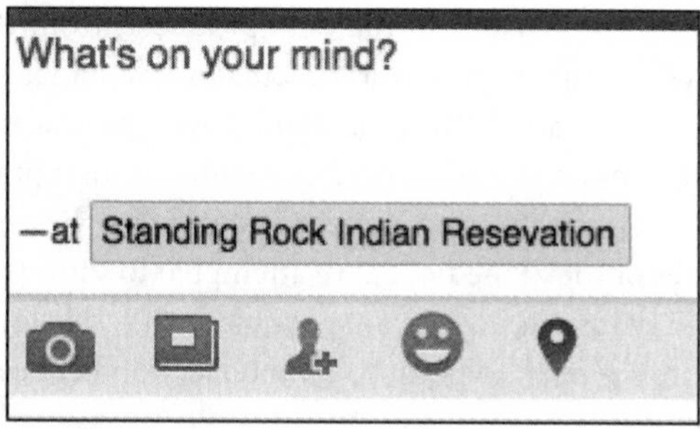

FIGURE 10.7. Screenshot of checking-in at Standing Rock Indian Reservation

because the pipeline protests were a failure in the sense of stopping the pipeline's installation.

On December 31, 2016, an unverified story ran about the Morton County sheriff tracking protestors who checked-in on Facebook. An example of this check-in can be seen in figure 10.6. In response to a call for support, people from around the world began to check-in to the Standing Rock Indian Reservation on Facebook's digital map. According to a November 1, 2016, NPR report, "More than 1 million people [have] 'checked in' on Facebook to the Standing Rock Indian Reservation page, in a show of support for the tribe that has been rallying against construction of the Dakota Access Pipeline." This social media activism, something that Stephanie Vie and others have labeled "slacktivism," was not successful in the traditional sense.[14] The protest did not block the pipeline.

However, as a case study, checking-in demonstrates collective action that uses dark interactions in savvy, unexpected ways. The Facebook digital demonstration disrupted possible tracking of physical protesters. Even if the reported story was false—and the Morton County sheriff denied any such tracking took place—users perceived this interface field to be a place of collective surveillance and treated the status update field rhetorically. Users engaged in a type of civic action that viewed dark interactions as integral to the protest. In this case study, users recognized the philosophy of design as surveillance and they acted upon it for the purposes of (perhaps unsuccessful) collective action.

CONCLUSION

In this chapter, I have argued that dark interactions can function for intelligence-gathering and tracking purposes. I have done so by drawing upon interface images and data visualizations because these figures illustrate a relationship between interfaces and the data produced from them. Interfaces and object arrays can function only as practical surveillance structures if users employ them as intended. The case of the DAPL protest is meant to show a disruption of intended use. This type of rhetorical disruption can occur if targeted individuals and groups develop strategies for viewing interfaces as rhetorical features of social media. I have attempted to show that surveillance, and challenges to that surveillance, are possible with respect to web design. In doing so, my aim has been to point to an intersection between rhetoric, web design, and intelligence operations.

I end this chapter, then, by addressing the middle ground of dark interactions, that is the process by which information entered into interfaces is turned into actionable databases. In addition to interfaces and databases, I suggest investigating publicly accessible APIs of platforms, which can help shed light on ways that interfaces are connected to backend databases. I think doing so will help trace more fully the lifecycles of information from interface to object array to database.

NOTES

1. Perzanowski and Schultz, *End of Ownership.*

2. For an extended discussion of interface, see Hookway, *Interface*; Bolter and Grusin, *Remediation*. For an extended discussion of the rhetorical role of interfaces, see Brooke, *Lingua Fracta*, 1–26.

3. See Scott Shane and Mike Isaac, "Facebook to Turn Over Russian-Linked Ads to Congress," *New York Times*, September 21, 2017, https://www.nytimes.com/2017/09/21/technology/facebook-russian-ads.html?_r=0.

4. See, for example, the discussion of the Islamic State's and digital monitoring, Laura Smith, "Messaging App Telegram Centrepiece of IS Social Media Strategy," BBC News, June 5, 2017, http://www.bbc.com/news/technology-39743252.

5. Gallagher, "Challenging the Monetized Template."

6. See Tokunaga, "Computers in Human Behavior."

7. Marwick, "Public Domain."

8. Marwick, 379.

9. Marwick, 380.

10. I'd like to thank Yinyin Chen, Xuan Wang, Zeng Zeng, and Alyssa Kong for creating figures 10.3 and 10.4. They used the ggmap package in the programming language R to generate these visuals.

11. See Barton and Barton, "Modes of Power in Technical and Professional Visuals."

12. Trice and Potts have taken up Brignull's work in "Building Dark Patterns into Platforms." While they focus on user experience, my companion term *dark interactions* focuses on the input information of user experience.

13. For instance, Twitter has an economic investment in amassing the most users, despite a particular user's detrimental rhetorical to worldwide health.

14. Vie, "In Defense of 'Slacktivism.'"

REFERENCES

Arola, Kristin L. "The Design of Web 2.0: The Rise of the Template, The Fall of Design." *Computers and Composition* 27, no. 1 (2010): 4–14.

Barton, B. F., and M. S. Barton. "Modes of Power in Technical and Professional Visuals." *Journal of Business and Technical Communication,* 7, no. 1 (1993): 138–62.

Beck, Estee N. "The Invisible Digital Identity: Assemblages in Digital Networks." *Computers and Composition* 35, no. 1 (2015): 125–40.

Bolter, Jay David, and Richard Grusin. *Remediation: Understanding New Media.* Cambridge, MA: MIT Press, 2000.

Branden Hookway. *Interface.* Cambridge, MA: MIT Press, 2014.

Brooke, Collin. *Lingua Fracta.* Cresskill, NJ: Hampton Press, 2007.

Dark Patterns. https://darkpatterns.org/.

Gallagher, John R. "Challenging the Monetized Template." *Enculturation,* no. 24 (2017). http://enculturation.net/challenging_the_monetized_template.

Gallagher, John R., and Steve Holmes. "Empty Templates: The Ethical Habits of Empty State Pages." *Technical Communication Quarterly.* Forthcoming. https://doi.org/10.1080/10572252.2018.1564367.

Gillespie, Tarleton. "The Relevance of Algorithms." In *Media Technologies: Essays on Communication, Materiality, and Society,* edited by Tarleton Gillespie, Pablo J. Boczkowski, and Kirsten A. Foot, 167–93. Cambridge, MA: MIT Press, 2014.

Marwick, Alice E. "The Public Domain: Social Surveillance in Everyday Life." *Surveillance and Society* 9, no. 4 (2012): 378–93.

Perzanowski, Aaron, and Jason Schultz. *The End of Ownership.* Cambridge, MA: MIT Press, 2016.

Tokunaga, Robert S. "Computers in Human Behavior Social Networking Site or Social Surveillance Site? Understanding the Use of Interpersonal Electronic Surveillance in Romantic Relationships." *Computers in Human Behavior* 27, no. 2 (2011): 705–13.

Trice, Michael, and Liza Potts. "Building Dark Patterns into Platforms: How GamerGate Perturbed Twitter's User Experience." *Present Tense: A Journal of Rhetoric in Society* 6, no. 3 (2018).

Vie, Stephanie. "In Defense of 'Slacktivism': The Human Rights Campaign Facebook Logo as Digital Activism." *First Monday* 19, no. 4 (2014).

11

DIGITAL SURVEILLANCE OF GANG COMMUNICATION

GRAFFITI'S RHETORICAL VELOCITY BETWEEN STREET GANGS AND URBAN LAW ENFORCEMENT

SETH LONG AND KEN FITCH

This chapter describes the surveillance of graffiti by urban law enforcement. Utilizing digital photography, geotagged databases, and social media, law enforcement tracks this form of subculture writing in support of criminal cases involving conflict between street gangs and the communities they inhabit. A twelve-year veteran of the Los Angeles County Sheriff's Department, Detective Ken Fitch has witnessed this form of digital surveillance in various contexts and cases, so this topic immediately suggested itself while we discussed the applicability of rhet ops to urban policing. It represents a nexus of digital technology, rhetorical action, and conflict between state and nonstate actors—all of which are central to the concept of rhetorical operations.

SURVEILLING GRAFFITI

In the predigital era, tracking gang graffiti was a laborious task. Graffiti contains complex signifying features, all of which must be deciphered and catalogued if law enforcement is to prosecute a vandalism case—or, more importantly, to tap into the inter- and intra-gang communication encoded therein.

For example, a tag in Los Angeles might say:

EL TOPO VAMPE
SCXV3ST

Here, the parent gang can be identified by the combination of XV (Roman numeral fifteen) and the English numeric three. Fifteen plus three equals eighteen, followed by the abbreviation ST, which combined together stands for

18th Street. The 18th Street gang is one of Los Angeles's largest; it has many cliques and subgroups. A clue to which clique wrote this particular tag is offered in the abbreviation *SC*, which stands for South Central. This clique is located in LA's South Central district. SCXV3ST thus stands for South Central 18th Street, the gang and clique responsible for the graffiti.[1]

This tag also displays the street names or monikers of the artists. Here, the artists are El Topo (Spanish for "the mole") and Vampe. While these monikers can be found in various gangs, a moniker is typically used by only one or two members of each gang. In this tag, then, we can locate the gang (18th Street), the clique (South Central 18th Street), and the monikers (El Topo and Vampe). If a gang, clique, and moniker can be identified, the graffiti can be tied to its creator(s). Identifying these features allows law enforcement to narrow the scope of a vandalism investigation. More importantly, if graffiti has been crossed out or added to by rival gangs, officers can anticipate specific gang conflict.[2]

Graffiti features are valuable, but tracking the tens of thousands of tags that occur every year in an urban area was obviously a Herculean task in the predigital era. When gang and graffiti investigation was in its infancy, an investigator had to have personal knowledge of the gang members in his or her area and what their monikers were. Some law enforcement organizations kept a paper file system documenting this information.

Today, software companies such as TAGRS offer database technology that turns graffiti tracking into an automated surveillance system. TAGRS expert Detective Scott Sorrow explains that these programs work as a data aggregate for all graffiti that occurs within designated areas.[3] When graffiti is reported, a photo of the graffiti is taken by a government employee. The photo is then uploaded to the TAGRS database, accompanied by a latitude and longitude coordinate, along with the graffiti's characteristics. These characteristics include when the graffiti was observed, what the graffiti said, the gang and clique associated with the graffiti, and the moniker/name of the tagger. Once in the database, these meta-tagged photographs facilitate automated search queries based on the characteristic criteria, such as gang name, moniker, location, and so on. In any particular vandalism case, the search results will provide enough information for an investigator to cross-reference the graffiti under investigation with the legal names and photos of individuals who have been linked to a particular gang, moniker, or location in the past. Self-admitting to using a moniker, having tattoos with the moniker, or being caught while tagging the moniker could all lead to an individual's being associated with the moniker in these databases.

If an investigator is unsuccessful at identifying a tagger through databases such as TAGRS, he or she can turn to social media. Social media has embraced the vanity of its user base to give them a platform to exhibit their achievements. In the fleshspace world, gang members tag in highly visible areas because they want a large audience to see it. Online, social media platforms provide access to an even wider audience. Social media sites such as Twitter or Instagram enhance a gang's public intimidation factor and aid in recruiting by allowing potential members to see a gang's lifestyle. While it may seem foolish for gang members to broadcast and amplify their criminal enterprise on social media, they often assume, rightly or wrongly, that only certain audiences will comprehend and thus be influenced by the coded language in which their broadcasts occur, while other audiences—such as law enforcement—will not have the requisite knowledge to understand these digital amplifications of gang activity. However, if an investigator does possess the requisite knowledge of cliques and monikers, he or she can use assorted social media search tools to locate the digital version of a tagged gang sign. If located, these digital monikers will often provide the investigator with a legal name; sometimes, he or she will even find photos of the graffiti under investigation. Because social media networks are usually left open, once the investigator locates a suspect, he or she can then examine his or her social media pages, identifying other gang members and associates. These associations can then be uploaded to and circulated within the TAGRS database.

Whenever a tagging culprit is identified, an investigator can return to TAGRS or similar databases to determine how much graffiti has been associated with that particular offender. Potentially, this could include hundreds of tags with tens of thousands of dollars in property damage—turning a misdemeanor case into a felony one. The program can generate a report with all the locations, times, dates, and photos of the tags, and an estimated amount of property damage. The investigator now has all the evidence he or she needs to initiate a prosecution of a tagger, having used nothing but digital resources. The investigator could even continue to utilize both commercial and government databases to locate the suspect's current residence and contact information. The investigator does not need to leave his or her office at all until it is time to arrest the accused tagger.

GRAFFITI AND GANG CONFLICT

Systems such as TAGRS seize the rhetorical features of graffiti and convert these physical, analog visual signs into digital signals that can be searched, analyzed, compared, and traced across time and space. TAGRS "recomposes" graffiti into metadata for purposes of surveillance and to enhance the state's prosecutorial power. In the next section, we explore in more detail the law enforcement databases in which graffiti circulates as a digital, meta-tagged artifact. However, before exploring the rhetoric of this analog-to-digital conversion, we must first examine the contexts and motives underlying the initial creation of graffiti as well as its circulation in gang-inhabited communities.

Since the mid-1800s street gangs have been a part of domestic conflict within the United States. What began as ethnic territorial policing between Irish, German, and English neighborhoods has morphed into a vast gang culture that divides up entire cities and states into informal boundaries. Gangs today are typically classified as white, Hispanic, black, or Asian, though other cultural or ethnic subsets exist.

While laws defining criminal street gangs vary from state to state, a street gang is typically defined by meeting the following criteria:

(1) A group of three or more people,
(2) Having a common name or common identifying sign or symbol,
(3) Whose members engage in a pattern of criminal gang activity.[4]

Many states provide a list of predicate crimes that gangs engage in to assist in classifying gang activity.[5] These could include illicit drug sales, human trafficking, vandalism, robbery, among others. These predicate crimes separate criminal street gangs from other groups that share similar characteristics. For example, an environmental group might have three or more members, have a common name or symbol, and engage in a pattern of criminal activity such as illegal protests. However, their members do not engage in any of the predicate crimes for the benefit of the group. This is a noncriminal social faction and not a gang.

With this categorization of gangs in mind, aforementioned criterion (2) provides a good definition of *graffiti* as opposed to street art or other illicit tagging: graffiti is a common identifying sign or symbol of street gangs. Not all tagging is gang-related. If taggers operate on their own, they are sometimes referred to as an oner.[6] Tagging by oners is typically more artistic than gang graffiti, and will often be accompanied by *1*, or the word *oner*—these are the street artists hailed in graffiti scholarship. On subjective grounds of creative appearance, however, it is sometimes impossible to differentiate between oners' tagging and graffiti. Nevertheless, tagging not associated with a street gang can be defined as *street art*, whether or not one finds artistic value in it.

Understanding graffiti as group sign/symbol allows us to highlight graffiti's deeply rhetorical nature. These signs communicate to specific audiences with specific goals in mind, yet they engender varying responses, which, in turn, may cause counter-responses from those who initially inscribed the

FIGURE 11.1. Gang graffiti crossed out by a rival gang

sign. What does graffiti communicate? In a word: intimidation. What response does it engender? In a word: conflict. Gangs engage in acts of violence to cause others to be too intimidated to interfere with their activities. This makes graffiti extremely important to the furtherance of gang activity. According to Detective Sorrow, graffiti's purpose is to intimidate other gangs, nongang affiliated criminals, law enforcement, and the community. Graffiti is tagged in highly visible areas, where it is sure to achieve its communicative end—and where it is easily surveilled and tracked by law enforcement.

Graffiti's intimidating message leads to several layers of conflict. The first is the conflict between various gangs. A gang sign tagged on a wall informs other gangs that they are entering someone else's territory. Violence against rival gang members entering a gang's territory is justified, because they are merely defending their territory against invaders. The ultimate act of aggression amongst gangs is to enter a rival gang's territory and cross out their graffiti (figure 11.1). The most defiant gang members will cross out their rival's graffiti and replace it with their own. Since gangs rely heavily upon intimidation to achieve their goals, they cannot allow the reputational loss incurred by not retaliating against others who tag in their territory. This often leads to assaults and murders against the violating gang. Oftentimes a vital clue in a murder or assault investigation is the graffiti in the area where the crime occurred. If two gangs are at war, it will be evident in the area's graffiti.[7]

The second layer of conflict is that between gangs and the community. Gangs do not own property in the communities they claim as their own. The property they tag belongs either to the local government or to local residents and business owners. Any edifice that is highly visible will be tagged in order to make the presence of the gang known. This tagging comes at a cost to the community. There will be increased gang activity near the site of the tagging, as gang members cross out the old tagging or add new tagging. This leads to decreased safety for community members, since it is likely that violent encounters will occur between rival gangs at the site of the graffiti.[8] When firearms are used in these confrontations, innocent residents are often caught in the crossfire. Additionally, rampant graffiti and its associated safety concerns can lead to a decrease in property values and lack of trust in the local government to keep citizens safe.

The final layer of conflict is between gangs and law enforcement. Law enforcement is tasked with abating graffiti through both proactive and reactive measures. Proactive responses include uniformed officers creating a visual deterrent by patrolling the community, conducting pedestrian and vehicle stops, and making arrests for observed crimes. However, the majority of the response to graffiti is reactive, investigating vandalism that has already occurred. In order to make an immediate arrest, a tagger must be caught in the act or a witness must come forward and identify the culprit. Because it takes only a few seconds to vandalize a surface with spray paint, and since most taggers utilize lookouts, it is extremely difficult to catch a tagger in the act.

Recognizing the impact that tagging has on the community—to say nothing of the danger it poses to youth involved in gang activity—many municipalities have empowered their officers with specialized digital resources such as TAGRS to combat graffiti. Private software companies have likewise recognized the market for tools to assist in anti-graffiti enforcement. While costly, these programs assist law enforcement in tracking and prosecuting graffiti crime.

GRAFFITI'S RHETORICAL VELOCITY: FROM GANG SIGN TO DIGITAL DATA

Rhetorical velocity offers a valuable framework for understanding the social and rhetorical facets of law enforcement's digital surveillance of urban graffiti with databases such as TAGRS.

Working from theories of circulation and remix, Jim Ridolfo and Danielle Nicole DeVoss note that all texts circulate beyond their initial site and medium of delivery.[9] A press release, for example, circulates among various news reports, where it will be excerpted and interpreted outside the control of the organization that originally wrote the press release. In digital contexts, the recomposition of text or image becomes an even greater concern. Ridolfo and DeVoss give the name *rhetorical velocity* to the set of strategies one might adopt in light of today's widespread circulation, appropriation, remix, and recomposition of text.

As its name suggests, rhetorical velocity is a function of time: how much time might be involved in the recomposition of an appropriated text? Does an author want to make it easy or difficult—in terms of time and effort—for others to recompose his or her text? The answer depends on whether the appropriations are expected to be positive, negative, or neutral in relation to the text's rhetorical goals. (For example, if an author does not want his or her text to be copied/pasted by its recipients, he or she could deliver it as a PDF without optical character recognition.)

We also want to suggest that rhetorical velocity is a function of direction. Velocity is direction-aware. If a person were to move forward and backward a million times, there would be much activity but zero velocity. Rhetorical velocity must likewise have a steady direction—a vector. *Circulation* might work as a rough synonym for *rhetorical vector*, but in addition to its unique Marxist connotations,[10] circulation often lacks a logic of directionality, assuming instead a "comprehensive picture of interaction" of texts across the many sites available in a complex society.[11] However, rhetorical velocity and vector suggest something like a first law of rhetorical motion: a text's rhetorical force will tend to move in a single direction (that is, toward a single goal) unless acted on by an outside force. Of course, in many cases, countless forces might act on or influence a text's vector at any time. Indeed, a key assumption of rhetorical velocity is that recomposition happens, as it were, in the wild, where multiple agents are presumed to have access to a text. However, we argue that graffiti's rhetorical velocity—on a vector from physical gang sign to meta-tagged digital signal in a law enforcement database—is an example of a vector on which outside forces can have little, if any, impact.

Graffiti, as spray-paint on architecture, is composed against recomposition. Graffiti emphatically does not invite appropriation and recomposition by non-gang-affiliated individuals. Both graffiti's intimidation factor and its fixed medium preclude its widespread circulation outside gang-sanctioned environments. Needless to say, concrete and intimidation cannot stop graffiti from being recomposed in the age of digital media. It takes no effort to take a high-definition digital photograph of graffiti and hardly any effort to upload the photograph onto a computer, where it can be remixed, tagged, and distributed in any number of ways. As mentioned, gangs themselves circulate their signs and monikers online. Gang signs have even become trending hashtags on Twitter, where they continue to meet the goal of intimidating rival gangs, often to deadly ends.[12] Whether in the form of a digital photograph or a hashtag, graffiti now circulates in digital spaces, where it is easily surveilled and appropriated by law enforcement for ends not intended by the individuals who created it.

We noted earlier that recomposition typically occurs in the wild, where multiple forces can act on any one of a text's rhetorical vectors at any given time. In the wild, a text appropriated for negative reasons can be reappropriated and realigned with the author's goals. Political memes offer a good example: they are constantly composed, recomposed via negative appropriation, then re-recomposed to renew the meme's original intent, before being re-re-recomposed via another negative appropriation, and so on ad infinitum. A simpler example: in the wild, a writer can respond directly to negative appropriations of his or her text, acting as his or her own outside force to divert a negative vector that his or her text may have been on.

However, in the case of graffiti surveillance (and surely in other cases), the closed nature of the rhetorical vector nullifies the writer's agency. Rhetorical velocity is still in play, but there are some vectors that authors cannot control or respond to. More complexly, there are spaces into which texts circulate that only a privileged few can access but in which texts are still recomposed for purposes of social influence. In the context of graffiti databases, the power of rhetorical vector means that, once a state investigator seizes graffiti in the form of a digital photograph, no outside force can stop it from circulating into a surveillance database and, eventually, into a dossier for a criminal case. Graffiti in this form is designed to meet new ends unlike those for which it was created, and in this state-controlled context, the first law of rhetorical motion is implacable. Graffiti takes on a new life when circulated into databases such as TAGRS. No longer a mark of intimidation, graffiti is first remediated into a digital image, then recomposed into a multilayered, geographically tagged database entry providing information to law enforcement about taggers, their activities, and their movements—eventually, this entry and others will be recomposed into a vital piece of evidence in a prosecutor's criminal case. Taggers are not given a chance to respond to this negative vector on which their texts have embarked (until they are given a court date).

Whether this is an ethical or unethical appropriation of graffiti writing is a subjective question. A more objective comment is that this digital seizure of physical graffiti—recomposed as a tool for surveillance—enhances law enforcement's prosecutorial power. As a San Diego city employee puts it: "When you catch somebody for tagging one location, you can tie them to everything they've done that's been reported through [the database]."[13] What once would have been a single charge of vandalism for taggers turns into multiple charges. In most municipalities, this is the difference between a misdemeanor and a felony. And, of course, with a tagger's whole oeuvre and gang associations now networked together in a single interface for easy browsing by law enforcement, a simple tag might lead to more serious criminal charges as well.

As a gang sign on street corners or social media, graffiti's rhetorical velocity can further the goals of the gang associated with the graffiti. However, as a meta-tagged digital photograph—circulated on the TAGRS database and, eventually, into a criminal case file—graffiti's rhetorical velocity moves along a very different vector, toward a very different goal. Its velocity cannot be diverted by any outside force, least of all the tagger's. Importantly, although it is closed, it remains a vector whose velocity still generates social influence—in this case, expanded prosecutorial power for the state. Without condoning gang activity or tagging, we nevertheless suggest that the digital surveillance of graffiti by urban law enforcement raises interesting rhetorical questions, particularly when viewed through the lens of rhetorical velocity and vector. What is the difference between free and controlled, open and closed circulation? As a matter of rhetorical velocity, how might texts or images be composed against surveillance? As citizens, what rights do we possess when it comes to the appropriation of our texts and images by—and the circulation of our texts and images among—state actors?

We leave these problems to future research. However, briefly bringing these questions together, we would first note that there is little individuals can do to influence the closed, one-way vectors upon which their texts or images embark when appropriated by state as well as corporate actors. We leave digital traces of ourselves online as readily as we leave physical traces of ourselves in every room we visit; and few people (or legal policies) question that these physical traces are up for grabs when it comes to surveillance. Perhaps the questions posed earlier—as well as our nascent theories of rhetorical vector and the laws of rhetorical motion—simply provide a new language to talk about the perennial tension between civil liberty and civil policing, or between individual privacy and the social commons. Regarding privacy, corporate actors have come clean recently about the existence of closed spaces into which our digital traces circulate and in which they promote goals and ends we may or may not align with. More widespread awareness about and rhetorical research into both corporate- and state-run spaces over which we have no control (e.g., the billion dollar NSA Utah Data Center) would be a good first step toward understanding one-way rhetorical vectors. In general, theories of remix and recomposition assume a free and open social space where all texts and writers interact in a complex ecology. Shining some light on the less open spaces of the internet—where our texts circulate, without our knowledge, to serve corporate and state interests—will be a valuable project in the coming years at the nexus of rhetoric, digital technology, and asymmetrical conflict.

NOTES

1. Alonso, "18th Street Gang in Los Angeles County."
2. Martinez, "Know Your Graffiti."
3. Sporrow, interview with Fitch.
4. US Department of Justice, "About Violent Gangs."
5. State of California, "Penal Code Part 1, Title 7, Chapter 11."
6. Tabb, "Misunderstanding of Graffiti."
7. Romero, "Graffiti Is Blooming in Los Angeles."
8. Los Angeles Police Department, "Why Gang Graffiti is Dangerous."
9. Ridolfo and DeVoss, "Composing for Recomposition."
10. John Trimbur, "Composition and the Circulation of Writing."
11. Ridolfo and DeVoss, "Composing for Recomposition."
12. Austen, "Public Enemies."
13. Garrick, "San Diego Graffiti Crackdown."

REFERENCES

Alonso, Alex. "18th Street Gang in Los Angeles County." StreetGangs.com, June 25, 2008. http://www.streetgangs.com/hispanic/18thstreet#sthash.Tv06vNfh.dpbs.

Austen, Ben. "Public Enemies: Social Media Is Fueling Gang Wars in Chicago." *Wired*, June 17, 2013. https://www.wired.com/2013/09/gangs-of-social-media/.

Garrick, David. "San Diego Graffiti Crackdown Includes More Staff, Centralization, Phone App." *San Diego Union-Tribune*, June 26, 2017. http://www.sandiegouniontribune.com/news/politics/sd-me-graffiti-enforcement-20170623-story.html.

Los Angeles Police Department. "Why Gang Graffiti is Dangerous." http://www.lapdonline.org/top_ten_most_wanted_gang_members/content_basic_view/23471.

Martinez, Jose. "Know Your Graffiti: Disses, Threats and the Mexican Mafia." Southern California Public Radio, March 7, 2012. http://www.oncentral.org/news/2012/03/07/know-your-graffiti-disses-threats-and-mexican-mafi/index.html.

Ridolfo, Jim, and Danielle Nicole DeVoss. "Composing for Recomposition: Rhetorical Velocity and Delivery." *Kairos: A Journal of Rhetoric, Technology, and Pedagogy* 13, no. 2 (2009). http://kairos.technorhetoric.net/13.2/topoi/ridolfo_devoss/velocity.html.

Romero, Dennis. "Graffiti Is Blooming in Los Angeles: Could that Mean Something?" *LA Weekly*, June 9, 2015. http://www.laweekly.com/news/graffiti-is-blooming-in-los-angeles-could-that-mean-something-5666143.

Sorrow, Scott. Interview with Ken Fitch. September 1, 2017.

State of California. "Penal Code Part 1, Title 7, Chapter 11." https://leginfo.legislature.ca.gov/faces/codes_displaySection.xhtml?sectionNum=186.22.&lawCode=PEN.

Tabb, Bryce. "The Misunderstanding of Graffiti." *Graffiti, Rap, Writing, Tattoos*, December 10, 2010. http://66wrtg1150.wikidot.com/the-misunderstandings-of-graffiti.

Trimbur, John. "Composition and the Circulation of Writing." *College Composition and Communication* 52, no. 2 (2000): 188–219.

US Department of Justice. "About Violent Gangs." https://www.justice.gov/criminal-ocgs/about-violent-gangs.

PART III

PRACTITIONER STORIES

12

DIGITAL AGE EDUCATION

PREPARING WARRIORS FOR HYBRID CONFLICT AT AIR FORCE CYBERWORX

JEFFREY COLLINS AND GARY MILLS

Upon graduation our students join in shaping global narratives swirling about cyberspace at digital speeds. This chapter is about the importance of preparing them as rhetorical operators, military officers, and citizens possessing the integrity and rhetorical maturity needed and about our attempts at Air Force CyberWorx to help them along their way with design thinking, applied in a project-based learning and maker space studio in Colorado.[1]

SURVIVAL NARRATIVES AND THE EXIGENCIES OF A LOOMING CYBERPOCALYPSE

Clint Emerson served on SEAL Team 3 and SEAL Team 6; he also worked with covert and special operations units, even the National Security Agency (NSA).[2] He has since retired and written three survival books. His second work, *100 Deadly Skills: The SEAL Operative's Guide to Surviving in the Wild and Being Prepared for Any Disaster*, includes not only defensive tactics to thwart physical attacks but also cyber-survival techniques for the wilds of the internet. Threats have changed and Emerson asserts that our networked society demands a new blueprint for the survival skills needed, including how to "escape a stadium or theater shooting" and how to "elude ransomware attacks."[3] *Surviving* cyberspace has made it into *100 Deadly Skills*, a top-selling doomsday prepper's guide, helping stabilize cyberattack's place within pop cultural disaster narratives. Granted, Emerson's concerns here may be read as hyperbolic salesmanship. The exigencies, however, are far from imaginary and motivate us to work to figure out ways to help prepare students for, what we argue, the rhetorical operations (rhet ops) world they will enter.

At the global level, monitoring world-changing threats is the focus of the advisors of the Bulletin of the Atomic Scientists. Established in 1945, the organization was founded by Manhattan Project scientists unwilling to distance themselves from the mass destruction they had created.[4] The Doomsday Clock has symbolized their findings since their first publication in 1947. Over the years, the Bulletin has explored an increasing range of threats with the potential to make the clock strike midnight (global destruction).[5] Their wide-ranging indicators include the status of global nuclear weapons, the security and handling of these weapons, sea level rise, carbon dioxide in the atmosphere, global temperature changes, Arctic ice melt, biosecurity, and emerging technologies.[6] Reports from 2016 and 2017 have included cyberattack as one of the key threats posed by emerging technologies. Cyberattack is not only part of the famous doomsday calculation—it is also a threat with the potential to ignite multiple catastrophes, including manipulation of networks and systems behind nuclear command and control.[7]

In early 2017 the Doomsday Clock was advanced from three minutes to two and a half minutes to midnight in part due to the volatile dialogue and posturing between key world leaders in response to North Korea's ongoing ballistic missile test flights and underground nuclear detonations.[8] So, within degrees, the Bulletin also tracks the ebb and flow of "official" narratives as part of the qualitative equation. It is more than counting warheads and measuring the rise of oceans—it is also the discourses these events ignite. The closest we have ever come to midnight was in 1953. Back then, the Doomsday Clock was at two minutes to midnight following the first-ever thermonuclear device tests by the United States in October 1952 and the USSR in August 1953.[9] Nearly seven decades later, we have managed to gain a thirty-second buffer from global doom. Unfortunately, even that narrow gap was eliminated on January 25, 2018.

In early 2018 the Doomsday Clock advanced again, this time to two minutes to midnight, placing the current global doomsday narrative on par with the perceived threat at the apex of the Cold War.[10] The Bulletin of the Atomic Scientists reveals how earlier indicators have intensified through "hyperbolic rhetoric and provocative actions by both sides."[11] Importantly, Mecklin's report points to disruptive and destabilizing discourse as a central catalyst for the shift. World leaders have failed to craft and "clearly communicate a coherent nuclear policy [narrative]."[12] This in turn has cloaked national intentions "more than ever," which has effectively blocked discourse and "reassurance" desperately needed by major stakeholders and their allies.[13] These gaps are amplified by the erosion of "public trust in political institutions, in the media, in science, and in facts themselves"[14] created by "internet-based deception campaigns."[15] This has created a narrative vacuum, devoid of stable and sustained political and policy intent, which is being infiltrated by sophisticated digital tools and discourses aimed at destabilization.

Our national strategies and those of the Department of Defense (DoD) share similarly dire assessments. The 2015 *National Security Strategy* advances "The danger of disruptive and even destructive cyber-attack is growing"[16] and, in response, the United States is "fortifying our critical infrastructure against all hazards, especially cyber espionage and attack."[17] We are reassured that through military operations and civilian industry the nation's critical infrastructure is being hardened to "decrease vulnerabilities and increase resilience."[18]

Bleakly, the most recent *National Security Strategy*, released on December 18, 2017, frames an "America First"[19] stance, with China and Russia spotlighted as direct challenges to American power and North Korea and Iran called out as destabilizing regional actors.[20] In the latest strategy, focus widens on the newest warfighting domains, space and cyberspace: "Cyberattacks have become a key feature in modern conflicts."[21] Russia's cyberattacks and "its influence campaigns blend covert intelligence operations and false online personas with state-funded media, third-party intermediaries, and paid social media users or 'trolls.'"[22] Previous national efforts to counter exploitation of information are positioned as being "tepid and fragmented" and lacking a "sustained focus" without "properly trained [cyber] professionals."[23] This is a shift from the previous assurances that help is on the way. Instead, "Weaponized Information"[24] sees its first use in a *National Security Strategy*, along with "overmatch."[25] Military overmatch is employed so that US forces can respond in "the combination of capabilities [and] in sufficient scale to prevent enemy success."[26] This overmatch advantage is to be preserved through advancing innovation, restoring major conflict readiness, and up-sizing military forces to "win across a range of scenarios."[27]

Such shifts in official discourse are noteworthy. They shape the ever-developing global narrative of the United States' leadership and policy development roles in the international community. Each iteration of the *National Security Strategy* over the better part of the last decade reveals how US positioning and priorities have changed:

2010: "Our national security strategy is . . . focused on renewing American leadership so that we can more effectively advance our interests in the 21st century."[28]

2015: "This National Security Strategy provides a vision for strengthening and sustaining American leadership in this still young century."[29]

2017: "This National Security Strategy puts America first."[30]

How different audiences, ranging from US citizens, foes and allies, perceive these nation-level survival narratives contributes to the evolving global narrative, shaping the rhetorical situation and exigencies for future political and military actions.

Turning to the US military's specific narrative about cyberwarfare, *The DoD Cyber Strategy* is equally alarming: "We are vulnerable in this wired world. Today our reliance on the confidentiality, availability, and integrity of data stands in stark contrast to the inadequacy of our cybersecurity."[31] Cyberwarfare has marched toward center stage: The director of National Intelligence has highlighted cyber threat as "the number one strategic threat to the U.S., placing it ahead of terrorism for the first time since the attacks of September 11, 2001."[32]

Many publications extend this prevailing narrative. However, Jerry Brito and Tate Watkins provide a countervailing view, asserting that the dominant discourse has escalated cyberwar artificially: "The rhetoric of 'cyber doom' employed by proponents of increased federal intervention in cybersecurity implies an almost existential threat that requires instant and immense action."[33] *Cyber* is rapidly fused to, as Brito and Watkins assert, culturally loaded language to intentionally amplify the doom surrounding cyberattacks: "cyber Katrina" (failed infrastructure aggravated by slow response); "digital Pearl Harbor" (equipped, but taken by surprise); and "Cyber 9/11" (threat identified, but no warning before horrific attack).[34] Such language used to describe cyberattacks places emphasis on tragedy over reflection and our eventual recovery.[35] However the rhetors using such language often go on to encourage us to close vulnerabilities and strengthen our resilience with such past disasters in mind.[36] Their messages fade and blur as attacks on corporate and military networks increase in number and sophistication, amplifying fears and implying a terrible breach is imminent—best to put down our books and get prepared.

In a *New Yorker* piece, Evan Osnos explores this alarmist evolution through preparation by business elites to survive "the crackup of civilization."[37] "Doomsday—as a prophecy, a literary genre, and a business opportunity—is never static; it evolves with our anxieties."[38] From underground survival condos built into decommissioned intercontinental ballistic missile silos to elaborate escape plans to New Zealand, Osnos explores our fascination with and preparation for calamity.[39] Importantly, Osnos underscores that these fears often ignite during dramatic political and technological shifts: "Historically, our fascination with the End has flourished at moments of political insecurity and rapid technological change."[40] The scholars David Miller, Piers Robinson, and Vian Bakir underscore the role global disaster narratives serve in shaping perceptions: "The world also faces an uncertain future: global climate change, resource wars and fear of superpower rivalry between the major global states are all major issues and ones in which propaganda and persuasion [carefully crafted narratives—some forged in truth, some designed to manipulate] are playing a central role," one serving to reheat a Cold War narrative.[41]

Adam Segal surveys what he sees as the start of the newfangled cyber Cold War: "Year Zero began with a newspaper article. In June 2012, government officials leaked details of a computer attack on Iran's nuclear program."[42] The cyber-techne took the form of a complex program called Stuxnet. According to public sources, this sophisticated offensive weapon brought a new capability to cyberwar: "Before Stuxnet, computer code had served primarily to steal or destroy data on other computers; now it was causing equipment to malfunction. It was creating physical outcomes."[43] Code can generate focused effects without the legal or political consequences of conventional kinetic (missile/bomb) attacks.

According to this emergent narrative, Stuxnet is the cyber equivalent to the Sputnik launch on October 4, 1957. Back then, the Soviets surprised the world with a technological leap into space by putting a satellite in orbit. The equally monumental cyber leap, according to public reporting, was launched in 2007, spawning kinetic effects (destroyed centrifuges) through computer code.[44] The cyberwar was underway, and the space/arms race of the millennium was taking shape in terms of innovations ("first use of new idea")[45] and still-developing issues surrounding digital forensics, accountability, and rules of engagement. Critically, how we talk about this conflict, define it, describe it, and visually/textually represent both military and civilian discourses will shape powerful narratives. This, in turn, will influence how we plan, project, prepare, and prevail (prevent or survive) future conflicts.

NARRATIVES AFFECTING (OR EFFECTING) MILITARY EXIGENCIES

Narratives play important roles in shaping society. Stories, even narrative fragments or tweets, build meaning and shape communal understanding. The acclaimed psychologist Jerome Bruner gives us a sense of the pivotal role narratives serve in our lives, especially our engagement in, survival of, and recovery from conflicts. Bruner starts with the role culture itself plays in giving "meaning to [our] action[s]" through the "interpretive system" of language and symbols, constructed from "forms of logical and narrative explication" and "patterns of mutually dependent communal life."[46] As Bruner argues, such collectively defined patterns are shaped by daily communication: "Indeed, the meaning placed on most acts by the participants in any everyday encounter depends upon what they say to one another in advance, concurrently, or after they have acted,"[47] "organiz[ing] experience into a narrative form, into plot structures, and the rest."[48] Narratives create powerful supports and "mitigates or at least makes comprehensible a deviation from a canonical cultural pattern."[49] In short, narratives teach, warn, restrain, and normalize—and we are drawn to use and personalize these templates. Narratives also give us reflexivity, allowing us to change the present in light of past lessons, and generating a "capacity to envision alternatives," and enhancing our ability to see through others' perspectives—building empathy.[50]

Narratives, clearly, play a pivotal role in warfare and, as we have experienced, cyberspace provides for expedient power projection tools. These can build or hijack existing narratives; they can also generate a new form of agency for the attacks themselves. The program CrashOverride is a useful illustration as, according to public reporting, this malware was used in Russian-sponsored cyberattacks against Kiev. "It was executed by a highly sophisticated, adaptable piece of malware . . . expressly coded to be an automated, grid-killing weapon."[51] It could "scan a victim's network to map out targets, then launch at a preset time, opening circuits on cue without even having an internet connection back to the hackers. In other words, it's the first malware found in the wild since Stuxnet that's designed to independently sabotage physical infrastructure."[52] CrashOverride takes on the narrative agency of a supervillain, wielding fear-inducing pathos while remaining ominously anonymous (if desired). Narratives help build appropriate (or not) political and military responses to perceived threats to ways of life. So, are we ready for this?

The cyber researcher Shane Coughlan joins many others in asserting we are building the aircraft while also piloting it, frantically racing to prepare for a concept of war that we do not understand: "Cyber warfare is the new wonder weapon, and the new unknown threat, and the technology on which it relies is beset by vague depictions of the dangers it presents, or the benefits it offers."[53] We are not only scrambling to build defenses for newly discovered vulnerabilities and changing tools, tactics and techniques, but also struggling to define the attacks Russians and other actors have already employed. Former Central Intelligence Agency director Michael Hayden concedes, "We are very sloppy with our language. My concern is not that [language is] going to lock us into an inappropriate response. My concern is it's just another reflection of [the fact that] we haven't gotten the deeper understanding required to really operate in this domain—what constitutes normal state-to-state activity, what constitutes a crime, what constitutes espionage, what constitutes war."[54] Within this language limbo, Hayden defines Russian involvement in the 2016 presidential race as the "most successful covert influence campaign" in history—not an "act of war."[55] This suggests a comfortingly wide divide between spycraft and influence/propaganda versus military attack and defense. Such comfort is suspect.

HYBRID WARFARE AND RHETORICAL ARSENALS

Influence campaigns are part of the "blend" of conventional, irregular, and/or guerrilla warfare strategies Williamson Murray and Peter Mansoor explore across a wide spectrum of historic conflicts.[56] This blend allows adversaries to strike a balance within their own "strategic cultures, historical legacies, geographic realities, and economic means."[57] Their book on hybrid war reveals assumptions across major conflicts that have crippled great armies and favored weaker opponents. As for gains, hybrid warfare allows disadvantaged nations "to extend wars in time and space to achieve their goals," testing an opponent's "political will" as persistent campaigns "work to achieve control over the population."[58] In such a way, "hybrid warfare magnifies the importance of perceptions . . . the battle over competing narratives plays out among three audiences: the indigenous population, the home front of the great power, and the wider international community."[59] Such hybrid analytical structures expose deep rhetorical roots: Narratives, perceptions, and influence are at the heart of rhetorical studies and awareness of the rhetorical arsenal amplifies understanding of cyberwar's hybrid nature.

As a start, rhetoric provides for lenses analysts could apply to explore the underlying "urgent need or demand; necessity; emergency"—exigency—cyberwarfare sparks.[60] Focusing squarely on the urgent need, Lloyd Bitzer asserts that exigencies shape the rhetorical response (discourse), and discourse can "completely or partially" fix the exigency, aided by understanding the exigency, audience, and constraints (rhetorical situation) surrounding the problem.[61] Rhetorical situations will appear "as a natural context of persons, events, objects, relations, and an exigence which strongly invites utterance [a response]."[62] But this reactive, emergency-driven approach has encountered resistance. For example, Arthur Walzer sees Bitzer's focus on "rhetorical exigencies" as being too restrictive, requiring "a kind of rhetoric Richter scale to measure and validate exigencies in terms of historic tremors they make"[63] A cyber 9/11 event might move the needle, but more subtle, nuanced exigencies ("shaping operations" in military parlance) leading up to a main attack probably would not. Walzer asserts Bitzer's vision "needs to be reformulated" and provides an alternative conception in which rhetorical exigency prompts "a writer's [cyberwarrior's/politician's] sense of 'why' [purpose and intent] relating to an urgent need. It would prompt questions as to 'where it is heading' [target audience] and 'how' [capability and effects]."[64] Providing a flipped view of exigency, Richard Vatz gives the rhetor even more control. The rhetorical discourse in this case will shape any resulting exigency.[65] So, our response to a cyberattack (malware, influence campaign, or "weaponized information")[66] either in public dialogue or in covert exchange, can redirect or interrupt the impact of the exigency.

Focusing beyond the emergency/response models, Barbara Biesecker calls for a more complex (and likely more useful in our cyber context) look at exigency through Derrida's lens of *différance.* This perspective focuses on "provisional limitations of a potentially unlimited and indeterminate textuality."[67] This adaptation of deconstruction helps to support "analysis of rhetorical events," which allows us to gain access to the "rhetorical dimension" (means of communication and context-centered, shifting production of meaning)—not through a static look at exigency, rhetor, and/or audience but through their moving, "provisional" influence on each other.[68] Biesecker inspires use of a metaphor to help see this rhetorical exploration in action.

Imagine filming a bird (discourse) in flight (action). Once the flight is captured, we can pause the video to permit view of its rhetoricity (influential and persuasive mechanisms)[69]—not through a focused study of the bird itself but through a look at how it is influenced by and influences the displaced "air" (ecologies, established narratives, etc.) all along its path. *Différance* serves as a way to better understand the bird—not by focusing exclusively on the avian mechanics but by examining the perception- and meaning-shaping elements surrounding and interacting with it. One can then hit pause and play to scrub along the video and learn that persuasion is, according to Derrida, "only within a topic [an orientation in space]" that, in turn, "corresponds to a condition of forces."[70] Stopping the video provides a provisional context that can be rewound to identify intertextual origins or fast-forwarded to scaffold potential and potentially innovative interactions.

In our digital, hyperconnected age, exigency is aptly aligned with the role narratives play within hybrid warfare. We see the blend of key elements in shifting ecologies of persuasion and potential outcomes through discourses shared with "one another in advance, concurrently, or after they have acted," as Bruner has written.[71] This becomes a new blueprint, drawing us to an arsenal of rhetorical tools able to serve to help understand cyberwarfare actions. As Laura Gurak warns in her examination of digital communications at the turn of the twenty-first century, with the speed, reach, anonymity, interactivity, and impact of cyberspace, each act comprises "social, rhetorical, and political features."[72] Without some frameworks within rhetors' arsenals, we will enter "cyberspace with only a limited understanding of both the power and the problems of this technology."[73]

In our conception, rhet ops specialists would have the maturity to guide and refocus the use of these tools. Rhetoric and conflict have reached a tipping point as cyber-techne, mastery of technology and code, has taken on kinetic effect. We have seen this with marked results in the Ukraine in 2015 and 2016.[74] More directly, information and narratives have been weaponized as part of complex campaigns to influence American perceptions—a form of cyberattack that challenges source credibility, government-industry response paradigms, and progressively fosters the construction of "information monocultures"[75] that unify then isolate ("capture" via mutually supported narratives) targeted audiences through social media platforms. Although the impacts are still under study, America's foundational dialogues and narratives were "hacked" in 2016. As a result, rhet ops awareness has become part of our cyber survival guide.

AIR FORCE CYBERWORX'S BLUEPRINT: PROBLEM-BASED LEARNING AND DESIGN THINKING

This brings us back to Emerson, our Navy SEAL. His call for warriors to establish a core skillset as well as a new blueprint for survival and success is not altogether wrong. Beyond providing coding skills, electrical and computer science acumen, math and engineering know-how, and access to a good library and the latest technology, how do we prepare officers to fight in a war that has been active for over a decade, but is still being defined? How best to address a type of warfare that is evolving at high velocity? How to help develop officers acting with integrity and character in the hybrid warfare environment? We ask such questions because we are responsible for enhancing the education and training of future Air Force cyberwarriors. When commissioned upon graduation, they will be responsible for the protection, maintenance, enhancement, and ethical use of cyber technologies—weapons capable of swiftly complicating or calming the doomsday narrative. More directly, their education must recognize "that the line between war and peace can be fractured in an instant. . . . The only elements of crisis under our control are our own preparation and response."[76] The cyber landscape demands continuous exploration and innovation, creativity, problem-solving, boundary spanning, and ethical decision-making.

The Air Force's CyberWorx program helps to answer these demands by focusing on the education of talented students, officers, government civilians, and enlisted personnel participating in problem-solving through the AF CyberWorx design studios and maker spaces at the US Air Force Academy (USAFA) in Colorado Springs, Colorado. By placing AF CyberWorx within the

USAFA's academic environment, and by allowing the organization to partner with experts from industry and academia, a more diverse, dynamic approach to problem-solving (exigency, audience, narrative, and invention) emerges, encouraging participants to approach problem-solving differently and more broadly, thereby changing the military culture from within. Developing and sustaining a culture of innovation—one that embraces rebel thinkers (intellectually fearless, ethical, creative, curious, open to theoretical and technical experimentation)—is needed. The freedom and flexibility to "fail fast and cheap" in maker spaces and design studios in order to tinker and prototype as many scenarios, solutions, and testable assumptions as possible—to scrub along provisional contexts in the Biesecker/Derrida formulation—hones a cyber force we believe is more prepared to reckon with the ongoing and future hybrid warfare that has emerged in our digital age.

NEW DESIGN THINKING WITH SOME OLD RHETORICAL SCAFFOLDING

At the center of each project, AF CyberWorx uses "design thinking" as its methodology.[77] Design thinking is an innovation-based, human-centric problem-solving method embraced by industry leaders and corporations such as Apple and Google, but not yet widely embraced within the Department of Defense (DoD). The design thinking process as applied at AF CyberWorx is a transdisciplinary method that breaks down organizational and academic silos, fostering discourse and collaboration. Large organizations across the DoD, major industries, and academia naturally form structures based on specializations to enable deep expertise. However, these structures often impede creativity, collaboration, and knowledge sharing—all vital to innovation. We deliberately reach across specialties to bring diverse perspectives to a problem in a nonthreatening, diversity-embracing, studio environment. This evokes ideas that would otherwise be missed or stifled. This transdisciplinary design approach to problem-solving encourages meaningful interactions and solutions that are intuitive and open to the vast opportunities available in the cyber realm.

The outcome of our collaborative design project "sprints" (time-sensitive, focused problems) is to develop low-fidelity/high-concept prototypes to forward fast solutions to the Air Force. Our semester-long projects allow deeper engagement with the end users of innovations, their concerns, and needs. These extended projects help refine USAFA cadets' understanding of exigency in relation to the intended audience, dominant or rising narratives, means of influence, and cultures into which the innovation may be employed. It teaches students to seek first the right problem to solve and questions to answer and then find meaningful solutions by exploring a wide range of possible answers to the design challenge, not an application of a particular technology solution favored by one silo of expertise or another, regardless of the rhetorical consequence.

Part of answering the problem is coming to terms with the surrounding narrative. Jonah Sachs addresses the power of narratives across effective marketing. Marketing wrestles with a different type of conflict, but his "story wars" are critical in both civilian and military realms.[78] Sachs aligns marketing conflict and warfare in terms of the ability of narratives to guide our decisions and "think differently": "Even if stories are not driving you into literal battle, they are still driving each of us to make decisions that will shape the future of our democracy and our planet. . . . They recruit people into their own definition of *us* to get them to share that sense of belonging with others."[79] Sachs's call for a dynamic shift in how we tell stories, whether it is ultimately for profit margins or military objectives, share a common thread—the messages they advance "will matter."[80] Using John Powers's narrative pillars as a scaffold, Sachs asserts that Powers's template is "still our best guides to success" in any war of competing stories: "Be interesting. Tell the truth. And if you can't tell the truth, change what you're doing so you can. In other words, live the truth."[81] This narrative-building blueprint aligns with Air Force core values ("Integrity First") and official guidance. Miller, Robinson, and Bakir amplify this focus on advancing truth by calling on practitioners "to help steer producers of persuasive communication toward communication strategies that are nonmanipulative and ethically grounded. Ideally, such persuasive communication would avoid all forms of deception and coercion."[82] Continuing, they address the shifting complexity of information warfare: "If deception and coercion are deemed unavoidable and the propaganda is seen as vital to furthering the 'national interest' . . . then there should be some form of post-event ethical reckoning."[83]

PROJECT DESCRIPTION AND OUTCOMES: BEST PREP FOR RHET OPS WARRIORS

An example illustrates the direction. AF CyberWorx's spring 2017 project brought together twenty-five cadets and industry partners to travel to locations across the Air Force for concentrated research visits with the airmen who are conducting command and control (C2) in the cyber domain. The Air Force and other organizations (both civilian and military) are just learning the full range of actions required to keep missions and essential services functioning ("resilience") in the face of unprecedented complexity, interconnectivity, and the ease of vulnerability exploitation. Furthermore, military and government organizations are striving to understand what will be needed to leverage wartime operational advantages from and through the cyber domain in digital age wars, such as scenarios envisioned by the "2018 Doomsday Clock Statement," 2017 *National Security Strategy*, and 2015 *DoD Cyber Strategy*.

The student/industry design teams needed to rethink how the Air Force does C2 to improve the user experience of airmen involved in cyber conflict and day-to-day operations in other warfighting domains at all levels. The goal was to develop a concept for an improved structure, including recommendations for technologies or processes, to present to policy leaders at the end of the semester. Their ideas would be shared with leaders at the Pentagon rewriting the Air Force instructions guiding C2 of cyber operations. Through their research, analysis, and assessment of their field experiences for Pentagon policymakers, students learn the professional practices officers must draw upon to gather diverse inputs and move large organizations forward differently, effectively, and more agilely (than past practices) in the digital age. Such moves do not happen in a vacuum, these future leaders learn, but are set in a time, place, and culture to which they must be constantly attuned and adjusting.

The design teams reached out to individuals from five Air Force bases located across the country—Texas, Colorado, Illinois, and Virginia—all involved in how the Air Force operates, prevents and responds to cyberspace events, both enemy-driven and unintended, such as a software patch or firewall adjustment applied to a system that accidentally breaks or impedes another system's possibly mission-critical function. A project officer at each location set up research interviews and visits for the design teams with organizations and airmen involved in C2 of cyber operations to observe action in the field at the bases using ethnographic and design research methods.[84]

The design team was originally asked to define and refine C2 for communications and (emerging) cyber squadrons, the lowest level "business units" of the Air Force where warfighting work is accomplished. The Air Force has been transforming its communications squadrons' missions from providing information technology (IT) services to providing active cyber defense of its missions while relying on commercial industry to provide the needed IT services. Results of the team's field research and in-depth user observations, however, led them to realize the need to broaden the areas of exploration beyond just the organizational structure of the squadrons. During the research phase of the design process, the teams developed a clearer understanding of the audience and issues through "empathy" and "defining" the problem.[85] The student-industry team visiting Langley Air Force Base, for example, decided to apply an "AEIOU framework." Described in our course text, this framework is an analysis heuristic: a user- and context-centric aid used by our students to observe "Activities, Environments, Interactions, Objects and Users" around them.[86] Using this framework, the students noticed the ramshackle physical spaces (environment) in which some of the personnel (users) were operating, and this led to a conversation with those users about the flooding that sometimes occurs during heavy rainfall, which caused mission impacts (activities) that must be mitigated—a literally wet cyber failure.

The empathetic drive to look not just at what someone is saying but at the context in which she is saying it, and additional conversations that may engender, is afforded by such methods. In this case, the team compared their findings with teams visiting other locations, concluding that the poor physical conditions not only hampered mission accomplishment (e.g., during heavy rain) but also reflected the implicit narrative about the lack of importance placed on the talented men and women carrying out the Air Force cyber mission from these facilities. Such affective connections between the elements within the AEIOU framework lead teams toward answers to design questions such as "How might we attract and keep the needed cyber talent to carry out the C2 missions for our digital age?" and "How do we convey the importance of a C2 mission to those conducting the mission?"

As the teams share observations and apply design-thinking methods, they worked to formulate potential solutions to help advance the Air Force along several thematic lines to combat current risks and extend operational advantages in its cyber operations. These proposed solutions within the groups were then prototyped and tested with users rapidly, using minimum viable product (agile) methodologies to indicate where the Air Force would likely be successful—narrowing to options with the potential to make the biggest impact on warfighting. Through reflection and writing user stories (narratives) and storyboarding solutions, students activate an empathetic approach to understanding the impact of their decision-making. This is a key skill for any leader, but, we argue, a core one for cyberwarriors.

AF CyberWorx projects do not aim to deliver a perfect solution to the tough operational problems taken on, but to deliver ways ahead to improve warfighting based upon design team findings/evidence. In the same way an apprentice hones his or her understandings and skills over time, our projects are intended to prompt follow-on interactions and agile implementations of promising ideas. A digital age education must ensure cyberwarriors use and modify a core process to analyze and organize information in a way to communicate new understandings with real people facing real problems that really matter. This rhetorical and design approach aids in heightening empathy, which is made more effective by the teams' development of personas—archetypal descriptions of user behavior patterns into representative profiles—to humanize the design focus and describe the results of their tests through proposed scenarios and prototypes. The resulting design changes affect Air Force operations at all levels of warfare (strategic, operational, and tactical) within the cyber warfighting domain.

Teaching students methods to rapidly and accurately envision problems; formulate good questions; project mission impacts; empathize with users; brainstorm ways to mitigate technical, cultural, and environmental changes going on around them and their missions; and prototype ideas rapidly are some of the core skills taught at AF CyberWorx. These abilities help answer the demands of the 2017 *National Security Strategy* for "properly trained professionals" for all modern warfighting domains.[87] More directly, these skills will help keep warriors anchored with empathy to the human element on all sides of the battlefront, and grounded to thoughtful analysis of the available blends of perspectives and influences made necessary through hybrid warfare. This is our current, but evolving, blueprint for honing rhet-ops-enabled warriors at AF CyberWorx.

NOTES

The views expressed in this work are those of the authors (Collins and Mills) and do not reflect the official policy or position of the United States Air Force, Department of Defense, or the U.S. Government.

1. Brown, *Change by Design*.
2. Emerson, *100 Deadly Skills*, about the author, Kindle.
3. Emerson, 85, 61, Kindle.
4. Mecklin, "It Is Two and a Half Minutes to Midnight."
5. Mecklin, 1.
6. "Doomsday Dashboard."
7. Stoutland, "Growing Threat."
8. Mecklin, "It Is Two and a Half Minutes to Midnight," 3.
9. Mecklin, 17.
10. Mecklin, "It Is Now Two Minutes to Midnight."
11. Mecklin, 2.
12. Mecklin, 4.
13. Mecklin, 4.
14. Mecklin, 5.
15. Mecklin, 2.
16. White House, *National Security Strategy*, 2015.
17. White House, 3.
18. White House, 9.
19. White House, *National Security Strategy*, 2017.
20. White House, 45.

21. White House, 31.
22. White House, 35.
23. White House, 35.
24. White House, 34.
25. White House, 28.
26. White House, 28.
27. White House, 28.
28. White House, *National Security Strategy*, 2010.
29. White House, *National Security Strategy*, 2015, 29.
30. White House, *National Security Strategy*, 2017, 1.
31. US Department of Defense, *DoD Cyber Strategy*.
32. US Department of Defense, 9.
33. Brito and Watkins, "Loving the Cyber Bomb?" 40,
34. Brito and Watkins, 83–84.
35. Brito and Watkins, 84.
36. Brito and Watkins, 84.
37. Osnos, "Doomsday Prep for the Super-Rich."
38. Osnos.
39. Osnos.
40. Osnos.
41. Miller, Robinson, and Bakir, "Propaganda and Persuasion in Contemporary Conflict."
42. Segal, *Hacked World Order*, chap. 1, Kindle.
43. Segal, chap. 1, Kindle.
44. Finkle, "Stuxnet Was Deployed against Iran in 2007."
45. Edgerton, *Shock of the Old*, ix.
46. Bruner, *Acts of Meaning*, 34.
47. Bruner, 18.
48. Bruner, 45.
49. Bruner, 49–50.
50. Bruner, 109–10.
51. Greenberg, "How an Entire Nation became Russia's Test Lab for Cyberwar."
52. Greenberg.
53. Coughlan, "Is There a Common Understanding of What Constitutes Cyber Warfare?" introduction, Kindle.
54. Michael Hayden, quoted in Chalfant, "Don't Call Russian Election Hacking 'Act of War.'"
55. Chalfant.
56. Murray and Mansoor, *Hybrid Warfare*, introduction, Kindle.
57. Murray and Mansoor, introduction, Kindle.
58. Murray and Mansoor, introduction, Kindle.
59. Murray and Mansoor, introduction, Kindle.
60. *Oxford English Dictionary*, s.v. "Exigency."
61. Bitzer, "Rhetorical Situation," 6.
62. Bitzer, 5.
63. Walzer, "Lloyd Bitzer's 'Rhetorical Situation.'"
64. Walzer, 4–5.
65. Vatz, "Myth of the Rhetorical Situation."
66. Miller, "Information Dominance."

67. Biesecker, "Rethinking the Rhetorical Situation," 111.
68. Biesecker, 112.
69. Biesecker, 116.
70. Jacques Derrida, quoted in Biesecker, "Rethinking the Rhetorical Situation," 120.
71. Bruner, *Acts of Meaning*, 18.
72. Gurak, *Cyberliteracy*, 11.
73. Gurak, 11.
74. Greenberg, "How an Entire Nation became Russia's Test Lab for Cyberwar."
75. Mecklin, "It Is Two and a Half Minutes to Midnight," 6.
76. Emerson, *100 Deadly Skills*, introduction, Kindle.
77. Brown, *Change by Design*, introduction, Kindle.
78. Sachs, *Winning the Story Wars*, prologue, Kindle.
79. Sachs, prologue, Kindle.
80. Sachs, prologue, Kindle.
81. Sachs, part 2, Kindle.
82. Miller, Robinson, and Bakir, "Propaganda and Persuasion in Contemporary Conflict."
83. Miller, Robinson, and Bakir.
84. Melles, Howard, and Thompson-Whiteside, "Teaching Design Thinking."
85. Brown, *Change by Design*, chap. 2, Kindle.
86. Martin and Hanington, *Universal Methods of Design*, 10.
87. White House, *National Security Strategy*, 2017, 35.

REFERENCES

Biesecker, Barbara. "Rethinking the Rhetorical Situation from within the Thematic of 'Différance.'" *Philosophy & Rhetoric* 22, no. 2 (1989): 110–30.

Bitzer, Lloyd. "The Rhetorical Situation." *Philosophy & Rhetoric* 25, no. 1 (1968): 1–14.

Brito, Jerry, and Tate Watkins. "Loving the Cyber Bomb? The Dangers of Threat Inflation in Cybersecurity Policy." *Harvard National Security Journal* 3 (April 2011): 39–84. https://www.mercatus.org/publication/loving-cyber-bomb-dangers-threat-inflation-cybersecurity-policy-0.

Brown, Tim. *Change by Design: How Design Thinking Transforms Organizations and Inspires Innovation*. New York: HarperCollins, 2009.

Bruner, Jerome. *Acts of Meaning*. Cambridge, MA: Harvard University Press, 1990.

Chalfant, Morgan. "Former CIA Director: Don't Call Russian Election Hacking 'Act of War,'" Hill, April 11, 2017. http://thehill.com/policy/cybersecurity/328344-former-cia-director-dont-call-russian-election-hacking-act-of-war.

Coughlan, Shane. "Is There a Common Understanding of What Constitutes Cyber Warfare?" Master's thesis, University of Birmingham, 2016.

"Doomsday Dashboard: Some of What We Consider, When We Set the Doomsday Clock." Bulletin of the Atomic Scientists, n.d. https://thebulletin.org/doomsday-dashboard.

Edgerton, David. *The Shock of the Old: Technology and Global History since 1900*. New York: Oxford University Press, 2007.

Emerson, Clint. *100 Deadly Skills: The SEAL Operative's Guide to Surviving in the Wild and Being Prepared for Any Disaster*. New York: Touchstone, 2016. Kindle.

Finkle, Jim. "Researchers Say Stuxnet Was Deployed against Iran in 2007." Reuters, February 26, 2013. https://www.reuters.com/article/us-cyberwar-stuxnet/ researchers-say-stuxnet—was-deployed-against-iran-in-2007-idUSBRE91P0PP20130226.

Greenberg, Andy. “How an Entire Nation became Russia’s Test Lab for Cyberwar.” *Wired*, June 20, 2017. https://www.wired.com/story/russian-hackers-attack-ukraine/.

Gurak, Laura. *Cyberliteracy: Navigating the Internet with Awareness*. New Haven, CT: Yale University Press, 2001.

Martin, Bella, and Bruce Hanington. *Universal Methods of Design*. Beverly, MA: Rockport Publishers, 2012.

Mecklin, John, ed. “It Is Two and a Half Minutes to Midnight: 2017 Doomsday Clock Statement.” Bulletin of the Atomic Scientists, January 26, 2017. https://thebulletin.org/sites/default/files/Final%202017%20Clock%20Statement.pdf.

Mecklin, John, ed. “It Is Now Two Minutes to Midnight: 2018 Doomsday Clock Statement.” Bulletin of the Atomic Scientists, January 25, 2018. https://thebulletin.org/sites/default/files/2018%20Doomsday%20Clock%20Statement.pdf.

Melles, Gavin, Zaana Howard, and Scott Thompson-Whiteside. “Teaching Design Thinking: Expanding Horizons in Design Education.” *Procedia: Social and Behavioral Sciences* 31 (2012): 162–66. doi:10.1016/j.sbspro.2011.12.035.

Miller, David. “Information Dominance: The Philosophy.” Global Policy Forum, December 29, 2003. https://www.globalpolicy.org/component/content/article/154/26581.html.

Miller, David, Piers Robinson, and Vian Bakir. “Propaganda and Persuasion in Contemporary Conflict.” In *Routledge Handbook of Media, Conflict and Security*, edited by Piers Robinson, Philip Seib, and Romy Fröhlich. London: Routledge, 2017.

Murray, Williamson, and Peter Mansoor, eds. *Hybrid Warfare: Fighting Complex Opponents from the Ancient World to the Present*. New York: Cambridge University Press, 2012. Kindle.

Osnos, Evan. “Doomsday Prep for the Super-Rich.” *New Yorker*, January 30, 2017. https://www.newyorker.com/magazine/2017/01/30/doomsday-prep-for-the-super-rich.

Sachs, Jonah. *Winning the Story Wars: Why Those Who Tell—and Live—the Best Stories Will Rule the Future*. Cambridge, MA: Harvard Business Review Press, 2012. Kindle.

Segal, Adam. *The Hacked World Order: How Nations Fight, Trade, Maneuver, and Manipulate in the Digital Age*. New York: Hachette Book Group, 2017. Kindle.

Stoutland, Page. “Growing Threat: Cyber and Nuclear Weapon Systems.” Bulletin of the Atomic Scientists, October 18, 2017. https://thebulletin.org/growing-threat-cyber-and-nuclear-weapons-systems11201.

US Department of Defense. *The DoD Cyber Strategy*. Washington DC: Government Printing Office, 2015.

White House, *National Security Strategy*. Washington, DC: Government Printing Office, 2010. http://nssarchive.us/NSSR/2010.pdf.

White House. *National Security Strategy*. Washington, DC: Government Printing Office, 2015. http://nssarchive.us/wp-content/uploads/2015/02/2015.pdf.

White House. *National Security Strategy*. Washington, DC: Government Printing Office, 2017. http://nssarchive.us/wp-content/uploads/2017/12/2017.pdf.

Vatz, Richard. “The Myth of the Rhetorical Situation.” *Philosophy & Rhetoric* 6, no. 3 (1973): 154–61. http://www.jstor.org/stable/40236848.

Walzer, Arthur. “Lloyd Bitzer’s ‘Rhetorical Situation’ and the ‘Exigencies’ of Academic Discourse.” *ERIC*, March 1987, 4. https://files.eric.ed.gov/fulltext/ED280059.pdf.

13

MAPPING THE RHETORIC-OPERATIONS DIVIDE

CONSIDERATIONS FOR THE FUTURE

ANGIE MALLORY

The Red Team (the enemy, in this case, Da'esh) was relentless in their communication efforts; not only were their messages culturally tailored in an effective manner, but there was an overwhelming amount of messaging, too. They had the ability to think quickly on their feet, twisting the messaging of the Blue Team (friendly forces) to benefit their cause and pushing it back out over the net before the White Team (local population) even had time to respond. When messaging from the Blue Team started to slow even more, I knew there was a problem. I switched screens in the war room and hastily scanned the behind-the-scenes conversations happening between members of the Blue Team. They were divided over what should be done, why, and if it was realistic; there was an edge to their words that indicated their disagreements were passionate. The Red Team, like the real-world adversary they represented, did not do time-outs: in the eight minutes I had not monitored their activities they had pushed out multiple effective messages. The local population was scattering as a result, some toward the Red Team. The Blue Team had been encouraging the population to fight for their children against Da'esh, but now much of the population was having public discussions about turning to Da'esh for protection.

Charged only with observation and analysis, I could not do anything but analyze and report, so I alerted the chain of command lest the Blue Team lose their one shot at persuading the White Team to stand up for themselves against Da'esh. However, before I was able to alert them, a message was volleyed by Da'esh and, as was my job, I opened it and analyzed it from a rhetorical-operations perspective.

Having spent several months analyzing Da'esh recruitment and beheading videos, I was steeled against emotional involvement and in analysis mode, but this message made me bolt from the war room to vomit: It was a picture of a local man, his child obviously dead from a chemical attack, hanging limply in his arms. I identified with the look on his face as what I might feel if I had utterly failed someone vulnerable who depended upon me. The caption urged the local population to stop fighting to that their children would be spared. It defied all logic, asking parents to surrender to the enemy to save their children from the enemy, but clearly it did not need logic: it cut right to the gut. I knew that theories of rhetoric could explain that power to circumvent logic, but did my field also have the methods to apply that knowledge to a battlefield? And did our Department of Defense (DoD) counterparts have the ability to cut through miles of outdated policy to let us assist? The quality of the Blue Team's debrief and the honesty with which they addressed the gaps in their teamwork would dictate, in part, how we moved forward. We were as united a front as they come, the Blue Team: handpicked members of academia and of the Psychological Operations (PSYOP) community, who had prepped for this exercise for weeks. But I was shaken.

NOT KNOWING ANYONE ON THE OTHER SIDE

My journey toward rhet ops started in my first year of graduate school when I realized that I wanted to get back into the fight, this time armed with knowledge, rather than the weapon and the wrench I had used in my time as an aircraft technician in the navy. I reasoned that there must be some intersection between rhetoric and the military, but I had no idea where to look. I did not feel qualified to poke my academic nose into anything remotely tied to operations, in part because I was not aware of rhetoric being used in real-time settings where lives were at stake. In true academic style, it was a research interest that drove me on.

Islamic State of Iraq and Syria (ISIS) videos were just becoming prominent and, shocked that anyone would fall for their message, one day I did some digging. I found every existing story on people who had joined ISIS and did some hasty analysis. I soon learned that I was not alone in my confusion: not even the experts could find patterns of similarity between the people who were joining ISIS. When I came across a video that the US government had made in a botched attempt to respond to the ISIS videos, I felt moved to act. I had been pursuing this out of curiosity, but a shift was occurring in my perspective.

As someone who had sworn to protect others, it occurred to me that in the past, terrorists would have had to take over a television or radio station to assault innocent onlookers with messages that framed their violent acts, but now they had unbridled access to the airwaves, coming at us from inside the devices we carried in our pockets. My sense of duty pricked now, in realizing that there was no way to protect those within US borders from the relentless videos without infringing on our freedoms. Instinctively, I did not turn to the uniform in which I had defended my country before, but to the new tools I had acquired since then: the very roots of rhetoric were tools of mass public persuasion. Of course rhetoric could give operations a leg-up on ISIS. I just had to find operations, get them to listen to me, and clearly explain what rhetoric was, and how it might be applied to this particular problem—a problem I still knew so little about that I could not answer any of the questions. The challenge that I did not expect to run into was that my field was not equipped with methods for analyzing videos in a way that would benefit operations, nor was my university prepared to publish and maintain video dissertations (at that time). I would eventually find the gap in rhetoric's methods was too big to be filled in the four years remaining in graduate school, but for at least a year I thought the gap was simply that I could not find or comprehend the methods.

WORDS MATTER: CONSEQUENCES OF NOT STATING THE "OBVIOUS"

A friend from my military days told me that I should check out Army Psychological Operations (PSYOP) units because rhetoric would intersect well with them. I discovered that psychology was involved with PSYOP, at least in theory, so I researched who in the psychology department might be best to talk to. Now, of course, I can articulate how a PSYOP unit attempts to use persuasion to avoid violence, but then, even though I felt it, I could not articulate it. Often the academic assumption was that I was going to take theories and methods that rhetoricians use to lift the downtrodden and use them to make war more destructive. Again, if I had the exposure to an actual military problem or challenge, I could have used it to articulate how rhetoric could play a part in negotiating meaning that lessened violence. I did not have that, though, so an additional chasm began forming, at least from my perception—apparently, I did not want the same things from rhetoric as my peers and faculty did, so maybe I did not belong in academia, or at least not in rhetoric. I came very close to quitting graduate school and even closer to giving up on doing a dissertation research project that combined rhetoric and operations. I was held fast by the fact that my department had taken a chance on me and I could not let them down. Plus, I would finish what I started. But I had exhausted all my leads.

One day, I read a news article about a researcher in my university's Psychology Department who was working on a defense-related project. It was not even remotely related to PSYOP, but it merged psychology and the DoD, and that was something. I contacted the professor, saying I had read his article and that "I was interested in studying persuasive communication in DoD problem sets" (a statement that had taken over a year of searching and learning to come up with). To my great joy, he not only answered, but agreed to meet with me, even during the busiest time of the semester. Walking across campus to his office, I became terrified: I was going to a stranger, a smart one, about my dreams, and I did not even know enough about what I wanted to do to have any additional language other than what I had emailed him. But I was desperate to take my research into an area where I thought it could make a difference in an area that mattered to me. What I know now that I did not know then was the importance of common motives: both of us wanted to decrease the chances of violent conflict, to help people solve problems without destroying each other. I would learn to rely on that shared motivation in the future, even with those who did not share any similar theories or words; however, in that moment, I just felt like I was walking to my last chance at attaining my dream.

When I got to his office, the words jumbled as they fell out of my mouth. He was calming, however, and repeated back to me my line of inquiry in a way that was almost what I was thinking, enough that I could clarify which parts were not. This marked the very beginning of my faltering ability to express the gap my research wished to fill. Finding research in my field to frame the gap was the next challenge.

UPON THE SHOULDERS OF WHICH GIANTS SHALL I STAND?

During this time, I needed access to established academic knowledge to know the shape of my research gap in academic terms. What journals should I read? What conferences should I attend? All the journals I knew of were discipline-specific, so even though the field of psychology was working with the DoD and publishing their work, I needed to find a way that my own field of rhetoric could insert itself into the conversation; as a grad student, I could not find one. The psychology faculty member became a mentor and friend, meeting with me on a regular basis and giving me some language from his discipline that might be a place of overlap. It was then that I realized how closely related rhetoric and psychology are, though perhaps neither side would celebrate that fact. Interestingly, I came to realize this by learning more about PSYOP: they were oblivious to rhetoric and drew their entire background from psychology, and yet rhetoric was all about persuasive communication, which is what PSYOP experts do. How could that be? I began to think about the (metaphorical) cost that industry pays for us guarding the borders of our academic fields so tightly.

CALLING SIMILAR THEORIES BY DIFFERENT NAMES

Da'esh had become prolific in messaging in English, and I began to watch their English videos avidly, with the scholarly intent to understand how the persuasion worked so well. Their messaging to local populations who might be suffering from lack of necessities involved promising to protect their families and give their children food, while messaging to US populations had to do with idealism: building your own sense of meaning based on contributing in a unique way. This reminded me of Maslow's hierarchy of human needs (which comes from humanistic psychology), which states that basic physiological needs for survival must be met prior to higher order needs being addressed. The fact that Da'esh employed this theory meant they were very good at audience analysis, which is a theory rhetoric has laid claim to since Aristotle; I wondered with a shudder, did Da'esh have rhetoricians on staff?

At that point, my goal and that of my department bifurcated: I wanted to use my dissertation research to decode Da'esh's power and stop them from killing any more innocent people; my department's job was to make sure I knew how to operate in my own field, with its existing theories and methods. I understand that goal and appreciate its intent and execution to this day. I also hope that someday organizational relationships between rhetoric and operations will mean that, within rhetoric departments, consideration is placed on the types of knowledge and skill necessary for a grad student to be effective when integrated with operations, because rhet ops grad students need different training in some areas, than a rhetoric graduate student who aims to stay in academia.

THE COST OF OPERATIONAL EDUCATION WITHOUT ORGANIZATIONAL RELATIONSHIPS

I continued to seek the bridge between rhetoric and operations, and in the spring of 2015 my mentor in the Psychology Department introduced me via email to a colleague of his who taught a course at a counterterrorism research center at the University of Maryland called the National Consortium for the Study of Terrorism and Responses to Terrorism (START). He was teaching an online course through the START Center that fall and said I should attend. I remember feeling both elated and devastated: this had nothing to do with rhetoric. This faculty member was still in psychology, and the course was at a completely different university. But it was the only bridge I could find to the work I wanted to do. I spent nights awake, trying to figure out how to connect that opportunity with my field. At long last I proposed to my graduate advisor a bold and daring plan, with a list of eight ways this plan would be good for our department and our university. I could take all twelve credits the START program offered as a graduate certificate in terrorism analysis through their Behavioral Science Department and transfer them back into my home university as my area of specialization. Everyone else used literature, journalism, women's studies, or the like, so why couldn't I use this? From my advisor on up through the graduate college, everyone signed off on my plan, and I was on my way. The only catch was that I would have to pay my own way. I added one online course in terrorism analysis to my graduate course load each year, along with a couple thousand dollars to my credit card for each course, and I was on my way. It would get me to operations, maybe, but the rhetoric part I would still have to carve out on my own.

By that time in my journey I expected to have to find and pay my own way, but when a potential graduate student asked me later how to go about doing the same thing, I realized just how steep the cost was to the student: our peers could specialize in any discipline on campus, and their tuition waiver from teaching would apply. Since we had no operational disciplines on campus, no counterterrorism, no organization ties with a university that did, we had to pay our own way.

FROM WHERE DO I DRAW MY RESEARCH?

In the START program, I reveled in knowledge, finding that there was an entire area of study called Terrorism Studies that had its own journals. For example, the *Journal of Terrorism Research* is published in the United Kingdom by the Centre for the Study of Terrorism and Political Violence. *Critical Studies on Terrorism* is an international journal with editors in New Zealand, the United Kingdom, and the United States. Although all the journals are peer-reviewed, this one is the only one claiming an initial blind peer-review process. *Studies in Conflict and Terrorism* is an open-access journal, and specifically oriented to bridge the divide between theory and practice. *Perspectives on Terrorism* is produced by a combined effort between the European-based Terrorism Research Initiative at the Universiteit Leiden, the Netherlands, and the US-based Terrorism and Security Studies. Founded in 2007, *Perspectives on Terrorism* is an open-access online and print journal with over 3,200 subscribers. All of these journals are peer-reviewed, interdisciplinary, and all attempt to represent the most emergent knowledge without being tied to any single funding organization that would drive their agenda.

The field of Terrorism Studies is not very old and is riddled with new-area challenges common to every interdisciplinary area. Instead of being done by field, literature reviews had to be done by topic: what interdisciplinary articles have been written on, say, how persuasion works in Da'esh videos? Doing secondary research in this way, one could never tell if they had really collected all that had been written on the topic. Since all articles were written in the jargon of other disciplines, you must become adept at understanding multidisciplinary approaches to research. The problem was not just a newcomer's challenge either, as coworkers would later tell me over conference dinners—even the veterans of Terrorism Studies experienced it. The result of this challenge is that you can never be sure you have found everything that has been published, therefore the size and shape of the research gap is tenuous.

MAKING OPERATIONS FIT IN A HUMANITIES GRADUATE DEGREE PROGRAM

Meanwhile, in my own discipline, while mostly everyone marveled at the unheard-of way I was earning my degree and the wild places I was taking rhetoric, we all struggled to connect my area of interest to current areas of inquiry in rhetoric. It was an important label to figure out, too, because I was coming up fast on the deadline for choosing my chair and dissertation committee, and to do that, I needed to know where in rhetoric or technical communication my research interests fit. The problem is complex, but basically comes down to access: if you are going to do research, you need a place, process, or artifact, first. I did not have any of those. I did have the Da'esh videos, but then it became a question of methods: what methods does my field have to analyze video? I could find none that got at what I wanted to analyze.

Video analysis exists in film studies, I discovered, and in marketing, but I was constrained to the theories and methods in my field. Why not perform plain old rhetorical analysis of a video? That came down to the output: to do a rhetorical analysis of a video for a dissertation, I would need to do a digital dissertation, and that was still problematic, both because the one faculty member we had who championed such advances had just moved to another university, and because the university was tenuous on how to store and publish such works. In my mind it was unthinkable to do an analysis of a video without the audience seeing the video, so that was out.

However, the main problem was that after hours of analyzing Da'esh recruitment videos, I believed that the power was not just in one layer: a visual rhetorical analysis would not be sufficient to decode the source of power, and neither would an analysis of the words. Besides, rhetoric's most common method for analyzing spoken language is to make it into a text to analyze it, and in my thinking, that removed it so far from the dynamic way in which it was used in the video that it would be pointless analysis. However, to analyze the spoken words as sound would be to divide them from the other sounds in the video, which meant I would also have to look at the setting: the wind, the music, the sounds of birds and later of gunfire. I was unaware of any model utilizing rhetorical theory to analyze those pieces of a video. However, I discovered that some of the genre for the video was similar to a video game, and I discovered game theory—but again, it was outside of my field, so I was discouraged from using it as my main source or method.

What I wanted to do was devise a way to analyze the video by layers, which would have meant analyzing each layer with a method and theory from a different discipline, and then pull in rhetoric to theorize why the way in which the layers meshed, along with the audience Da'esh intended for the video, gave it the persuasive power it held. However, the amount of interdisciplinary learning and support that project would have required would have extended well beyond the time constraints of a dissertation, so I let it go.[1] What we could support in our department, I was told, was a workplace study, and that Terrorism Studies could fit under that umbrella. Terrorism communication used technical tools and communication to accomplish tasks, so it fit under the umbrella of technical and professional communication. Wanting to graduate in the twenty-first century, I found words for my interests, chose a faculty member I admired and who appreciated my subject, and was on my way. To somewhere unknown. With no journal, no previous research in my field, and no access to a research site to gather data. To say there was a gap in the area where rhetoric and operations intersected was an understatement: the gap was the size of the Grand Canyon and I was a solitary hiker, ill-prepared but eager to begin the journey.

ONE CONNECTION LEADS TO ANOTHER

As all this was going on, I volunteered to be the assistant conference chair for a technical communication conference in Ireland (SIGDOC). I did not know what it had to do with my research interests, but it was a way to make connections. So, a year later, assistant chair duties successfully discharged, I found myself lost in Ireland, sitting at a pub with an also-lost, well-known researcher in rhetoric and technical communication. He asked what my area of research interest was, I managed not to grimace in frustration, and when I half-heartedly spilled a few words about persuasion in military communication, he picked up the conversation like he knew what he was talking about. I perked up! After we had found our way back to our respective rooms, I had a promise that he would connect me with an old rhetoric instructor who had worked in Army PSYOP. He fulfilled his promise a couple weeks later, and the dear professor connected me to the US Army Special Operations Command (USASOC).

Some of USASOC's senior persons ran a brainstorming/information-sharing platform called the Futures Forum (UF2), where they invited experts from academia and operations to come share their ideas and get connected. I wrote up a semi-coherent description of how I saw rhetoric being able to contribute to counterterrorism efforts and presented it at the forum. Several people who had called in from other locations asked to be connected with me after the presentation, and as a result I found that I was a reviewing editor on a new, nearly complete joint doctrine called the *Joint Concepts of Human Military Operations (JC-HAMO).*[2]

I was elated at the work the joint publication was doing, mostly because it did such a good job of tying lived experience and physical events to communication theories and persuasion. Their basic tenet is that war is a primarily human endeavor, so those who are interested in war must understand humans. Simply put, the *JC-HAMO* was an official way of saying, *rather than bomb your way to persuading a population to act, find the leader, figure out their culture, communicate with them in a way that is culturally persuasive, and let them in turn communicate to others, and then see what other actions are possible.* However, it never separated words from images or actions—on the contrary, it worked very hard to unite words, deeds, and images, saying that we could not effectively maneuver in any human endeavor without utilizing all three. This spoke to me on a deep level, confirming my instinct that persuasion was multilayered, living in actions as much as how they were framed, captured, and disseminated. I felt more strongly than ever that to be of value to operations, rhetoric must advance our methods to be able to account for human action, not just processes and texts. It also gave me a point of intersection more solid than persuasion: humanity. War is a human endeavor. It is about beliefs and family, food and resources. No one could ever again tell me that rhetoric was a very different thing than operations, for we both were concerned with humans, and with how humans make sense of and advance their world. War is engaged in that very task just as much as a university is, no matter how vastly our political differences may say otherwise.

I was shocked when the head editor of the *JC-HAMO* incorporated many of my editing suggestions. I had gained a glimpse of my people—people who knew persuasion, humans, and operations. The UF2 asked me to come back and talk again, and this time an army soldier who had been deeply involved in the conceptual forming of the *JC-HAMO* asked me to contact him. His work focused on narrative, and I was delighted to hear that he used all the same concepts as rhetoric, even though he called them something else.[3] He connected me with an organization within the Pentagon, the Strategic Multilayer Assessment (SMA) group, who worked for the joint chiefs of staff, operations. The SMA regularly brought academics and practitioners together to try and solve military problems, and they added me to their roster. I almost dropped the phone one day when a call came in from the Pentagon, asking me for my feedback on a concept the SMA was developing. Eighteen months of searching was starting to pay off, and I had become the bridge I had been seeking for between rhetoric and operations. Soon I was wargaming the effectiveness of Da'esh messaging, where analyzing the Blue Team's internal communications made me realize that operations and rhetoric experts have a lot of work to do still, even once we find each other. At least now, though, we can do it together.

EPILOGUE

From my position as an operational rhetorician, I leave you with the following words, penned by my mentor and his mentor, as they, too, wrestled with the rhet ops complexities you and I have and will continue to wrestle with.

> Finally, and perhaps most important, rhetoricians explore and explain how knowledge and power work, how they are created and circulated. We write about how institutions create and use knowledge and how power relations are reproduced or realigned in the process. As we go out into the field to do this sort of research, as we gather materials, analyze them, and build theory, we sometimes intervene in practice. Research in institutional sites such as LANL might be part of the "worldliness" that Hall (1989) described as the necessary complement to theoretical work, part of the move from "the clear air of meaning and textuality and theory to the something nasty down below."[4]

Those of us in operations know that it can be a place "nasty down below," but I, for one, say it is time that rhetoric dirtied its proverbial hands here, and operations welcomed the new perspectives. If my experience since bridging the chasms and reaching operations is any indicator, immersing rhetoric in operations creates an opportunity for increased relevance in complex times that demonstrate more than ever the need for rhet ops experts.

NOTES

The views presented in this chapter are those of the writer and do not necessarily represent the views of the US Department of Defense and its components.

1. I would later learn, too late to use on my dissertation research, of John Oddo's 2013 article in Written Communication, "Discourse-Based Methods across Texts and Semiotic Modes: Three Tools for MicroRhetorical Analysis." Oddo's work, published just the year before I needed it, would have given me the basic methods I needed to do my analysis, but I had not been exposed to his work, nor had any of my exhaustive searches returned it, which is a plight I credit partly to my field's use of differing terminology for similar concepts. However, for the results of that research to be valuable to operations, as a researcher, I would have to be working closely with operations experts to translate it into actionable knowledge.

2. Office of the Joint Chiefs of Staff, Joint Concept for Human Aspects of Military Operations.

3. Today we work for the same unit, though it would take two years from the time we met, and another instance of being at the right place at the right time for that to happen.

4. Herndl and Wilson, "Reflections on Field Research and Professional Practice."

REFERENCES

Herndl, Carl G., and Greg Wilson. "Commentary: Reflections on Field Research and Professional Practice." *Journal of Business and Technical Communication* 21, no. 2 (2007): 216–26. https://doi.org/10.1177/1050651906297171.

Joffe, H. "The Power of Visual Material: Persuasion, Emotion and Identification." *Diogenes* 55, no. 1 (2008): 84–93. https://doi.org/10.1177/0392192107087919.

Kendall, Elisabeth. "Jihadist Propaganda and Its Exploitation of the Arab Poetic Tradition." In *Reclaiming Islamic Tradition: Modern Interpretations of the Classical Heritage*, edited by Elisabeth Kendall and Ahmad Khan. Edinburgh: Edinburgh University Press, 2016.

Lemieux, A., and R. Nill. "The Role and Impact of Music in Promoting (and Countering) Violent Extremism." Strategic Multilayer Assessment White Paper Series. 2001.

Mallory, A., and D. Downs. "Uniform Meets Rhetoric: Excellence through Interaction." In *Generation Vet: Composition, Student Veterans, and the Post-9/11 University*, edited by Sue Doe and Lisa Langstraat. Logan: Utah State University Press, 2014. https://doi.org/10.7330/9780874219425.c002.

Office of the Joint Chiefs of Staff. *Counter-Da'esh Influence Operations: Cognitive Space Narrative Simulation Insights.* Washington, DC: Government Printing Office, 2016.

Office of the Joint Chiefs of Staff. *Joint Concept for Human Aspects of Military Operations.* Washington DC: Government Printing Office, 2016.

14

SOCIAL MEDIA STRATEGY FOR THE MILITARY-ENGAGED AMERICAN RED CROSS

LAURA A. EWING

I joined the American Red Cross Service to the Armed Forces (SAF) in 2015 while living in Okinawa, Japan. Coming from a background in academia, I now had to switch gears into nonprofit operations and policies. Organizational culture, mission requirements, funding, and the necessary adherence to an approved memorandum of understanding (MOU) with the Department of Defense (DoD) dictated the actions of our SAF station. Understandably, these factors also created the tendency to avoid massive change in practices. Upon returning to the United States in the summer of 2017, I was invited to become the strategic communications advisor to the vice president of Service to Armed Forces for a one year term. This role came with a rather specific charge: provide recommendations for a social media strategy for the American Red Cross SAF mission—what I consider a large-scale change to current practice on the ground.

In what follows, I will provide my approach to this task and address the following questions: (1) why should nonprofit organizations be concerned with current scholarship in social media implementation; (2) is it possible to create a single, unified strategy for the varied needs of SAF; and (3) how does the American Red Cross SAF acknowledge that staff and volunteers are in place as civilians, while still maintaining trust with the DoD and local military authorities? My task is met with a variety of obstacles including concerns from the communication teams regarding the inability to control messages, and the necessity to maintain operations security (OPSEC) specifically when dealing with Red Cross stations operating on American military bases overseas.

NONPROFIT SOCIAL MEDIA USE

To address my first obstacle and best convey to my colleagues the useful nature of social media, I called on current scholarship in the academic field. In many professional settings, but especially the nonprofit sector, there is often push back on social media, as communication professionals are concerned with the inability to control postings. This concern is completely understandable as these organizations need to maintain a positive, trusting reputation within the community to encourage support and giving.

Current research, however, points to an ever-increasing portion of the public receiving its information from social media outlets. According to the Pew Research Center, 67 percent of Americans receive some of their news from social media, while 20 percent do so frequently. The same report also pointed to an increase in Americans over the age of fifty receiving news from various social media platforms—55 percent in 2017 over 45 percent in 2016.[1]

While these numbers are encouraging to those already confident working with social media, they do little to allay those who are fearful of losing control over their organization's messaging. Social media offers users the opportunity to converse with an organization in real time but also opens the door for messaging errors and unwarranted criticism.[2] But with communication consistently trending toward online interactions, social media managers must use these platforms to their best abilities while acknowledging the potential for risk.

In the process of creating my strategies, it became apparent early that while nonprofit organizations (NPOs) have specific concerns that differ from their for-profit counterparts, many elements of the approach to social media strategies are similar. For example, both organization types operate within the parameters of their stakeholders; a business may find itself beholden to investors, while a nonprofit may need to appease board members. For-profit investors may look to financial return on investment the same way nonprofit stakeholders are concerned about seeing social impact demonstrated.[34]

OVERSIGHT OF SOCIAL MEDIA USE

A factor influencing concern over social media is the difficulty posed in gauging how well postings demonstrate social impact and actually reach a desired audience.[5] While metrics, like those available through Facebook, offer some insight into page views and visits, the large-scale impact can involve a bit of guesswork. For this reason, dialogue between an organization and social media users becomes increasingly important when determining if a message is being received.[67] Staff and volunteers on the NPO side, then, need to be trusted, with appropriate training and oversight to appropriately engage with users and provide clear and correct messages.

If the NPO is to trust those in its organization to take this role, it is imperative that oversight structures be put in place since a misphrased comment or inappropriate image risks severe damage to the organization's stakeholder relationships.[8] At an American Red Cross SAF station these structures need to be clearly dictated since volunteers, due their military association, turn over every two to four years, and mobile staff may only be on site for three years. It may seem obvious that such structures be put in place, or even that those presenting the information be already checking their comments, but a clear procedure on how to respond to a user and what information to post maintains the credibility of the NPO online and may reduce professional concerns. Providing resources that maintain consistent messaging assists those managing the online presence by providing easy access to accurate information.

SOCIAL MEDIA STRATEGY AND OPSEC CONCERNS

The mission of American Red Cross chapters in the United States differs slightly from that of SAF stations overseas. Local chapters and US-based programs that most Americans are familiar with include—but are not limited to—disaster assistance, biomedical services (blood donations), and health and safety education (e.g., CPR and first aid training), among other local programs. SAF, whose mission hails from that of the original American Red Cross established in 1881, "serves as a critical line of communication between the U.S Armed Forces and their families."[9] SAF stations in the United States and abroad utilize large components of volunteer staff made up of military, retirees, and dependents, and offer services ranging from emergency communication messages between active duty members and family at home to workshops helping families deal with deployment scenarios. During my time in Okinawa, I witnessed the Red Cross participating in military exercises, managing professional development training for military spouses, and hosting family-friendly events to engage the community.

Since SAF stations operate on military installations and in accordance with a DoD memorandum of understanding, the importance of adhering to military policies and structures is paramount. In the area of communication, this is most clearly seen in the need to uphold OPSEC procedures. The US Air Force defines OPSEC as "a process of identifying, analyzing and controlling critical information indicating friendly actions associated with military operations and other activities."[10] Translated for daily use, this usually means taking care to not share troop movements, deployment locations, training exercise plans, and other details that may hinder the effectiveness and safety of a military operation. Active duty members are routinely given training in OPSEC to avoid providing the enemy with information regarding how the US military fights or gives indicators about upcoming operations, but in many cases civilian dependents lack this guidance. With individuals interacting with our SAF station on a daily basis, staff and leadership volunteers were concerned with the type of information being disseminated online. Volunteers, both active duty and civilian, took great pride in their work with the nonprofit, and were quick to share their actions online. Additionally, the station itself frequently employed social media to market its offerings to the base community, resulting in a highly active social media presence.

CREATING THE STRATEGY

In creating an effective strategy, I needed to be concerned with a variety of factors. SAF stations work with a varied population of active duty military members, dependent families, retirees, and government civilians. On top of this, those populations may reside in the United States or on installations abroad. SAF stations worldwide do not have a unified social media strategy; each station has its own Facebook, Twitter, Instagram, etc., as well as its own locally created and managed web presence. Red Cross national headquarters provided social media tools to stations, but they were very basic. A quick overview showed that some stations use social media to a large extent, including posting volunteer and education opportunities and accounts of events conducted by the station. Other SAF stations, meanwhile, barely used social media at all. These factors create a situation where a one-size-fits-all approach to social media implementation is ineffective. As such, concern with being too prescriptive in social media use was a definite concern.

As demographics differ considerably between stations, the communication needs differ as well. For example, a post located in the United States may cater to a large number of retirees and their families, for whom social media is not effective. Meanwhile, an overseas station will serve active duty and their families, many in their twenties and thirties, and find social media to be the easiest way to reach a large community. Since building a script for all stations is not effective, the communication team provides guidelines and templates they can pull from, referred to as the "Hero Care Tool Kit." However, two distinct problems existed with the current tool kit: (1) there were no recommendations for when and how to effectively engage social media to ensure the American Red Cross SAF mission was appropriately represented, and (2) there was no guidance to assist stations, especially those overseas, in understanding and adhering to DoD rules regarding operations security. Since unifying stations under a single strategy is not possible, the best option was to instead support and not overwhelm the staff on the ground with too much information.

PROBLEM SCENARIO

From 2015 to 2017 I was a leadership volunteer at the Red Cross Kadena Station in Okinawa, Japan. I held the role of station chair, partnering with the regional program manager to oversee all station activities. One of two large stations on the island, Kadena Station provided support to a population of approximately 31,000 active duty military members; DoD civilians; DoD contractors, retirees, and dependents; and over the course of fiscal year 2016, our station engaged 318 volunteers in various activities. While working from home one day, I noticed a flurry of posts to our station's Facebook page from volunteers who were acting as "patients" during an exercise at the base medical facility. The images showed, in real time, the actions of the exercise, the location of personnel, and indicated the kind of emergency the active duty members were preparing to encounter. These images were a potential violation of OPSEC policies and were quickly removed from the page by Red Cross staff.

The following day, I spoke to a volunteer regarding the images. She stated that she had been given permission to take pictures by the officer leading the volunteers; however, a time line for posting the images was not discussed. Being a civilian dependent, she was largely unaware of the OPSEC policies and how they impacted her choices regarding what to post on Facebook. When I asked the opinion of the officer who granted permission, he informed me that his unit's typical time frame for posting such images was twenty-four hours after the exercise's conclusion—a time frame volunteers were not aware of. Unknowingly, the volunteers, who were very excited about their role and thrilled to be trusted with these duties, had potentially violated OPSEC guidelines.

SAF STATION SOLUTION

Thankfully, the aforementioned scenario was a very small infraction and did not damage the relationship between the Red Cross station and Kadena Air Base. Air Force guidance on social media was shared with volunteers, and the following month's station advisory council meeting included OPSEC training. The station staff implemented policies to avoid confusion in the future. Before participating in base events, volunteers were reminded to not post pictures of active duty members in uniform without express permission, and images from all exercises required permission from military counterparts and a twenty-four-hour waiting period

MOVING FORWARD AND MAINTAINING TRUST

The scenario at Kadena Station demonstrated a gap in social media training for Red Cross volunteers. Taking on the role of strategic communication advisor at Red Cross National Headquarters, I faced this question of how to develop a plan that advocated the mission of the American Red Cross SAF while maintaining OPSEC and respecting our trusted relationship with the DoD. When developing guidelines for SAF stations, it is not enough to simply provide a definition of OPSEC—rather, a social media toolkit must include plain language descriptions of DoD, Air Force, army, navy, and Marine Corps communication policies. Access to social media policies from all branches, documents which are publicly available, should be provided to those conducting online communication for the American Red Cross SAF.

In line with maintaining the trust of our military counterparts, the Red Cross needs to also demonstrate a clear and focused mission statement for communication personnel working for the stations. Without being prescriptive, a social media tool kit provided by the American Red Cross National Headquarters needs to include language that defines the role of the Red Cross SAF and answers common questions and concerns regarding the organization on military bases (i.e., the difference between a station's response to a disaster versus a US-based chapter's response). Stating the mission of the American Red Cross SAF in all public online spaces provides stakeholders with a clear indication of the organization's impact. Finally, as the tool kit is developed further, it will be necessary to create documents explaining social media policies (those of both the Red Cross and the DoD) and offering Red Cross staff and volunteers links to acquire more info, contacts for questions, etc.

The new social media tool kit for the American Red Cross SAF was in development as of 2018. In working with the communication team, I encountered reluctance to present too much information as stations may view it as overly prescriptive. Since my personal experience matches current concerns at the DoD, I recommended military documentation and the MOU to support my push for further social media guidance. As the nonprofit sector continues to produce data on effective social media use, it is imperative that large organizations like the American Red Cross take these findings into account.

The tool kit itself needs to meet the needs of the staff and volunteers in the SAF stations. At a busy station like Kadena, there is minimal time for detailed training, and much of it is done on an individual basis. With this in mind, tools need to be quickly digestible and provide simple explanations with links to further knowledge as needed. This format also leaves guidelines open to the individual needs of each station. To assist in oversight, a tool kit should provide guidance on how to address common user questions and where to seek assistance if unsure of how to proceed with a question or request. These tools may also provide tips on how to stay on topic and not impose personal views on the station's social media platforms. Over time, tools can be reevaluated in accordance with Red Cross and DoD policy, and situational changes at the station level.

CONCLUSION

The three questions addressed in this task need to be done so concurrently, with stakeholder engagement at the forefront of the social media strategy. The mission of the American Red Cross SAF is straightforward, but risks being misconstrued, and ensuring consistent messaging is an ongoing struggle in such a large organization. My sense is that strong tools can assist in detracting from errors on the part of American Red Cross staff and volunteers, and impart a culture of communication oversight. The tool kit, while not foolproof, will show over time where gaps remain. As stations follow American Red Cross and DoD guidelines, questions can come back to national headquarters and situational concerns can be addressed. Additionally, demonstrating active oversight also serves to maintain a trusted relationship with the DoD.

The role of strategic communication advisor pulled me into the duties of social media strategist. The tasks I encounter in this role taught me quickly the importance of engaging with varied stakeholders and recognizing their differing concerns. The role imparted on me the necessity of remaining informed of current scholarship in the field of NPO social media usage, as well as the ongoing changes to policies that impact an organization's ability to demonstrate social impact.

NOTES

1. Shearer and Gottfried, "News Use across Social Media Platforms."
2. Bowdon, "Tweeting an Ethos."
3. Guo and Saxton, "Tweeting Social Change."
4. Arvidson and Lyon, "Social Impact Measurement and Non-Profit Organisations."
5. Goldkind, "Social Media and Social Service."
6. Go and You, "But Not All Social Media Are the Same."
7. Guo and Saxton, "Tweeting Social Change."
8. Turley, "High (Risk) Society."
9. American Red Cross, "Service to the Armed Forces."
10. US Air Force, *Operations Security*.

REFERENCES

American Red Cross. "Service to the Armed Forces." 2017. http://www.redcross.org/local/washington-dc/programs-services/military-families-services.

Arvidson, Malin, and Fergus Lyon. "Social Impact Measurement and Non-Profit Organisations: Compliance, Resistance, and Promotion." *VOLUNTAS: International Journal of Voluntary and Nonprofit Organizations* 25, no. 4 (2013): 869–86. doi:10.1007/s11266-013-9373-6.

Bowdon, Melody A. "Tweeting an Ethos: Emergency Messaging, Social Media, and Teaching Technical Communication." *Technical Communication Quarterly* 23, no. 1 (2013): 35–54. doi:10.1080/10572252.2014.850853.

Go, Eun, and Kyung Han You. "But Not All Social Media Are the Same: Analyzing Organizations' Social Media Usage Patterns." *Telematics and Informatics* 33, no. 1 (2016): 176–86. https://doi.org/10.1016/j.tele.2015.06.016.

Goldkind, Lauri. "Social Media and Social Service: Are Nonprofits Plugged In to the Digital Age?" *Human Service Organizations: Management, Leadership & Governance* 39, no. 4 (2015): 380–96. doi:10.1080/23303131.2015.1053585.

Guo, Chao, and Gregory D. Saxton. "Tweeting Social Change." *Nonprofit and Voluntary Sector Quarterly* 43, no. 1 (2013): 57–79. doi:10.1177/0899764012471585.

Shearer, Elisa, and Jeffrey Gottfried. "News Use across Social Media Platforms 2017." Pew Research Center, September 7, 2017. http://www.journalism.org/2017/09/07/news-use-across-social-media-platforms-2017/.

Turley, Susan. "High (Risk) Society: Easing the Anxiety for Institutional Clients." *Air Force Law Review* 43 (2013): 44–72.

US Air Force. *Operations Security (OPSEC): USAF AFI 10–701.* June 1, 2012. http://static.e-publishing.af.mil/production/1/afgsc/publication/afi10-701_afgscsup_i/afi10-701_afgscsup_i.dpdf.

15

CHANGING TECHNOLOGIES AND WRITING FROM AND ABOUT WAR

D. ALEXIS HART AND CHERYL HATCH

Rhetoric, whether discursive or visual, has real power in the way events play out.

—CORI E. DAUBER

Writing for the *Seattle Times* in 2008, the reporter Chris Tomlinson noted that "wars have often been defined by the new technologies that shaped them," and went on to list technologies that have fundamentally changed reporting from and about war: photography in the Civil War, newsreels in World War II, television in the Vietnam War, and satellite broadcasting in the first Gulf War. Unlike these other technologies, however, twenty-first-century digital technologies have "done more than quicken reporting from the battlefield; [they have] made war interactive."[1] In other words, technologies available not only to journalists but also to military members themselves have rhetorically reframed war reporting and the public's reception and engagement with war. Web 2.0 technologies, as well as email and blogs, now offer the public unfettered access to more diverse texts and a wider range of perspectives regarding military engagements and the experiences of being at or in war than in previous periods of conflict. Indeed, in modern warfare, anyone with a smartphone can quickly distribute details about military missions through unfiltered and unedited texts, images, and videos, unlike in past wars, when communications from military personnel could be more strictly controlled and daily communication from the war zone was typically limited to professional journalists.

During war, in addition to the fight to achieve the military objective, there is also a fight to control public opinion. As Andrew Hoskins and Ben O'Loughlin write in the introduction to *War and Media*, "The mediatization of war matters because perceptions are vital to war—the perceptions of a public who can offer support to a war, of government trying to justify a war, and of those in the military themselves, who are trying to perceive and understand exactly what is happening as war is waged. It is through media that perceptions are created, sustained, or challenged."[2] With each advance in technology, the manner and speed by which the media reports from war shifts. In this chapter, the authors—one a navy veteran and writing studies teacher-scholar, the other a former war correspondent and current photojournalist and educator—trace these shifts in technology and access to the battlefield through a combination of rhetorical analysis, personal narrative, and practitioner accounts from Sonja Pace, Nick Utt, and Larry James. Our analysis begins with the Vietnam War, continues through the first Gulf War and Somalia, and ends with the post–9/11 Global War on Terrorism (GWOT).

THE VIETNAM WAR

The Vietnam War is often described as the first "living room war" since civilians no longer had to go to the cinema to watch the official newsreels but could view nightly updates on the television in the comfort of their own homes. These nightly newscasts were watched with particular attentiveness by family members of military personnel, in part because they offered the tantalizing promise of seeing absent loved ones, whose personal communication technologies were much slower to arrive.

Cheryl Hatch, Childhood

I am a military brat and the daughter of a career officer who served thirty years in the US Army, including two tours in Vietnam.

As a child, I grew up with the Vietnam War. The images and stories from the war have stayed with me. They likely shaped my choice of profession as a journalist, who for nearly a decade covered conflict in the Middle East and Africa.

I was five years old when he served his first tour. I don't remember much of my life or his absence that time.

I was in second grade when my father deployed the second time. I remember plenty from that deployment.

I remember watching the news broadcast every night on our small black-and-white television set. I watched the photos play across the screen and scanned the faces of the soldiers, hoping to catch a glimpse of my father. I dreaded the possibility that I'd find his face among the dead.

The TV broadcasts offered the most immediate news. I'd have to wait weeks for a handwritten letter from my father. I remember that I wanted a puppy and my mother told me I had to ask my father. I wrote him a letter and told him I'd saved my allowance and I had $5 to get a puppy at the shelter. Weeks later, my father's response arrived. He wrote that I could get a puppy if I promised to take care of it, feed it, and walk it. He said my mom had a lot to do since he was away and I would need to help her.

The real treat was the day a tiny yellow box would arrive in the mail. These were rare events and special occasions. We'd race to my mother's bedroom and gather on her bed to listen to the reel-to-reel message Dad had taped for us. We'd hear our father's voice as he spoke to each one of us. He'd tell us to be good and help our mother. And then he'd say he was going to talk to Mommy and we'd leave our mother alone with my father's recorded message from distant Vietnam.

One of the most compelling aspects of televised coverage of the Vietnam War was the proliferation of images from the combat zone. As Hoskins and O'Loughlin explain, "The image has a special status in the study of warfare. . . . As a tool of persuasion and, indeed, revelation or exposure of truth . . . [the] visual is taken as instrumental to the maintenance or loss of public and political support for military interventions and campaigns."[3] The rhetorical power of visuals was not confined to moving pictures, however. Still images significantly impacted public understanding of and support for the war, as well.

Practitioner Story: Nick Ut[4]

On July 20, 2017, Cheryl interviewed her former Associated Press (AP) colleague and Pulitzer Prize–winning photographer, Nick Ut, by phone at home in Los Angeles, just months after he retired from the AP after fifty-one years. They talked about the photo that's come to be known as "Napalm Girl."

Ut said it was easy to get to the war. He'd go by car with a driver from the AP office in Saigon. He took "The Terror of War" photograph in the village of Trảng Bàng, twenty-five miles southwest of Saigon; a twenty-minute drive.

"Nobody moved the picture," Ut said, explaining that some had expressed a concern about running a photo of a naked girl.

"Oh my god, who took this picture," Ut said, recalling what his photo editor, Horst Faas, had asked: "Nicky, what happened?"

Ut explained the fighting and the people fleeing the napalm strike. The AP sent ten photos, and Faas fought to have the AP publish the photo of Phuc.

They sent the photo to Tokyo then on to New York.

"We sent it as a radio photo," Ut said. Since it was a black-and-white image, it took only ten minutes to transmit. "Fifty years ago transmission was not like today."

It could take two hours or more to transmit one image.

Access to the war was also dramatically different in the Vietnam era of media coverage.

"In Vietnam, it was so easy. We were so welcome," Ut said about covering the war. "You go everywhere you want. They wanted media then."

FIGURE 15.1 South Vietnamese forces follow after terrified children, including nine-year-old Phan Thi Kim Phùc, center, as they run down Route 1 near Trang Bang after an aerial napalm attack on suspected Viet Cong hiding places on June 8, 1972. The children from left to right are: Phan Thanh Tam, Phan Thanh Phouc, Kim Phùc, Ho Van Bon, and Ho Thi Ting. Behind them are soldiers of the Vietnam Army 25th Division. Credit: Nick Ut/Associated Press.

> "In Vietnam, you could shoot pictures of dead bodies. You could talk to anybody you want. We showed them the war. Wounded. Dead. No one stopped us."
>
> "They show you everything. You're free," Ut said. "We sleep at camp with Marines and soldiers. We stand by in lounge. They welcome media."
>
> Ut said after the Vietnam War, the government never allowed the media the same freedom or access to the military or the battles.

Media scholars concur with Ut's claim. As Philip Seib explains, "War coverage has always involved considerable tension between the press and the military. The erroneous but still widely held notion that news coverage was a key factor in the loss of the Vietnam War led to increasingly restrictive coverage rules imposed by the Pentagon in conflicts such as the Persian Gulf War of 1991."[5]

THE FIRST GULF WAR

On June 1, 1980, Ted Turner launched the Cable News Network (CNN), a media company based on a bold idea: news available around the clock. He intended to challenge the model of the three major networks and their hold on news coverage with their nightly broadcasts and morning shows. CNN heralded the era of the 24/7 news cycle, irrevocably changing the media landscape and the traditional approach to and pace of coverage.

In August 1990 Saddam Hussein sent the Iraqi army into Kuwait. During the coverage of the buildup to the Gulf War in the fall of 1990, CNN dispatched its news teams to major cities in the Middle East, broadcasting from Riyadh and Dhahran, Saudi Arabia; Amman, Jordan; Cairo, Egypt; the Suez Canal; Jerusalem; and Baghdad, Iraq.

On January 17, 1991, when the US military started dropping bombs on Baghdad, the CNN news team made broadcast history when they transmitted a live report of the US attack from the Al-Rasheed Hotel. Twenty-five years later, Ingrid Formanek recalled the moment this way: "'Something's happening outside . . . the skies over Baghdad have been illuminated,' CNN anchor Bernie Shaw urgently intoned over the 4 WIRE."[6]

While the American public could tune in nightly to television coverage of the Vietnam War, live images of the first Gulf War could be accessed at any time on the twenty-four-hour news channels, adding to an illusion of "access" to news about the war. However, many of the images that audiences saw were Pentagon-produced videos. As Torie Rose Deghett of the *Atlantic* points out, "some of the most widely seen images of the air war were shot not by photographers, but rather by unmanned cameras attached to planes and laser-guided bombs. . . . The images were taken at an altitude that erased the human presence on the ground," resulting in what Deghett refers to as a "'video-game war'—a conflict made humane through precision bombing and night-vision equipment."[7]

Images were not the only "scripted" aspects of the reporting coming from the war. According to Shahir Fahmy and Thomas Johnson, "Coverage of the Persian Gulf War in 1991 was tightly controlled through censorship, pool reporting, and press conferences 'bleached of meaningful content.' . . . Military officers accompanied pool reporters and reviewed stories for sensitive information. Much of the press information on the war came from frequent military briefings."[8] Despite these restrictions, journalists persisted in following their professional imperative to "be there" and report from the scene.

Practitioner Story: Sonja Pace[9]

On Sunday, September 24, 2017, Cheryl interviewed the retired radio journalist Sonja Pace at her home in Washington, DC.

In the run-up to the ground war in Kuwait and Iraq, access to the story was limited.

"The US military had learned their lesson in Vietnam," Pace said. "Your best bet is to control the message."

In order to do so, the military offered briefings at the Pentagon and at hotels in Riyadh and Dhahran, Saudi Arabia.

Journalists could participate in pool coverage or embed with troops or take their chances and travel with the Arab coalition forces. If journalists traveled with the coalition troops, they were in Kuwait for ten days to two weeks.

"Very dicey," Pace said, of the security of traveling with coalition troops. Journalists were also hampered by poor communications, both access to technology and language skills. "You were stymied if you didn't speak Arabic."

Shortly before the ground war began, Pace participated in pool coverage. She spent four days on an aircraft carrier in the Red Sea, where she could interview pilots, the commander, and sailors.

Despite the access to the fighting forces, Pace had no way to transmit her stories. She had to ship cassette tapes to the mainland.

"Most of my cassettes never arrived," Pace said, of her collection of tapes that contained her interviews and natural sound from her days reporting on board. The compact cassettes she used for her sound were the same used for recording music in the 1990s. She said she has no idea or proof why her cassettes didn't make it back to land. With this older technology, delayed, misplaced, or lost tapes or film meant lost reporting.

SOMALIA

As in Iraq at the beginning of the first Gulf War, news reporters were already on the ground in Somalia when US troops landed on the beach in support of the humanitarian mission dubbed Operation Restore Hope.

Cheryl Hatch, Early Journalism Career

Nearly two years after CNN's historic broadcast from Baghdad, I was on the beach near the airport at Mogadishu, Somalia, in the predawn hours of December 9, 1992.

Some reporters asserted they'd been told the date and time of the landing. I had not. I listened to the rumors and made my best guess. A few reporters went to the port; however, most dispersed in the dark along the strip of sand between the Indian Ocean and the airport.

I was alone. I had sneaked across the tarmac earlier in the evening, about 10 p.m., and I planned to camp on the beach and wait for the arrival of US forces. I'd carried my camera gear, notebooks, some water, and two grapefruits. I was afraid Somali bandits might discover me.

Disembarking from Zodiac launches, the first troops arrived wearing camouflage face paint and night-vision goggles. TV cameramen turned on their white-hot lights and trained their lenses on the navy special operation forces and Marines, temporarily blinding the troops and revealing their position. As the forces attempted to establish a perimeter, a gaggle of international journalists surrounded them.

More than once, a Marine yelled, "Kill the lights." A French journalist replied, "Fuck you." Eventually, an officer came to the beach and held an impromptu press conference, informing the journalists that we were delaying their landing. For our safety, we needed to leave the landing area and report from the far ends of the beaches. No one complied.

CNN broadcast a live feed of the landing.

As an independent journalist, I did not have a satellite phone or the means to transmit my photos and story. I returned to Nairobi to ship my film to my agency in Paris and filed my story by telex before returning to Somalia to continue my coverage.

When I traveled, I had no way to communicate regularly with my agency in Paris or my family in the United States. When I went to Somalia, I told them I'd be in country about three weeks and I'd contact them, usually by telex or phone, when I returned to Nairobi.

I remember my brother discovered my whereabouts by chance after the troops deployed on the beach on December 9, 1992. He said he was in a 7–Eleven late one night when he saw a photo on the front page of the *News & Observer* (Greensboro, NC) that featured the troops, lit by a flash, coming ashore. In the background, there was a woman photographer in khaki trousers and white T-shirt with her hair tied back with a red bandana. My brother recognized my travel attire. He called my parents and let them know I was okay.

A couple of weeks later, I was in Baidoa, in central Somalia, covering the unrelenting death and disease as the famine raged unabated. The US military was slow organizing the logistics and safety protocols needed for the humanitarian convoys that would carry food and supplies to the interior. It was Christmastime and a radio reporter for CBS let me use his satellite dish to make a call home for the holiday. As I recall, the line cost approximately $25 a minute, and I spoke for a few minutes, grateful to have the opportunity to reassure my parents that I was well and safe and to hear their voices from half a world away.

Unlike the distant aerial images devoid of human presence that accompanied the start of the first Gulf War, the early reporting on the military operations in Somalia contained human-centered images "focused overwhelmingly on young American Marines with smiling Somali children."[10] However, the most well-known images from the Somali operations may be those of American military corpses being dragged through the streets of Mogadishu.[11]

As Cory Dauber argues, the United States did not cease the humanitarian operation in Somalia "because of what happened, but [they] pulled out because of the *photographs* of what happened. It is the reaction to the images, not the news of the event per se, which is represented as having raised the ire of the nation."[12] Once again, as in Vietnam, when human suffering and casualties became the visual rhetoric suffusing the American public's consciousness, the public's support for (or ambivalence toward) the operation turned into public outrage that impacted military policy.

IRAQ AND AFGHANISTAN

Mindful of the criticism resulting from the use of reporting pools during the first Gulf War and in order "to avoid a head-on collision with the news media, the Pentagon devised the embedded journalist program for use in Iraq."[13] These embedded reporters were attached to military units and accompanied them on their missions. As a result, "viewers at home enjoyed privileged access to action from the front line on an unprecedented scale."[14] Cheryl was one of those embedded reporters.

Cheryl Hatch, Embedded Reporting

In 2010 I was teaching journalism at the University of Alaska Fairbanks as the Snedden Chair. As a class project, we began documenting the soldiers and their families at the neighboring military base, Fort Wainwright, as the 1/25 Stryker Brigade prepared for deployment to Afghanistan. After following them for the entire academic year, they invited us to continue our coverage downrange, with the 1st Battalion 5th Infantry Regiment in Kandahar Province.

I embedded with the 1–5 for one month with the photographer J. R. Ancheta from December 2011 through January 2012. Our focus was following the troops over the holiday season. I returned from February through March 2012 to continue my coverage for the *Christian Science Monitor* on a piece about the female soldiers.

When I agreed to embed, I signed a pile of documents, well over an inch thick. The paperwork outlined the rules of engagement, including policies for photographing and reporting on those killed in action. I was also required to have insurance that would cover the costs of my medical expenses and evacuation, in the event of an injury or death. The army would provide immediate medical care in theater and then it would send me a bill.

In my entire career, I had never done an embed. I had maintained my independence. In my opinion, embedding with the military is fraught with ethical

Figure 15.2 Spc. Malecia James, twenty-five, from Jamaica, New York, kneels and lowers her rifle to speak to Afghan children during a two-day air assault joint mission of American and Afghan National Army soldiers in Molla Dust, Kandahar Province, Afghanistan, on December 28, 2011. Reproduced by permission from Cheryl Hatch.

challenges; and yet, it has become the only way to have direct access to the troops and document their lives and missions.

An embed offers 24/7 access to the soldiers' lives. We ate with them, went on patrols and an air assault mission, and spent downtime with them. It was both a blessing and a curse as a journalist.

After patrols, soldiers would sit around talking and smoking cigarettes. I remember young men would tell me about their wives and girlfriends. They trusted me. I realized they might forget that I was a reporter, although many times I was simply listening as a human being, as a woman.

I discovered the boundaries blurred between work and personal space, between a reporter's interview and a casual conversation.

I eventually made my own decision regarding boundaries. Perhaps it was my own military background that influenced my decision. On smoke breaks after a patrol, I let the soldiers know that if they didn't see my notebook and pen, we weren't on the record.

Often I would file my stories in the Morale Welfare Recreation (MWR)

> center, which was a cold, mud-brick building at Forward Operating Base Shoja. Ancheta and I never wanted to preempt the time the soldiers had to communicate with their families, so I would frequently find myself typing on a computer in the middle of the night, my face lit by the glow from the screen, my fingernails blue, and my breath visible in the frigid air.
>
> There were approximately twelve computers and four landlines. Soldiers could call home when they returned from a patrol or early in the morning before they reported for duty. They could chat in real time on Facebook. There was no privacy in the room. We could all hear each other's conversations.
>
> As a soldier's daughter, I recognized and deeply felt that those exchanges between loved ones were intimate and private conversation. Even though there was no privacy in the MWR, I felt it was a sacred place, a sanctuary. I made my own rule, enforced my own ethical boundary: I would not use anything I overhead in the MWR without permission. If I heard something interesting or important, I would make a note and then ask the soldier later, outside the MWR.
>
> It was a difficult decision. A decision another journalist might not have made.
>
> The embed allowed me to share stories from the front lines with soldiers' families on the other side of the globe. And that embed remained a delicate, ethical balancing act.

As Cheryl's experience shows, unlike in the 1990s, when the cost of satellite phone calls and limited access to email restricted journalists' professional and personal communications, "the 2003 War in Iraq was the first war to emerge in the electronic informational space as a fully coordinated 'media spectacle,' complete with embedded reporters, interactive Websites, and 3D models and maps all at the ready."[15] In addition, "the enthusiasm over using the Internet to communicate War information was not limited to large news corporations; citizen journalists, independent news Websites, bloggers, and online commentators of every variety entered into the emerging infosphere."[16] Even the US military allowed deployed service members to create and publish blogs, which eventually became referred to as "milblogs." Military leaders such as Army Lieutenant General William Caldwell, the military's media spokesperson for the Multi-National Force–Iraq during Operation Iraqi Freedom, characterized these blog posts as being "100% real and personal. It isn't messaged. That is the point . . . the American public wants to hear those stories so that they can connect with those who serve their country."[17] The milblogger Matthew Burden agrees that many service members used blogs to "chronicle their experiences" and "keep their families informed" but also suggests that since they had the same access to this online venue as journalists, they could also publish "expert on-the-ground accounts from the war zone."[18] In such an environment, the web ostensibly became "a space where news seekers could acquire and exchange helpful information from a wide variety of sources, all of which aided the public's ability to sift through the complexity of the War and better understand its intricacies."[19] These web spaces also enabled the public to respond and comment immediately, as well, adding yet another layer of complexity.

According to Tim Markham, these technological affordances "transformed the journalist's experience of conflict . . . more than embedding, pooling and other strategies for managing journalists' access to and movement around war zones."[20] Markham also notes that "the changes wrought by new technologies can also be understood in a specifically corporeal way. First, and most obviously, the mobility of journalistic hardware changes the manner in which war reporting is lived as a body: devices are worn, rather than the body addressing itself to larger pieces of equipment that are either immovable or transported mechanically."[21] Such was the experience of the radio and print journalist Larry James.

Practitioner Story: Larry James[22]

On Sunday, September 24, 2017, Cheryl interviewed the retired Voice of America (VOA) journalist Larry James in his home in Washington, DC.

In 1990 James and I literally crossed paths in Liberia. After three weeks of travel documenting the civil war, I was leaving the country to carry out my film and ship it to Paris from Abidjan, Ivory Coast. James was on his way into the country, carrying a bulky satellite ground station so he could file reports in real time from the field. The dish was three meters in diameter and had to be bolted in place.

When James set up VOA's office in Baghdad thirteen years later, he said the differences in technology were "like night and day."

"Everything would easily fit into a bag going over your shoulder," James said.

It was the miniaturization of technology. He had a Broadband Global Area Network (BGAN) satellite system with what looked like a small umbrella. James said the satellite dish offered "instantaneous broadband audio, video, anything."

He remembered a writer/photographer who worked for the *Christian Science Monitor* filing a story. "He was talking to his photo editor in the United States, sending pictures and listening to a live feed NPR radio report."

CONCLUSION

As mobile technologies become more ubiquitous, the delivery speed quicker, and the quality of transmitted sounds and images sharper, more and more "reporting" is likely to be coming from "citizen journalists" who happen to be on the scene. For professional journalists reporting from war zones, the question becomes how to "deal with those new forms of 'unprofessional' war reporting via social media, because these reports are often subjective and do not rely on journalistic quality criteria."[23] In this new era of war, as David Patrikarakos points out, people are no longer "seeing the same footage, the same reality, produced by media organizations with professional journalists."[24] Instead, 'Twitter contain[s] more up-to-date information than the *New York Times* or NBC.'[25] For the American citizenry, the question may be how to apply their own quality controls as they are bombarded with increasing amounts of discursive and visual rhetoric from conflicts overseas and violent acts of terrorism here at home.

In the twenty-first century, while wars are still fought on the ground with personnel and weapons, these conflicts are rarely fought between major state actors or sovereign states. Instead, the enemies are more nebulous and, as Patrikarakos argues, "the narrative dimensions of war are arguably becoming more important than its physical dimensions."[26] In other words, control of the narrative, winning "the hearts and minds" of the people and recruiting more supporters—not decimating the other side's troops or capturing their territory—is often the larger objective, and in the twenty-first century the narrative of war is being delivered via social media and is "aimed at a global audience, as opposed to the 'enemy' population."[27] Thus, who controls the war narrative and how rhetorically savvy the audiences receiving the information are may matter more now than ever.

NOTES

1. Tomlinson, "In Iraq."

2. Hoskins and O'Loughlin, *War and Media*, 5.

3. Hoskins and O'Loughlin, 20.

4. Huỳnh Công "Nick" Út won both the 1973 Pulitzer Prize for Spot News Photography and the 1973 World Press Photo of the Year for "The Terror of War," a photograph of a naked nine-year-old girl, Phan Thị Kim Phúc, running after a South Vietnamese napalm attack on North Vietnamese troops in a village twenty-five miles southwest of Saigon.

5. Seib, *Beyond the Front Lines*, 30–31.

6. Formanek, "Operation Desert Storm."

7. Deghett, "The War Photo."

8. Fahmy and Johnson, "How We Performed," 302.

9. Sonja Pace began her career at Voice of America (VOA) in 1976, after completing graduate school at American University. In her thirty-eight-year career with VOA, she filed radio reports and managed foreign bureaus in Abidjan, Cairo, Jerusalem, Moscow, London, and Washington, DC.

10. Dauber, "Shots Seen 'Round the World," 665.

11. Selwyn-Holmes, "U.S. Soldier Dragged Through Mogadishu. "

12. Dauber, "Shots Seen 'Round the World," 667; emphasis in original.
13. Seib, *Beyond the Front Lines*, 30–31.
14. Gunter, "The Public and Media Coverage," 42.
15. Jordan, "Disciplining the Virtual Home Front," 276.
16. Jordan, 277.
17. Edwards and Hart, "A Soldier Interacting."
18. Burden, *Blog of War*, 4.
19. Jordan, "Disciplining the Virtual Home Front," 289.
20. Markham, *Politics of War Reporting*, 140.
21. Markham, 141.
22. Retired after thirty-six years as a radio and print journalist, Larry James has reported stories in more than fifty countries, often covering conflict. He worked at Voice of America for twenty-five years, at the Associated Press for three years, at Agence France-Presse for a year, and at other radio stations for several years.
23. Köberer and Sehr, "Telling About War," 97.
24. Illing, "War in 140 Characters."
25. Patrikarakos, *War in 140 Characters*, introduction, Kindle.
26. Patrikarakos, introduction, Kindle.
27. Patrikarakos, introduction, Kindle.

REFERENCES

Burden, Matthew. *The Blog of War: Front-Line Dispatches from Soldiers in Iraq and Afghanistan*. New York: Simon & Schuster, 2006.

Dauber, Cori E. "The Shots Seen 'Round the World: The Impact of the Images of Mogadishu on American Military Operations." *Rhetoric and Public Affairs* 4, no. 4 (2001): 653–87.

Deghett, Torie Rose. "The War Photo No One Would Publish." *Atlantic*, August 8, 2014. https://www.theatlantic.com/international/archive/2014/08/the-war-photo-no-one-would-publish/375762/.

Edwards, Mike, and D. Alexis Hart. "A Soldier Interacting, Without Mediation." *Kairos: A Journal of Rhetoric, Technology, and Pedagogy* 14, no. 3 (2010).

Fahmy, Shahira, and Thomas Johnson. "'How We Performed': Embedded Journalists' Attitudes and Perceptions Towards Covering the Iraq War." *Journalism and Mass Communication Quarterly* 82, no. 2 (2005): 301–17.

Formanek, Ingrid. "Operation Desert Storm: 25 Years On." CNN.com, January 19, 2016. https://www.cnn.com/2016/01/19/middleeast/operation-desert-storm-25-years-later/index.html.

Gunter, Barrie. "The Public and Media Coverage of the War on Iraq." *Globalizations* 6, no. 1 (2009): 41–60.

Hoskins, Andrew, and Ben O'Loughlin. *War and Media: The Emergence of Diffused War*. Malden, MA: Polity, 2010.

Illing, Sean. "War in 140 Characters." *Vox*, December 8, 2017. https://www.vox.com/world/2017/12/8/16690352/social-media-war-facebook-twitter-Russia.

Jordan, John. "Disciplining the Virtual Home Front: Mainstream News and the Web during the War in Iraq." *Communication and Critical/Cultural Studies* 4, no. 3 (2007): 276–302.

Köberer, Nina, and Marc Sehr. "Telling About War in the Digital Age: Media Ethical Reflections on New Forms of War Reporting and the Role of Recipients in New Communication Scenarios." In *Controversial Matters on Media Ethics*, edited by Luis Alfonso Guadarrama Rico, 91–111. Madrid: Dykinson, S. L., 2016.

Markham, Tim. *The Politics of War Reporting: Authority, Authenticity and Morality.* Manchester: Manchester University Press, 2012.

Patrikarakos, David. *War in 140 Characters: How Social Media is Reshaping Conflict in the Twenty-First Century.* New York: Basic Books, 2017. Kindle.

Seib, Philip. *Beyond the Front Lines: How the News Media Cover a World Shaped by War.* New York: Palgrave Macmillan, 2004.

Selwyn-Holmes, Alex. "U.S. Soldier Dragged Through Mogadishu. " Iconic Photos, March 10, 2010. https://iconicphotos.wordpress.com/2010/03/10/u-s-marine-dragged-through-mogadishu/.

Tomlinson, Chris. "In Iraq, Soldiers' Lives Are On the Line—and Online." *Seattle Times*, March 17, 2008. http://seattletimes.com/html/iraq/2004286903_iraqnet17.html.

16

MILITARY WIVES AS RHETORICAL INSURGENTS

RESISTING ASSIMILATION AS "FORCE MULTIPLIERS"

ELISE DIXON

At the 241st Marine Corps Birthday Ball for my husband's reserve unit, a speaker thanked all the military spouses in the room, stating that we "were truly force multipliers." I shifted uncomfortably in my chair and picked at the chicken on my plate; for years I have felt as if the Marine Corps treated spouses—wives especially—as free labor, both in terms of work and in birthing new potential legacy military members. What did this speaker mean by "force multipliers"? I mentioned my annoyance at the term to my husband's company commander, who suggested I should be honored by such a compliment as it meant that wives increased the Marines' overall efficiency as a force. As he spoke to me about this supposed honor, he slid his hand down over my backside before I could move away. The moment this marine violated me was the moment in which I knew—not just intellectually but viscerally—that the military sees me as government property, as less-than, as support staff, as a woman allowed into the military world as free aesthetic, reproductive, and service-oriented labor. Force multiplier indeed.

This chapter discusses the rhetorical strategies used by the military to assimilate military wives as *force multipliers*—a military term commonly referring to an attribute that can dramatically increase a group's efficacy, like weather, technology, or diplomacy. In response, wives have developed rhetorical tactics via online and print publications to work with and against this interpellation. Using Michel Foucault's concept of docile bodies and Michel de Certeau's conceptions of strategies and tactics, I argue that the characterization of the military wife as force multiplier is a rhetorical strategy used by the military-industrial complex to perpetuate the production and reproduction of military members by positioning wives as women whose main purpose is to support military careers. As a response, military wives co-opt and subvert these narratives by writing blogs, survival guides, Pinterest boards, and Facebook groups where they assert their own individual identities. Drawing on Helène Cixous's call for women to enact écriture feminine as a "new insurgent writing,"[1] I discuss the ways in which military wives enact what I term *rhetorical insurgency*—communication acts that subvert large ideological state apparatuses like the military—through the creation of these texts as a way to transgress the institution that seeks to assimilate them.

STRATEGIES OF ASSIMILATION

The US military could not function without the production of what Foucault calls "docile bodies" through disciplinary labor of military training. Military personnel are produced through training aimed at stripping their individuality in the interest of assimilating them as parts of a larger whole. Those in the United States with political power may pursue control over military members, "not only so that they may do what one wishes, but so that they may operate as one wishes, with the techniques, the speed, and the efficiency that one determines. Thus, discipline produces subjected and practiced bodies, 'docile' bodies."[2] This intention to assimilate personnel through discipline in order to continually reproduce the system enacts what de Certeau delineates as a *strategy*: "the calculation (or manipulation) of power relationships that becomes possible as soon as a subject with will and power (a business, an army, a city, a scientific institution) can be isolated. . . . It makes this knowledge possible and at the same time determines its characteristics. It produces itself in and through this knowledge."[3] Thus, the US military strategically produces itself and its own territories (and, consequently, any colonized territories won through military action) by the production of docile bodies enculturated by ideologies.

While docile bodies within the US military system comprise service members of all genders, the common cultural conception of military members is that they are male. In *Discipline and Punish* Foucault's discussion focuses nearly entirely on the discipline of the male body. Foucault's omission of women in his argument leads Bartky to ask, "Where is the account of the disciplinary practices that engender the 'docile bodies' of women, bodies more docile than the bodies of men?"[4] Indeed, to leave female bodies out of the discussion of the practices that subjugate individuals is to exclude an even more complex consideration of discipline. Furthermore, in the case of the military, it is important to consider how those connected to military personnel, particularly their spouses, are also implicated and disciplined for the same

FIGURE 16.1. Front cover of the *4th MCD's Resource Guide to Recruiting*

purposes of reproducing the system of power. Just as the military heavily relies on hypermasculinity to justify and legitimate the violence and force used against enemies, so too does the military rely on what Enloe refers to as the "feminized silence" of wives in order to allow such violence to continue to be justified.[5]

Many of the military wives I know were enculturated into the military system first through their marriages to military personnel. Friends who are or were military wives got married in their late teens or early twenties, and were then quickly whisked away to their spouse's duty station. In military spouse support groups, wives often discuss the isolation from the civilian world experienced on base. Many wives, myself included, have found themselves further alienated when their spouses are away for weeks or months at a time on deployment or for training. Enculturation into military life often occurs through sheer necessity: the need to connect with other wives either on base or digitally becomes imperative. Then, once wives are invested in the military system through marriage and socialization, the military also provides informational packets that assume, among other things, that the wife

FIGURE 16.2. Front cover of the Relocation Assistance Program brochure

"A DAY IN THE LIFE OF A MARINE CORPS RECRUITER"

Have you ever wondered what the day of a Recrutier looks like? The following article provides you with an example of what a typical day in the life of a recruiter might look like.

4:00 a.m. Hunter awoke to the sound of a local morning radio program as the disc jockey was telling his listeners about the rainy day outside. His wife Ann was already up and he could smell the aroma of frying bacon. Hunter shut off the clock radio (opportunity clock) and listened to the rain beating on the roof. Today would be tight, and he wanted to make the most of every minute.

4:10 a.m. "I hope the eggs aren't too hard," Ann said. She set the plate of bacon and eggs on the table and poured a cup of coffee. She yawned. "Do you feel like going back to bed?" Hunter asked. "You were up all night with the baby." Their two year-old-son had been awake all night, sick with the flu. "I may do just that," Ann responded. "I don't think he has a fever," she said, as if anticipating Hunter's next question. "I felt his forehead this morning and he is cool and sleeping peacefully."

FIGURE 16.4. Excerpt from the *4th MCD's Resource Guide to Recruiting*, "A Day in the Life of a Marine Corps Recruiter."

FIGURE 16.5A. Front cover of the commandant's wife's reading list

1. Separated by Duty, United in Love
   - Shellie Vandevoorde
2. 1001 Things to Love about Military Life
   - Crooks, Henderson, Hightower, Scherer
3. Help! I'm a Military Spouse--I Get a Life Too
   - Hightower, Scherer
4. Confessions of a Military Wife
   - Mollie Gross
5. The Military Spouse's Employment Guide: Smart Job Choices for Mobile Lifestyles
   - Janet Farley
6. The Road Home: Again. Smoothing the Transition Back from Deployment
   - Elaine Gray Dumler
7. Transformation: The Mindset You Need. The Body You Want. The Life You Deserve
   - Bill Phillips
8. Faith Deployed **- Jocelyn Green** Faith Deployed Again **- Jocelyn Green**
9. Courage After Fire: Coping Strategies for Troops Returning from Iraq and Afghanistan and Their Families
   - Keith Armstrong
10. Wounded Warrior, Wounded Home
    - Waddell, Orr
11. The 17 Day Diet
    - Dr. Michael Moreno
12. Service Etiquette, 5th Edition
    - Cherlynn Conetsco, Anna Hart
13. A Family's Guide to the Military for Dummies
    - Sheryl Garrett, Sue Hoppin
14. The Day After He Left for Iraq
    - Melissa Seligman
15. Eating For Life
    - Bill Phillips

FIGURE 16.5B. Commandant's wife's reading list

is a stay-at-home mother, is unemployed, heterosexual, financially dependent on her spouse, has experienced multiple deployments, and has lived on base.

For example, in 2013, when my husband became a recruiter for the Marine Corps, he and I were separated for eight weeks while he was away at recruiter school. On his graduation day, (and incidentally on my first day of teaching for the fall semester), I received a call from the station's Family Readiness Officer (FRO), who informed me that I would be receiving an informational packet about the transition to recruiting duty in the mail. Before we concluded our conversation, the FRO asked, "What are you up to while hubby is gone? Just waiting around for him to come home?" I informed him that I was late for work and said good-bye.

I received the *4th MCD's Resource Guide to Recruiting for Marines and Families* from my FRO just a few days later. The packet contains information on the military resources available for moving, health insurance, employment assistance, family member disability care, marriage and family counseling. It includes moving checklists, insurance checklists, emergency supply lists, tips for supporting a spouse on recruiting duty, a personal organizer, a day in the life of a recruiter, a family fact line, and financial management tips. The packet also includes a reading list written by the First Lady of the Marines Corps, the commandant's wife.

Among the list of fifteen recommended books are three diet books and one etiquette book. Furthermore, the packet contains a manual for coping throughout recruiting duty. Some of the tips for coping include:

> Bring lunch to your spouse's office once in awhile.
> Have family dinners as often as possible.
> Tell your spouse how wonderful he/she looks in uniform.
> Tell yourself "what a great job you are doing."
> Have pillow talk and don't get upset if he/she falls asleep while talking.
> Put a love note into his/her briefcase, a picture from one of the kids, a bag of baked cookie [*sic*], or some of his/her favorite snacks (include a note).

If these tips, which seem as if they might come straight out of *Leave it to Beaver*, and the absurdity of the diet books recommendations were not strong enough promotional discourse of the military wife as support staff, the fact that this entire packet is mailed to spouses and not the military member suggests an assumption that military spouses are responsible for all household tasks. The implicit assumption made here is that spouses—and, statistically speaking, a majority of them are women—are expected to act as unpaid support staff. Acting as support staff is the means by which military wives become force multipliers, as their unpaid and silent assistance allows military mem-

Tips for Spouse's Staying Connected

- With the long working hours it is important that you and your spouse stay connected. At times, you have to be clever and /or very selfless. Stay flexible and be spontaneous when a break comes, be ready to take advantage of it.

- Reserve time once a week (even if only an hour or two) as family time.
- Support your spouse with constructive solutions to problems.
- Leave phone messages for each other on the answering machine.
- PT together. It's another opportunity to see him/her and stay in shape.
- Bring lunch to your spouse's office once in a while.
- Get up early or stay up late to see each other.
- Have family dinners as often as possible.
- Coordinate calendars regularly to find opportunities for family time.
- Be creative with the time you do have to spend with each other.
- Have a white board (dry erase) or chalkboard for notes.
- Have a "drop box" for notes, gifts, jokes, etc...

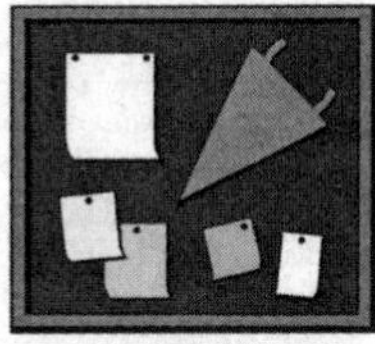

- Have pillow talk and don't get upset if he/she falls asleep while talking.
- Tell your spouse how wonderful he/she looks in uniform (often).
- Tell yourself "what a great job you are doing" (just as often).
- Leave encouraging notes on the car steering wheel, bathroom mirrors, and on the desk at the office.
- Make each success a family celebration.
- Put a love note into his/her briefcase, a picture from one of the kids, a bag of baked cookies, or some of his/her favorite snacks (include a note).
- Write on a calendar at home how many mission months are left.
- Communicate! Understand/acknowledge each other's stress.
- Keep a family journal, or start a "Gratitude" journal. It may keep you more focused on the positive things in your life. Remember that you are IMPORTANT.
- Expect your spouse to work long hours-sometimes 12-16 hours a day, if not more. Consider giving your Marine a half hour "wind down" time upon their arrival home.

Be *flexible* and be *positive*!

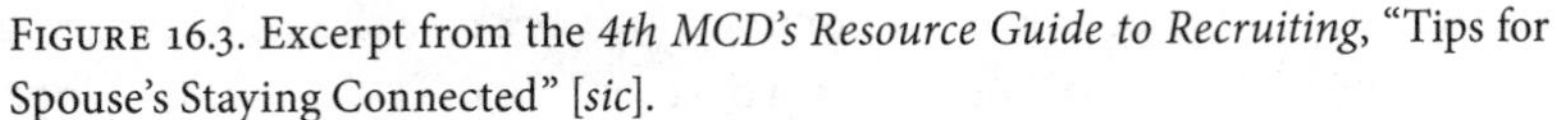

FIGURE 16.3. Excerpt from the *4th MCD's Resource Guide to Recruiting*, "Tips for Spouse's Staying Connected" [*sic*].

bers to focus entirely on their careers while their spouses maintain all other aspects of the marriage and family.

Military wives' inculcation into the military system forces them into disciplinary practices (such as base dress codes), socialization, and military information that covertly serves as propaganda that suggests wives exist as always already in service to the military member, and therefore to the military itself. The use of this propaganda is, as is the creation of docile bodies through boot camp, a de Certeauian strategy used to perpetuate the mission of the US military through the body of the military wife.

FORCE MULTIPLIER = SUPPORT STAFF

Playing the required role of supportive wife and force multiplier often means unquestioningly remaining silent about ongoing and gendered problems in a military lifestyle: domestic violence, sexual assault and harassment, and of course the precarious ethical problem of war itself. Enloe writes, with regard to wives' protests of divorce laws within the US military in the 1980s, "Feminized silence, it became clear, was a pillar of U.S. National security."[6] The silence of military wives is not necessarily a strategy that was always employed by the US military itself—in fact, military wives were not truly considered to be part of the military community until after World War II, when thousands of GIs arrived home to marry stateside, or with spouses from overseas already.[7] By the 1960s, military bases began to design neighborhoods, complete with white picket fences, in order to mimic the privileged mystique of domesticity in order to keep "soldiers' wives happy or, if not happy, at least silently resigned."[8] The US military was originally intended for men only, and when women began inserting themselves into the military system through marriage or work, the US government begrudgingly complied. Thus, the US military's ideal regarding women was enforced female invisibility.

The encouragement of feminized silence as complicity in military-endorsed nationalism is likely primarily employed "to ensure population, to reproduce labor capacity, to perpetuate the form of social relations: in short, to constitute a sexuality that is economically useful and politically conservative."[9] Just as certain sex acts and sexualities have been subjugated in the interest of perpetuating capitalism through new capitalist bodies (as Foucault asserts), so too does the US military ignore or avoid those military families, and especially wives, that do not ascribe to the metanarrative of wife as force multiplier. She is not worth the time or effort because she will not create as many potential military bodies. Indeed, according to Hyde, "what a gendered analysis again reveals, is the degree to which women's role and investment in the military institution is repeatedly understood in terms of their reproductive labour."[10] Force multiplier, then, takes on a new meaning: not simply as someone who can increase the military's efficiency through support but also as a producer of (potentially) future military members through reproduction. Indeed, according to Enloe, "military wives' unpaid labor has been the glue that has made many a base a working 'community.'"[11] The military benefits when military wives assimilate into these archetypal and supportive roles, and so it is no wonder that the disseminated representation of wives privilege a particular kind of woman.

COOPTING MILITARY NARRATIVES AS A CLAIM OF OWNERSHIP

While the US military disseminates multiple narratives about a spouse's role, military wives especially have co-opted these messages in the form of self-help and advice blogs, books, and support groups, Pinterest boards, quotes, and checklists of their own. Many of the narratives in these publications perpetuate similar iterations of the military wife as a force multiplier, yet because these narratives come from the wives themselves, they serve as radical acts of self-representation in an environment that treats military wives like their husbands: nameless and faceless. In essence, military wives "write themselves" into being as Cixous calls women to do.[12] The simple choice to engage with that discourse as a rhetor instead of as an audience is also a de Certeauian tactic: an insurgent rhetorical strategy of an assertion of agency, a diversion of the oppressive military space. Any time a woman makes the discourse her own, it is a small tactic used against the military-industrial complex—a small act of rhetorical insurgency.

There are multiple self-help manuals and "survival guides" written by and for military spouses.[13] For the purpose of this chapter, I will focus on the 2nd edition of Meredith Leyva's *Married to the Military: A Survival Guide for Military Wives, Girlfriends, and Women in Uniform* (2009).[14] This book, with pink and purple camouflage cover art, provides a guide for military wives, or, as Leyva describes them, "CinCHouse" or "Commander and Chief of the House."[15] The chapters discuss, among other topics. taking advantage of family resources, navigating military protocol, how to have a "portable" career, personal finances, health-care benefits, and working through marital conflict. Much of these chapters mirror the information that might be provided in a government packet or website. For example, Leyva dedicates just one paragraph on what to do if one needs to separate from an abusive spouse, citing the 1995 DoD Authorization Act.[16] Beyond logistics, Leyva offers no words of sympathy or commonality; in this way, her text co-opts the same military coldness reflected in the informational packet I received.

However, in other sections, Leyva co-opts military information with her own subtle personal critiques of military life. For example, while the concept of "CinCHouse" comes from military jargon, and essentially reiterates the military's assumption that military wives should act as force multipliers through their unpaid support, Leyva implies through her use of the term that military spouses are the members of the household who are actually in charge, regardless of who the breadwinner may be. Leyva writes, "You are the CinC of your house because, while your husband is off playing G.I. Joe, you are primarily responsible for raising the kids, maintaining the household finances, and establishing yourself and your family in the community. This is no job for the faint of heart."[17] Instead of framing these tasks as service work, Leyva frames this work as supervisory. Leyva later describes some of this work, especially in terms of navigating relocation, as "controlling one's destiny." She notes, "at some point your service member will be deployed and your family will relocate, possibly at the same time. The key is learning to *control your destiny* to the extent you can by understanding the military system and choosing a strategy that works best for your family."[18] While the military often frames relocation as a task that must be completed by military spouses for efficiency's sake, Leyva frames relocation as a means for seeking and gaining some control from within an oppressive system. Other examples of Leyva co-opting and then transgressing military terms and concepts are littered through *Married to the Military.* She suggests that becoming close to other military families is a wise professional and social move for one's spouse instead of merely a necessity;[19] advises creating a coded language to use when sending sexual emails to one's spouse on deployment;[20] and concludes *Married to the Military* with a chapter entitled "Really Stupid Acronyms and Jargon." The chapter is a list of important military lexicon unfamiliar to a civilian, but the title transgresses its import, implying first and foremost that outside of the military, the jargon simply doesn't matter.[21] Essentially, Leyva complicates the government-sanctioned notion of military spouse as force multiplier by offering tactics of resistance and asserting the individual agency of the military wife.

RHETORICAL INSURGENTS

Leyva's rhetorical choices in *Married to the Military*, alongside other military wives who author books and blogs, curate Pinterest boards, and speak their minds via online support groups, all act as de Certeauian tactics to subvert military strategies of assimilation. According to de Certeau, "The more a power grows, the less it can allow itself to mobilize part of its means in the service of deception. . . . Power is bound by its very visibility. In contrast, trickery is possible for the weak, and often it is his only possibility."[22] Precisely because the US military is such a vast, all-encompassing system, military wives, as weaker members, can move relatively freely as individuals using tactics of subversion. Tactics, according to de Certeau, can comprise of "clever tricks of the 'weak' within the order established by the "strong," an art of putting one over on the adversary on his own turf, hunter's tricks, maneuverable, polymorph mobilities, jubilant, poetic, and warlike discoveries."[23] Thus, a military wife's tactics to individualize and delink from the military strategies to assimilate her can be as small as performing acts of individuality daily as an insider and outsider in the military community—the simple act of choosing to identify as a military wife is a tactic that disrupts the intentions and mission of the military-industrial complex.

The most effective tactics military wives use within the military system to navigate around oppressive metanarratives is to simply assert their identities, regardless of whether those identities fit in with the military's chosen metanarrative for wives as force multipliers. For instance, Judith Butler asserts that when people choose to congregate in public spaces, particularly as individuals who are resisting or protesting large governmental or capitalist regimes, those same people are simultaneously consciously exercising their rights to protest, and unconsciously exercising their rights to their gender identities. She writes, "When we exercise the right to appear as the gender we already are—even when we feel we have no other choice—we are still exercising a certain freedom. . . . When one freely exercises the right to be who one already is and one asserts a social category for the purposes describing that mode of being, then one is, in fact, making freedom a part of that social category."[24] Thus, when a military wife interacts with the military in the varying ways she is allotted, she enacts her own identity freely, regardless of whether that identity meets the military's needs. Of course, when she interacts with the military in the ways in which she is not necessarily allotted or encouraged (for instance, in my own writing of this chapter), she also freely enacts her identity, sometimes directly against the military's needs. Both of these acts are acts of rhetorical insurgency because when she speaks and acts within the heteropatriarchal military-industrial complex, she sends ripples of disruption throughout it. She is an insurgent through her mere existence within a system she was never meant to be in. Military wives "trouble the boundaries intended to keep military power contained."[25] Insurgencies are often powerful not simply because they do damage, but because the symbolic act of insurgency suggests possibilities and alternatives to the governing system in power. The US military's intentional assimilation of wives as force multipliers means that military wives are always seen both as a disruption and as powerful. Thus, military wives and the US military system exist in a perpetual cycle of simultaneous disruption and limitation of each other.

A NEW INSURGENT WRITING

The work of military spouses to assert their own identities is not the only space where women are acting as rhetorical insurgents; indeed, likely anytime a woman asserts her individual identity in spaces that seek to assimilate her, she writes herself. A woman's writing of herself becomes "a new insurgent writing which, when the moment of her liberation has come, will allow her to carry out the indispensable ruptures and transformations in her history."[26] Thus, military wives who construct their identities in text and online in support groups, blogs and Pinterest boards enact rhetorical insurgency from within the military system by simply articulating their individuality instead of their military-sanctioned roll as nameless, faceless force multipliers. In other words, the simple act of expressing oneself online and in printed text ruptures the US military's intention to assimilate and anonymize military wives as force multipliers; for this reason, these are acts of rhetorical insurgency against the military from within it. Because of their identities as rhetorical insurgents, women are potentially more capable of enacting tactics of disruption from within traditionally masculine frameworks such as the military through the inherently rhetorical presence of their bodies, their genders, and through speech and written acts. Women are constantly creating indispensable ruptures and transformations in their histories through their mere existence.

Examining how military wives navigate the various representations of good spousehood impressed upon them by the military and media provides a fruitful contribution to an ongoing feminist rhetorical project outlined by Royster and Kirsch, who assert that studying the rhetorical practices of women's groups sheds light on the weight and importance of meaning-making practices of women. Jacqueline Jones Royster and Gesa E. Kirsch assert, "We look at people whom we have not looked at before . . . and we think again about what women's patterns of action seem to suggest about rhetoric, writing, leadership, activism, and rhetorical expertise."[27] Examining the discourse provided to and created by military wives may be an important first step to providing an illustration of the complexities of gender and identity negotiations that take place when weaker members of a powerful network are implicated in a system that they both reinforce and resist. Put another way, "If one fails to pay close attention to women—all sorts of women—one will miss who wields the power and for what ends."[28] Military wives' enactment of rhetorical insurgency can be applied to women's tactical resistance in multiple oppressive systems.

NOTES

1. Cixous, "Laugh of the Medusa," 880.
2. Foucault, *Discipline and Punish*, 138.
3. De Certeau, *Practice of Everyday Life*, 36–37.
4. Bartky, *Femininity and Domination*, 27.
5. Enloe, *Bananas, Beaches and Bases*, 147.
6. Enloe, 147.
7. Enloe, 142.
8. Enloe, 142.
9. Foucault, *History of Sexuality*, 37.
10. Hyde, "Inhabiting No-Man's Land," 90.
11. Enloe, *Bananas, Beaches and Bases*, 145.
12. Cixous, "Laugh of the Medusa," 875.
13. Gross, *Confessions of a Military Wife*; Sloan, *Today's Military Wife*; Leyva, *Married to the Military*.
14. The first edition of *Married to the Military* was published in the early years of the war in Afghanistan and the first year of the Iraq War, and was then revised in 2009 "to reflect the reality of military and economic unrest around the world" (back cover).
15. Leyva, *Married to the Military*, 1.

16. Leyva, 178.
17. Leyva, 1–2.
18. Leyva, 16; emphasis added.
19. Leyva, 44.
20. Leyva, 163.
21. Leyva, 190.
22. De Certeau, *Practice of Everyday Life*, 37.
23. De Certeau, 40.
24. Butler, "Bodies in Alliance and the Politics of the Street," 134–35.
25. Hyde, "Inhabiting No-Man's Land," 150.
26. Cixous, "Laugh of the Medusa," 885.
27. Royster and Kirsch, *Feminist Rhetorical Practices*, 72.
28. Enloe, *Bananas, Beaches and Bases*, 9.

REFERENCES

Bartky, Sandra Lee. *Femininity and Domination: Studies in the Phenomenology of Oppression*. London: Routledge, 1990.

Butler, Judith. "Bodies in Alliance and the Politics of the Street. *Sensible Politics*. New York: Zone Books, 2012.

Cixous, Helène. "The Laugh of the Medusa." *Signs* 1, no. 4 (1976): 875–93.

De Certeau, Michel. *The Practice of Everyday Life*. Berkeley: University of California Press, 1988.

Enloe, Cynthia. *Bananas, Beaches and Bases: Making Feminist Sense of International Politics*. Berkeley: University of California Press, 2014.

Foucault, Michel. *Discipline and Punish: The Birth of the Prison*. 2nd ed. New York: Vintage, 1995.

Foucault, Michel. *The History of Sexuality*. 1st ed. New York: Vintage, 1980.

Gross, Mollie. *Confessions of a Military Wife*. Auburn Hills, CA: Savas Beatie, 2015.

Hyde, Alexandra. "Inhabiting No-Man's Land: The Military Mobility of Military Wives." PhD diss., London School of Economics and Political Science, 2015.

Leyva, Meredith. *Married to the Military: A Survival Guide for Military Wives, Girlfriends, and Women in Uniform*. 2nd ed. New York: Simon & Schuster, 2009.

Royster, Jacqueline Jones, and Gesa E. Kirsch. *Feminist Rhetorical Practices: New Horizons for Rhetoric, Composition, and Literacy Studies*. Carbondale: Southern Illinois University Press, 2012.

Sloan, Lydia. *Today's Military Wife*. 7th ed. Mechanicsburg, PA: Stackpole Books, 2014.

US Marine Corps. *4th MCD's Resource Guide to Recruiting for Marines & Families*. 5th ed. Harrisburg, PA: USMC, 2012.

AFTERWORD

INVENTING A CRITICAL PRAXIS OF ENGAGEMENT ON SOCIAL MEDIA PLATFORMS

JIM RIDOLFO AND WILLIAM HART-DAVIDSON

As the work in this collection has proceeded from the initial call for papers to the published chapters collected here, we have been increasingly asked: what comes next? This question, as we noted in the preface, has been made all the more urgent by recent events in US national and international politics. To close this collection, we share a framework that emerged for us as we engaged with the authors and their works collected here. In light of the more visible, more sophisticated, and more widespread weaponization of rhetorical knowledge, the framework we propose represents for us one of the most urgent professional trajectories for teachers and scholars of rhetoric and writing studies.

We call, specifically, for a critical praxis of engagement on social media platforms such as Facebook, Instagram, Twitter, WeChat, and Sina Weibo. One outcome should be a deeper and more widely shared understanding of how these platforms enable state and non-state actors to build and host networks of influence, to enroll individuals as actors in these networks and specific influence campaigns, and how algorithms and humans spread messages. Reading the chapters by Marcelino and Magnuson alongside the analysis of GamerGate by Trice, we see startling similarities in recruitment and grooming tactics employed by militant insurgent groups such as IS and by online coalitions such as GamerGate. Gallagher shows us how relatively innocuous user actions—liking and sharing—can facilitate herding and targeting to drive influence campaigns, while Dixon shows us how state actors have motives beyond sales and marketing to mobilize affinity networks on social platforms. Gagnon's chapter on the Minerva reveals that in higher education generally and in the humanities and social sciences more specifically, we are already seeing large-scale efforts to recruit the skills we aim to cultivate in our students for RhetOps.

A critical praxis of engagement on social platforms would, ideally, find its way into our rhetoric and writing curricula where we ask students to learn to evaluate the credibility of source material. However, this evaluation would not merely focus on where the source and its information came from but also where it is going not only in terms of its potential future circulation but also its influence. With every Facebook click, there is the material potential to contribute to someone else's influence campaign. Liking or favoriting someone else's post algorithmically groups you with others who have positively engaged with that post, as well as others that share metadata descriptors, enrolling you in affinity groups that are immediately made available for targeted content sharing. To this end, every bit of content shared similarly carries the potential to algorithmically group and herd others—people in your immediate friend group and their second-order contacts—into similar targeted groups.

The mechanics of influence networks on social platforms vary and will continue to change based on the way they are designed, who inhabits them, and whose resources move through their networks as "content." For this reason, the development of a critical praxis of engagement specific to identifying and understanding real time influence campaigns is not merely an effort to instruct or document known risks. This rhetorical work must also be a holistic program of inquiry into the human motivations and dynamic effects of influence campaigns as well as the work supporting influence campaigns on specific platforms and beyond. The issues at stake put productive pressure on helpful frameworks such as Salvo's "information architecture as critical practice."[1] The challenge of real-time analysis, likewise, calls for critically engaged action of the sort described by Walton and Rose, an approach that moves swiftly and deliberately between inquiry and intervention.[2] This real-time investigative work seeks to understand how social media influence campaigns work and what their medium and short-term effects may be on our social institutions, state and political entities, and individuals. As we have learned from congressional hearings in April 2018, the impact of these campaigns is not yet well understood even by those who have built social media platforms and are therefore called to regulate activity on social media platforms.[3] The result is a dearth of evidence to support a patchwork of policy and pedagogy, all of which is seemingly struggling to keep up with the volume of use and the pace of change.

AN INVITATION TO ENGAGE

We hope this book facilitates many productive conversations about the weaponization of rhetorical knowledge and how we—both as a field and as individual scholars and teachers—contribute to and/or resist this trend. We've tried to include a range of academic educator, theorist, and practitioner voices. We hope that these chapters have prompted readers to reflect on the relationship of rhetorical studies to modern warfare and conflict. After reading the accounts by operators, by researchers whose work enables sophisticated operations, and by those charged with training and educating operators, we invite you to engage.

Since June 11, 2013, and with the much appreciated support of a dozen colleagues, we have "slow sourced" examples of how digital rhetoric intersects with asymmetrical conflict.[4] In doing so, we have documented approximately two hundred examples under the Twitter and Facebook hashtag #RhetOps. These examples point to the ways rhetorical knowledge is weaponized in conflict situations, with practices that include but are not limited to hashtag policing, data-mining initiatives such as Cambridge Analytica, physical and electronic attacks on network infrastructure, state and military use of social media for the dissemination of propaganda, and more. Our Twitter hashtag #RhetOps is one way to follow instances and commentary related to the topics in this book as well as to share your own examples. We hope, though, that these topics make it into your own scholarship and on your syllabi as well. As a community of scholars, our work lies at the center of activities that are remaking our social worlds and civic structures, and reshaping values in a very public way. If we hope to have more peaceful exchange, more productive dialogue, and more inclusive engagement with the public, we must be prepared to look carefully at rhetoric and what it has become in an age of networked warfare.

PROVOCATION

We want to end this afterword with a provocation to our peers. In the growing fog of digital rhetoric, a crisis of authorial origins, authenticity of speech and distributive means and strategies, do we as scholars in rhetoric and composition acknowledge that we once again have the capability to undermine civilizations and cultures if we don't establish some ground rules and limits for deploying weaponized digital rhetoric? We argue that our discipline is not neutral in this future but rather our field knowledge is already being put to use by state and non-state actors, and our students will be too. Will influence campaigns require a future "Potsdam Conference"? Thinking back to Steve Katz, will our students be trained to think about the ethics of expediency in relationship to RhetOps?[5] This is the new market for our field's expertise. Whether we each choose to sit at the table or not, rhetorical studies is already there.

NOTES

1. Salvo, "Rhetorical Action in Professional Space."
2. Walton and Rose, "Factors to Actors."
3. "Transcript of Mark Zuckerberg's Senate Hearing."
4. Ridolfo, "@billhd We should use a new hashtag."
5. Katz, "Ethic of Expediency."

REFERENCES

Katz, Steven B. "The Ethic of Expediency: Classical Rhetoric, Technology, and the Holocaust." *College English* 54, no. 3 (1992): 255–75.

Ridolfo, Jim. "@billhd We should use a new hashtag for this kind of news - #rhetops." Twitter, June 11, 2013, 1:54 p.m. https://twitter.com/ridolfoj/status/344558181810307072.

Salvo, Michael J. "Rhetorical Action in Professional Space: Information Architecture as Critical Practice." *Journal of Business and Technical Communication* 18, no. 1 (2004): 39–66.

"Transcript of Mark Zuckerberg's Senate Hearing." *Washington Post*, April 10, 2018. https://www.washingtonpost.com/news/the-switch/wp/2018/04/10/transcript-of-mark-zuckerbergs-senate-hearing.

Walton, Rebecca, and Emma J. Rose. "Factors to Actors: Implications of Posthumanism for Social Justice Work." In *Posthuman Praxis in Technical Communication*, edited by Kristen R. Moore and Daniel P. Richards, 91–117. London: Routledge, 2018.

CONTRIBUTORS

JEFFREY COLLINS is a colonel in the United States Air Force who directs Air Force CyberWorx, a unit comprising a public-private research and design center located at the Air Force Academy in Colorado Springs. His research is focused on cyber capabilities and disruptive technology, melding military, academic, and industry expertise with the latest technology, policy thinking, and user-centered design to solve tough operational problems for US Air Force and Joint Forces Command commanders. He holds a PhD from Carnegie Mellon University.

ELISE DIXON is a PhD candidate in rhetoric and writing at Michigan State University. Her research focuses on the disruptive tactics of writing centers, queer populations, and military spouses. Drawing from feminist and queer theories, she is interested in the ways in which people use discursive practices to seek legitimacy from and simultaneously disrupt the institutions to which they belong.

MIKE EDWARDS is an associate professor of digital rhetorics in the Department of English at Washington State University. His research focuses on the intersections of economics, technology, and rhetoric and composition, and has appeared in *Rhetoric Review* and *Pedagogy*, as well as in several edited collections. He likes cats.

LAURA EWING holds a doctorate in rhetoric and composition theory from the University of South Florida, and her research focuses on intercultural digital communication. She frequently engages with nongovernmental organizations and nonprofits to consult on matters of program development and volunteer management.

KEN FITCH is a ten-year law enforcement veteran of the Los Angeles County Sheriff's Department. He currently works as an advanced training deputy, teaching and designing training for law enforcement agencies throughout California. Ken holds a bachelor of science in criminal justice management and a master's degree in public administration. He also works as an adjunct faculty member in the criminal justice programs of several Los Angeles area community colleges.

JOHN GAGNON is an assistant professor of rhetoric and composition in the Department of English at the University of Hawaii at Manoa, where he teaches courses in composition studies, rhetorical theory and history, and argumentation. He is a cultural rhetorician whose work on topics such as weaponized rhetoric and the rhetorical framing of human rights issues is informed by his former role as a program manager in the federal government.

JOHN R. GALLAGHER is an assistant professor of English and writing studies at the University of Illinois at Urbana-Champaign. He has investigated template rhetoric and digital writing, and has published in the journals *Written Communication*, *Computers and Composition*, *Enculturation*, *Technical Communication Quarterly*, *Rhetoric Review*, and *Transformations*.

BILL HART-DAVIDSON is a professor in the Department of Writing, Rhetoric, and American Cultures and associate dean for research and graduate education in the College of Arts and Letters at Michigan State University. He has worked previously with Jim Ridolfo on the coedited collection *Rhetoric and the Digital Humanities* (University of Chicago Press), which won the Computers and Composition Outstanding Book Award for 2015.

CHERYL HATCH is a journalist and photojournalist who has worked in the United States, the Middle East, and Africa. The daughter of a career soldier and Vietnam veteran, Hatch is also an educator and the founder and president of the nonprofit the Women's Education Initiative, which offers scholarships to women overseas who have the desire but not the resources to pursue a college education.

D. ALEXIS HART is an associate professor in English and the director of writing at Allegheny College. Her research focuses on veteran studies and has appeared in *College Composition and Communication*, *Composition Forum*, *Pedagogy*, *Writing on the Edge*, and *Kairos*, as well as in several edited collections.

NATE KREUTER is an associate professor in the Department of English Studies at Western Carolina University. He formerly worked as an imagery analyst with the National Geospatial-Intelligence Agency.

SETH LONG is an assistant professor in the English Department at the University of Nebraska Kearney. His work has appeared in *Rhetoric Review*, *Computers and Composition*, and the edited collection *Rhetoric and the Digital Humanities*.

ELIZABETH LOSH is associate professor of English and American studies at William & Mary with a specialization in new media ecologies. Before joining William & Mary, she directed the Culture, Art, and Technology program at the University of California, San Diego. She is the author of *Virtualpolitik: An Electronic History of Government Media-Making in a Time of War, Scandal, Disaster, Miscommunication, and Mistakes*, *The War on Learning: Gaining Ground in the Digital University*, and *Hashtag*.

BRAD LUCAS is an associate professor of English and director of graduate studies at Texas Christian University, where he teaches courses in technical writing, research methodologies, and social movement rhetorics. He is former editor of *Composition Studies* and author of *Radicals, Rhetoric, and the War* (Palgrave Macmillan, 2006).

MADELINE MAGNUSON is a former research assistant at the RAND Corporation, specializing in Arabic language and Middle East political analysis. She is a currently a student at Stanford Law School.

ANGIE MALLORY holds a PhD in rhetoric and professional communication from Iowa State University. She works with military and paramilitary organizations, applying communication principles to the challenges of relationship building, trust, and perception in operational environments.

BILL MARCELLINO is a social and behavioral scientist at the RAND Corporation and a professor at the Pardee RAND Graduate School. Marcellino was trained as a sociolinguist and corpus linguist, and received his PhD in rhetoric from Carnegie Mellon University.

GARY MILLS is an associate professor of English in the Academic Success Center at the United States Air Force Academy. His research explores the role of digital and traditional rhetoric in the enhancement of college-level reading and writing practices.

RYAN M. OMIZO is an assistant professor in the Department of English at Temple University. His research focuses on computational rhetoric, the digital humanities, and professional writing, and his work has appeared in the *Journal of Writing Research* (with Bill Hart-Davidson), the *Journal of Interactive Technology and Pedagogy*, and *Enculturation*.

JIM RIDOLFO is an associate professor in the Department of Writing, Rhetoric, and Digital Studies at the University of Kentucky. He has published several books and edited collections, and his work has appeared in the journals *JAC, Enculturation, Kairos, Pedagogy, Language, Composition, and Culture, College English*, and *Rhetoric Review.*

MICHAEL TRICE is a lecturer in the Writing, Rhetoric, and Professional Communication program at the Massachusetts Institute of Technology. His research addresses the role of rhetoric and digital governance in knowledge-making practices, and his work has appeared in the journals *IEEE Transactions on Professional Communication* and *Present Tense.*

INDEX

academia, 47, 54–55, 59–60, 192, 201, 204, 208; and military funding, 79, 80, 82, 87
"AEIOU framework," 194, 195
Afghanistan, 34, 54, 125, 226–27; war in, 70, 73, 81, 244n14
algorithms, 128, 158, 160
Al Qaeda, 68, 71, 74, 75, 134
alt-right, 108, 142, 143, 144, 148
American imperialism, 22–23, 24, 25, 28
American Psychological Association (APA), 54, 55, 60–61
American Red Cross Service to the Armed Forces (SAF), 211, 213–17
Ancheta, J. R., 226, 228
anonymity, 144, 188, 190, 243; and GamerGate, 107, 109, 115, 117
anthropology, 44, 54–55, 67, 85
anti-racism, 91, 142, 144
application programming interfaces (APIs), 159, 165, 168
Arab Spring, 5, 71
Associated Press (AP), 221, 231n22

Back, Les, 144, 145
Bakir, Vian, 186, 193
Baldwin, Adam, 109, 115
battlespace, 69, 79, 81
Bean, Hamilton, 37, 61, 62–63
Biesecker, Barbara, 190, 192
Bitzer, Lloyd, 93, 189
Black Panthers, 95, 96, 97
blogs, 68, 219, 228, 234, 240
bots, 6–7, 9, 10, 115
Brignull, Harry, 159, 164
Bruner, Jerome, 187, 190

Cable News Network (CNN), 127–28, 222, 223, 224, 225
Calhoun, Craig, 81, 82
Carey, James, 20, 21
Caribbean, 19, 20, 28
cartoons, 25, 26, 27–28, 74–75
Central Intelligence Agency (CIA), 11, 42, 44, 47–48, 61, 93, 188; extraordinary rendition program of the, 11, 34, 35, 54–58, 60, 61
chan boards, 109, 116; 4chan, 108, 109, 110, 114
China, 24, 26, 41, 185
Christian Science Monitor, 226, 229
civil rights, 85, 91, 93
Cixous, Helène, 234, 241
Clausewitz, Carl von, 40, 42, 44
climate change, 106, 184, 187
Cold War, 46, 184, 187

collaboration, 43, 45–46, 57, 92, 163, 192; authorship and, 8, 49, 94, 97; with IC, 54, 55, 64
communication, 24, 202, 207, 212, 216; networks, 27, 84, 85
computerization, 36, 73, 85, 92
counterinsurgency, 34, 35, 90
cyberattacks, 184, 186, 188, 190
cyberspace, 188, 190
cyber-techne, 187, 191
cyber warfare, 72, 164, 185, 186–89, 194, 195, 196
CyberWorx. See US Air Force, CyberWorx

Dabiq magazine (ISIL), 69, 70, 73, 74
Da'esh, 139n2, 200–201, 204, 206, 207, 209
Dakota Access Pipeline (DAPL), 159, 166, 168
Daniels, Jessie, 144, 145
dark interactions, 159, 164, 166, 168n12
data: -bases, 171–72, 175, 177, 178; mining, 10, 248; self-reported, 159, 163–64, 165
Days of Rage, 98, 100
de Certeau, Michel, 233, 234, 239, 241
defense: Defense Intelligence Agency, 42; Defense Technical Information Center (DTIC), 83, 88n30; National Defense Intelligence College, 63. *See also* US Department of Defense (DoD)
DeVoss, Danielle Nicole, 9, 71, 86, 175–76
Dillon, Michael, 38, 42
discussion forums, 143, 144, 145; "Have a Rifle? Now Learn How to Shoot It!," 146, 148–52; "Reloading for the AR," 146–52; Stormfront, 142, 149
disinformation, 48, 79, 85, 138, 158, 162; campaigns, 4, 6
dissentivism, 12, 106, 119
Dohrn, Bernadine, 96–97
Doomsday Clock, 184, 194

Eckstein, Arthur M., 100, 101
Edwards, Mike, 5, 11
Emerson, Clint, 183, 191
Enloe, Cynthia, 235, 239, 240
ethics, 36, 56, 57–58, 59, 61
exploratory factor analysis (EFA), 126, 133

Facebook, 9, 105, 119, 212, 228, 234, 246; actions taken on, 247; check-in case study, 159; interface, 163; profiles, 160; repurposed, 108; and SAF, 214, 215; targeted advertising, 158, 162; wireless apps for, 30
Faciloscope, 12, 143, 145, 146, 149–50, 151, 153n25
fake news. *See* disinformation
Fantasy Industrial Complex (FIC), 49–50
Federal Bureau of Investigation (FBI), 91, 96, 100, 143
feminism, 96, 101n1, 107, 235, 239–40, 243, 244; écriture féminine, 234, 241
Filipinos, 19, 25, 26, 28
firearms, 142, 143, 144, 147, 151, 175
Fitch, Ken, 12, 170
Foucault, Michel, 37, 38, 42, 61, 233, 234, 240; *Discipline and Punish*, 62–63, 234
Fountain, Benjamin, 11, 49
Free Speech Movement, 92, 94, 95, 96, 98, 99
FROWN Corpus of Contemporary English, 127, 128, 139n8

GamerGate, 10, 105, 108, 115, 117–19, 246; GitHub and, 110, 114; Imgur and, 109; weaponizing, 71, 78
gaming, 111, 114, 207
gang activity, 171, 173–74
Gates, Robert, 79, 81
gender identity, 243, 244
GitGud, 114, 116, 117
GitHub, 108, 109, 110, 114
Global War on Terrorism (GWOT), 220, 226–29
Google, 30, 45, 152
graffiti, 6, 171, 173
Greely, Adolphus Washington, 19–24, 28
groupthink, 45–46
guerilla warfare, 27, 99, 189
Gulf War, 38, 70, 219, 220, 222–24
Gurak, Laura, 4, 190

Hall, Simon, 101n1, 209
Hart, D. Alexis, 5, 13
Hart-Davidson, Bill, 12, 86
hashtags, 127, 165, 166, 177: GamerGate, 109, 111, 115, 116; #NoDAPL, 166–67; #RhetOps, 4, 7–10, 248
Hatch, Cheryl, 6, 13, 220–21, 223–24, 226–27
hate: crimes, 142; speech, 10, 110, 165
Hoskins, Andrew, 219, 221
Human Terrain System (HTS), 34, 35, 36, 54, 55–58, 79
Hussein, Saddam, 39, 40, 223

Indigenous peoples, 22–23, 24, 26, 27, 28
information, 8, 79, 81; capabilities, 83, 86, 87; as commodity, 159, 160, 185; freedom of, 117; warfare, 84, 85, 193; weaponized, 191
Information Operations (IO), 71, 72, 76n21
infrastructure, 19, 20–21, 22, 23
Inspire (Al Qaeda), 69, 70, 73, 74–75
Instagram, 172, 214, 246
insurgency, 29, 69, 80, 94; counter-, 34, 35, 67, 90; rhetorical, 234, 241, 243–44
intelligence: analysis, 33, 39, 40, 44, 49, 57; counter-, 61; doctrine, 36–37; head of National Intelligence, 186; military, 34, 37, 61; operatives, 161, 162, 164; organizations, 158, 165, 166; production, 58–59, 61, 63, 64; Secret Compartmented Intelligence Facilities, 43; Senate Intelligence Committee, 55
intelligence community (IC), 11, 36, 37, 40, 42; and theories, 34, 54, 56
interactive interfaces, 158, 159–60, 168, 228
Internet, 142, 184–85, 228; Internet Relay Chat (IRC), 109
Iran, 135, 185, 187
Iraq, 3, 35, 45, 54, 81, 134, 135; war in, 38–39, 42, 57, 223, 228
Islamic State (IS), 6, 7, 10, 73, 139n2
Islamic State of Iraq and Syria (ISIS), 71, 76n10, 84, 125, 133–34, 139n2, 246; language, 135; videos, 201. *See also* Da'esh
Islamic State of Iraq and the Levant (ISIL), 68, 69, 73, 75, 139n2

Jacobs, John, 96–97
James, Larry, 220, 229–30, 231n22
Jervis, Robert, 39–40, 49
Jessen, Bruce, 55, 60
journalism, 8, 205, 223, 226, 229–30; photo of napalm attack, 221, 222, 230n4; undermined, 10, 107, 119
journalists, 3, 70, 100, 106, 108, 225, 227;

"citizen," 229–30; and GamerGate, 116, 118; William Randolph Hearst, 24; international, 26–27, 223, 224, 230; and milblogs, 228; Evan Osnos, 186; Jim Tankersley, 68; Chris Tomlinson, 219
Judge, 26, 28

Katz, Steven, 4–5, 147, 248
Kaufer, David, 129, 139n15
Kent, Sherman, 48, 57, 61
keyness testing, 127, 128–29, 140n21
Kharijites, 125, 139n4
kinetic domain, 71, 72, 73, 81, 187, 191
knowledge work, 57–58, 102, 106, 108, 119, 209
Kreuter, Nate, 11, 34, 35, 36–37

language, 127–28, 134, 135, 143; English as a Second Language (ESL), 129; gang coded, 171, 172
Lanham, Richard, 56, 63–64
law enforcement, 11, 171, 172–74, 175; LA County Sheriff's Department, 6, 170; Morton County sheriff, 167; NYPD buildings targeted, 100; surveillance of user-generated content, 159; Walker Commission investigation and "police riot," 96
Log-Likelihood (LL), 128, 130, 140nn20,21

machine, 21, 126, 138; learning, 6, 9–10, 128, 143–45; mimeograph, 94–95, 96. *See also* Faciloscope
Magnuson, Madeline, 10, 12, 109–11
malware, 188, 190
Marcellino, William M., 5, 10–11, 12
Marconi device, 27–28, 29
Marr, Colonel Jack, 34, 35, 36
Marwick, Alice, 159, 162–63
Marxism, 67, 69, 70
Mason, Julia, 111, 114
mass shootings, 143, 183; Charleston, SC, 144; *Charlie Hebdo*, 74–75; Columbine, 3; Virginia Tech, 3, 4
media, 19–20, 68, 92, 98–99, 106, 107, 117; CBS, 225; NBC, 230; Radio Free Europe/Radio Liberty, 3; scholars, 222; SDS and, 95, 96, 97; traditional and online, 105; and war, 219–20
military, 10, 67, 78, 134, 142, 185, 234; bases overseas, 211; commandant's wife's reading list, 237; funding academic research, 79, 80, 82, 87; *Joint Concepts of Human Military Operations (JC-HAMO)*, 208; Information Support Operations (MISO), 69, 71–72, 76n21; intelligence analysis, 34, 37, 61; Kadena Station, Okinawa, Japan, 215; *Married to the Military*, 244n14; National Reconnaissance Office (NRO), 46; operations abroad, 90; policy and public opinion, 226; recruiting, 235, 236, 238, 239; telegraph, 19, 20, 21, 23. *See also* Minerva Research Initiative
Miller, Carolyn, 9, 48
Miller, David, 186, 193
Mills, Gary, 11, 12, 37, 61–63, 84
Minerva Research Initiative, 79, 82–83, 84, 85
Mitchell, James, 55, 60

narrative, 187–88, 189, 190, 191, 195, 230, 240; declension, 90, 91, 101n1
National Security Agency (NSA), 46–47, 73, 93, 178, 183; *National Security Strategy*, 185, 194, 196
Native Americans, 28, 166

Nazis, 4–5, 147
Neal, Andrew, 38, 42
networks: Advanced Research Projects Agency Network (ARPANET), 93; automated, 6–7; Broadband Global Area Network (BGAN), 229; cable, 21, 27; communication, 27, 84, 85; Computer Network Operations Squadron (CNOS), 73; ecology, 110; Imzy, 165; influence, 189, 190, 247; infrastructure, 248; mesh, 20; nonhuman agents in digital, 6; technology, 5; telephone, 92; terrorist, 159, 164
New York Times, 159, 163, 230
Newton, Huey P., 95, 96
Noble, Safiya Umoja, 144, 152
nonprofit organizations (NPOs), 212, 217

O'Loughlin, Ben, 219, 221
object arrays, 158, 159–60, 162–65, 168
Office of Strategic Services (OSS), 44, 61
Omizo, Ryan, 9, 12, 86
open source, 43–44, 45, 46, 49, 147
operations: Operation Disrespectful Nod, 117; Operation Iraqi Freedom, 228; offensive, 61; Operation Restore Hope, 224; security, 211, 213, 215; shaping, 189; Operation Vulcan, 117
Otis, General, 25–27

Pace, Sonja, 220, 223–24, 230n9
Pacific Ocean, 19, 23, 24
pacifism, 90, 96
Pedahzur, Ami, 6, 7
peer review, 40, 45, 59, 64, 205
Pentagon, the, 7, 79, 96, 100, 194, 222, 223, 224, 226; Strategic Multilayer Assessment (SMA) group, 209
Peters, John Durham, 20, 21
Philippine archipelago, 19, 20, 21, 24, 26–27
Pinterest boards, 234, 240
platforms, 106, 160, 164, 168, 172, 191; and information, 162, 163, 165; and misinformation, 107; social media, 9, 84, 105, 107–9, 144, 212, 216, 247; Futures Forum (UF2), 208; Voat and Gab, 110; WeChat and Sina Weibo, 246. *See also* chan boards; Facebook; GamerGate; Instagram; Reddit; Stormfront; Twitter; Youtube
Port Huron Statement, 90, 94
Potts, Liza, 86, 107
Powell, General Colin, 42, 46
presidents: G. W. Bush, 42, 70; McKinley, 19, 24, 27; Nixon, 100, 101; Obama, 7, 8, 143; Truman, 41
press, 109, 224; Agence France-Presse, 231n22; *Atlantic*, 223; *Charlie Hebdo*, 74–75; *Collier's Weekly*, 26; *Harper's Magazine*, 26; *Intercept*, 8; *Journal of Terrorism Research*, 205; *Military Review*, 35; *Nation*, 83; *National Geographic*, 21; *New Left Notes*, 95; *New Yorker*, 186; *News & Observer* (Greensboro, NC), 225; *Philadelphia Press*, 26; *Punch*, 25; *Record*, 27; *Seattle Times*, 219; and the Vietnam War, 220, 221–22; *Washington Post*, 68. *See also* journalism; journalists
propaganda, 78, 82, 114, 138, 187, 189, 248; armed, 90, 97, 99, 100, 101; counter-Russian, 128; disinformation and, 6; Facebook, 158; and information, 193, 239; ISIS and, 7, 84; rumors, 107, 114
psychological operations (PSYOP), 71, 72, 201, 202, 203, 208

psychology, 54–55, 58, 64, 203
Puck, 28, 29

racism, 147; cyber-, 144; ideologies, 152; Nazi, 147. *See also* anti-racism
RAND Corporation, 6, 128
Reddit, 109, 110, 111, 114
rhetoric, 91, 203, 204, 206, 244; digital, 4, 6–9, 126; and ethics, 4, 6, 57–58, 63; laws of motion and, 178; operations, 125, 183, 191; Orientalist, 68–69; religious, 73, 74, 135, 136; social movement, 90, 93–94, 99; studies, 9, 10, 79, 82–83, 85, 86; visual, 221, 226, 230; weaponization of, 87, 246
rhetorical insurgency, 234, 241, 243–44
rhetorical moves (staging, evoking, inviting), 145, 146, 149, 150
rhetorical theory, 19, 33, 56, 82, 207
rhetorical velocity, 86, 175–76, 177, 178
Ringler, Kristine, 81, 83–84
Robinson, Piers, 186, 193
Russian agents, 105, 158, 185

Salazar, Philippe-Joseph, 5, 136
satellite imagery, 46, 48, 49
scholars whose work is discussed: Thomas Asher, 87; James Arnt Aune, 69; Peter Baker, 83; Vian Bakir, 186; Sandra Lee Bartky, 234; Ulrich Beck, 70; Heidi Beirich, 143; Dan Berger, 91; Albert Beveridge, 25; Lloyd Bitzer, 93; Grant Bollmer, 21; Jerry Brito, 186; Catherine Chaput, 93; Deep Kanta Lahiri Choudhury, 24; Coleman and Blumler, 106; Jeffrey Collins, 12; Shane Coughlan, 188; Cory Dauber, 226; Jack Davis, 47; Derrida, 190; Elise Dixon, 13; Laura A. Ewing, 13; Theo Farrell, 6; James Fleming, 23–24; John Gagnon, 11; John Gallagher, 12; Henry Giroux, 80; Matthew Gold, 22; Laurie Gries, 93; Hugh Gusterson, 80; Franklyn S. Haiman, 99; Michael Halloran, 4; James E. Hansen, 74; Heather Ashley Hayes, 99; Katherine Hayles, 20; Stephen Heidt, 100; Sue Hum, 75; Lynette Hunter, 9; Alexandria Hyde, 240; Suguru Ishizaki, 129; Harold Jacobs, 100; William James, 29; Henry Jenkin, 105; Chaim Kaufmann, 39; Gesa E. Kirsch, 244; Phil Lapsley, 92; Benjamin Lee, 93; Yasha Levine, 93; Edward LiPuma, 93; Alan Liu, 22; Seth Long, 12; Bernadette Longo, 4; Elizabeth Losh, 11; Brad Lucas, 12; Arabella Lyon, 75; Adrian Mackenzie, 29; Angie Mallory, 12; Peter Mansoor, 189; Tim Markham, 229; John McMillian, 95; Brian McNely, 86; Stephen Paul Miller, 92; Williamson Murray, 189; Sean Naylor, 73; Cathy O'Neil, 5; Sean O'Rourke, 93; Lester Olson, 93; Laura Otis, 21; Lisa Parks, 19; David Patrikarakos, 230; James Petras, 79; Thomas Piketty, 68; John Powers, 193; Krista Ratcliffe, 75; Alexander Reid, 86; Ridolfo and Devoss, 9, 71, 86, 175–76; Jacqueline Jones Royster, 244; Jonah Sachs, 193; Kirkpatrick Sale, 94; Jennifer Sano-Franchini, 86; Adam Segal, 187; Raka Shome, 70; Lewis Sorley, 42; David Spurr, 83; Leigh Star, 20; Nicole Starosielski, 19; Mary E. Stuckey, 93; Christa Teston, 86; David Thorburn, 105; Richard Vatz, 93; Deb Verhoeven, 22; Stephanie Vie, 167; Arthur Walzer, 189; Bo Wang,

75; Mark Ward, 4–5; Tate Watkins, 186; Jeffrey White, 44; Robin Winks, 44; Langdon Winner, 4; Alan Wolf, 80–81; James Zappen, 4; Joanna Zylinska, 29–30
scholarship, 19, 33, 44, 108, 184, 212, 246; classroom instruction, 152, 154n45; rhetorical, 9, 10, 79, 82–83, 85, 86, 106–7; Strategic Studies Institute, 78
ScienceBuzz, 151–52
Selber, Stuart, 147, 148, 151
social media, 82, 105, 162, 167, 178, 215–17, 248; Am I interacting with a real person? 9; and disaster communication, 86; disinformation within, 105; influence campaigns, 246, 247; platforms, 84, 107, 144, 161, 191; and the Red Cross, 211–12; *Social Media Handbook*, 71; and surveillance, 170, 171–72; tool kit, 214, 216; war reporting on, 230
sociology, 58, 64, 67
Somalia, 220, 224–26
Sorrow, Scott, 171, 174
stance comparison, 128, 130–31, 137
Standing Rock Indian Reservation, 159, 166, 167
STEM education, 47, 80
Stormfront, 142–46, 149, 151, 152
Students for a Democratic Society (SDS), 90, 93–97, 102n24
Stuxnet computer program, 187, 188
support groups, 240, 243–44
surveillance, 24, 78, 90, 159, 162, 170, 178; database, 159, 177; federal repression and, 97; government 101, 158; -militancy, 99; and self-surveillance, 92–93; social, 162, 163
survival, 204; Air Force's Survival, Evasion, Resistance, and Escape (SERE), 55; GamerGate effective at, 110; guides, 191, 234, 241; narratives, 183, 186, 187

TAGRS database, 171–72, 175, 177, 178
technologies, 27–28, 147, 184, 219, 229–30; drones, 48, 49; telegraph, 19–27, 28, 30
terrorism, 68, 69, 70, 74, 165, 186, 204–7; defense against, 71–72; global war on, 220, 226–29; international, 57, 134; and online networks, 159, 164
text analysis, 126, 127, 128, 129, 138
torture, 54, 55, 60. *See also* Central Intelligence Agency (CIA), extraordinary rendition program of the
Trice, Michael, 10, 12
Tufecki, Zeynep, 5, 115
Twitter, 9, 108, 114, 187, 214, 230, 246; amassing users, 168n13; and analysis work, 10–11; and dark interactions, 164; and GamerGate, 109, 110; and gangs, 172, 177; and GitGud, 116. *See also* hashtags

universities: American, 80; Arizona State, 84; Carnegie Mellon, 129; Columbia, 96, 97; Cornell, 84; Georgia State, 84; California, Berkeley, 92; California–Davis, 84; Exeter, 84; Maryland, 84; Memphis, 84; Stanford's Literary Lab, 130; of Virginia, 84; Virginia Tech, 3, 4; US Air Force, 61
US Air Force, 55, 94, 192, 194, 213; CyberWorx, 12, 183, 191–92, 193, 195, 196
US Army, 67, 73, 76n21, 93, 208; Signal Corps, 19, 21, 24, 28; War College, 70, 71, 72, 78, 86. *See also* military

US Department of Defense (DoD), 127, 185, 201, 202, 211, 213, 214; and Minerva, 79, 82; publications, 76n21, 78, 85, 186, 194
US Department of State, 127, 139n6
user actions, 10, 196, 246
US Marine Corps, 233, 238
Ut, Nick, 220, 221–22

vandalism, 171, 173, 175
Vatz, Richard, 93, 190
video, 3, 8, 190, 201, 219, 223, 229; Da'esh and ISIS, 200, 202, 204, 206–7; games, 10, 114, 207; YouTube, 109, 111; Zylinska's essay, 29–30
Vietnam War, 41, 80, 91, 96, 219, 220–22; antiwar movement and, 90, 95, 102n24
Voice of America (VOA), 229, 230n9, 231n22

Waldman, Thomas, 40–41, 42, 49
war, 6, 96, 187, 219, 228, 239; Balkans conflict, 38; Battle of Manila, 26; in Cambodia, 91; hybrid, 189, 190, 191, 196; Inchon landings, 41; India occupation, 24; "Philippine Insurrection," 25; Spanish-American, 19; Sun Tzu's *The Art of War*, 44; Tet Offensive, 41, 42. *See also* Afghanistan, war in; Cold War; Global War on Terrorism (GWOT); Gulf War; Iraq, war in; Vietnam War; World War II
warfare, 79–80, 188, 193. *See also* cyber warfare; guerilla warfare; information, warfare
weapons, 39, 40, 57, 85, 184. *See also* firearms
Weatherman, 94, 96–99, 101
Weather Underground Organization (WUO), 12, 90, 98, 99, 100
Westmoreland, General William, 41, 42
white supremacism. *See* alt-right
Wikipedia, 106, 108, 109, 110–11, 119
Woodard, Nathan, 63–64
World War II, 41, 44, 80, 94, 219

Yiannopoulos, Milo, 107, 108
YouTube, 9, 108, 109, 110

Zittrain, Jonathan, 106, 111, 119